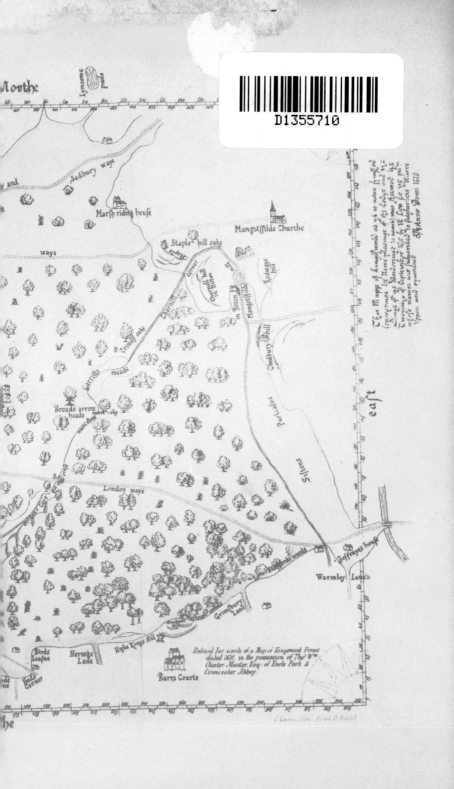

Reduced Fac-simile of a Map of Kingswood Forest dated 1610, in the possession of Thos Wm Chester Master, Esq. of Knole Park & Cirencester Abbey.

THE FOUNDER AT KINGSWOOD SCHOOL IN THE LAST
YEAR OF HIS LIFE
Detail from an engraving by James Heath, 1790 (see p. 100)

A. G. IVES

Kingswood School in Wesley's Day and Since

LONDON
EPWORTH PRESS

© *A. G. Ives* 1970
First published in 1970 *by*
Epworth Press

Printed in Great Britain at the
St Ann's Press, Park Road,
Altrincham

SBN 7162 0163 1

To the memory of
OWEN SPENCER WATKINS
my father's friend and mine
and to whom
Kingswood owes a debt
inadequately reflected in these pages,
and but for whose steadfast faith in the
school I might never have gone to it
or essayed the writing of this history

CONTENTS

LIST OF PLATES

Numbers refer to facing pages

FOREWORD

THIS ACCOUNT of Kingswood School differs from most school histories in what may seem to some readers the disproportionate amount of space accorded to the school in Wesley's life time, and a word of explanation may not come amiss.

The last history of the school was published in 1898. A fascinating volume, it has long been out of print; and as nearly a century has elapsed since the eighteen seventies with which to all intents and purposes it ended, it seemed that there was room for an account of the school which should bring the story down, if not quite to the present, at any rate to more recent times. I thought that all that would be needed would be to rehearse the earlier story of the school, for which the material appeared to lie ready to hand; perhaps to modify somewhat the perspective over the middle period; and to bring the story, as far as might be, up to date.

Only when I had begun did I realise that, striking as are the well known passages about the early days from Wesley's pen, they left large areas of the history of the school untouched; that sources of information did exist, and that no sustained attempt to piece them together had ever been made. It was not long before I was in close touch with Mr. Sackett, then already retired from the headmastership. As it happened that I too had recently retired, we had the leisure needed to pursue sundry time-consuming researches. Together we visited the site of Old Kingswood and its environs on the outskirts of Bristol; read musty registers in St. George's Kingswood, and St. Philip and St. Jacob in Bristol; drove up to Brecknockshire pursuing the footsteps of our almost wholly neglected first headmaster, Dr. John Jones; found our way to Fonmon Castle beyond Cardiff, where is the portrait by Reynolds of one of our earliest boys; returned time and again to the distracting files of the Bristol press room of Wesley's friend Felix Farley; wrestled with the near illegible writing of the Countess of Huntingdon in the Methodist Archives in London; read in the records at the Bodleian of the expulsion of the Methodist students from Oxford, finding that one of them, and perhaps the most prominent, *had* been at Kingswood; and so on. As we read on and on, and pieced this and that together, our concept of early Methodism, decade by decade, and of early Kingswood cradled within it, underwent considerable changes. If this has led us here and there—for example in our references to Dr. John Jones, and his almost equally neglected successor, the Rev. James Rouquet—to some disproportion in our account, we must plead guilty. If too from what we have written Wesley's weaknesses are all too apparent, so also we would hope is his stature and enduring achievement. We do not for a moment assume that our researches have been exhaustive, and it seems indeed probable that further light may yet be thrown on the complex story of early Methodism as time goes on.

In dealing with the story of the school since Wesley the historian is on much firmer ground. Minute books and other records are available, and the *History* of 1898 is a mine of information. The difficulty is to choose amid so much of such varied interest. I have tried to keep the narrative clear, to set the school to some extent in its context, and to avoid overloading the text with the names and achievements of old boys, except where a mention serves to illustrate a trend or a point under discussion. With many sections here also I have enjoyed Mr. Sackett's co-operation and advice.

A task such as this could never have been undertaken without help on every hand. The Governors and the present Headmaster, Mr. A. L. Creed, have most generously placed the school's records freely at my disposal, and I have derived much help also from the Methodist Archives in City Road now so attractively organised under the direction of Dr. J. C. Bowmer. Among so many to whom I am indebted it is not easy to single out individuals. In the early stages I was privileged to read a stimulating study of the school by Dr. W. G. Moore, of St. John's College, Oxford, and a careful thesis dealing with Wesley and Bristol, and including early Kingswood, by the Rev. Gordon T. Brigg. Both of these alerted me to aspects of the school's history which I might otherwise have overlooked. Mr. Warren Derry drew my attention to the entertaining reminiscences of Thomas Maurice about his stay at the school. I have had frequent recourse to the guidance of the Rev. Rupert Davies, especially in keeping me straight with regard to the history of Methodism; he has indeed most kindly read almost all in draft or in proof form. The Rev. Gomer Roberts has helped with references to be found among the unpublished Trevecka papers and Dr. John Walsh of Jesus College, Oxford, and Dr. Geoffrey Nuttall of New College, London, have saved me from various errors I might easily have made in territory with which I am not familiar. The loan of a complete set of the Proceedings of the Wesley Historical Society, formerly the property of the late Rev. E. G. H. Bryant, has been of the greatest possible assistance. To many most helpful and patient librarians, archivists, and personal friends (including several members of the past and present staff of the school) I also owe my warmest thanks.

With the appendices I have included a note on sources where will be found further indications of indebtedness.

Tonbridge, Kent
November 1969

Kingswood School
in Wesley's Day and Since

I

THE SETTING

The Religious Revival of the Eighteenth Century

KINGSWOOD SCHOOL was founded by John Wesley towards the end of the first decade of the religious revival of the eighteenth century, and some account of the events of those years, however brief, is essential to place his school in its proper setting.

We cannot here trace the diverse origins of the movement, nor rehearse the story of all that had gone before in Wesley's eventful life; his upbringing in the rectory at Epworth, his years at Oxford and his Fellowship at Lincoln College, his leadership there in the thirties of the little group sometimes known as the Holy Club and sometimes as Methodists, his chequered spell as chaplain in the colony of Georgia, the impact upon him of the piety and traditions of the Moravians, or his oft-described spiritual experience in Aldersgate Street in 1738. Nor can we touch here in more than the broadest terms upon the religious issues of the day. The Reformation and its reverberations, we must remind ourselves, were much nearer than they are today. Over all there still hung like a back-cloth across the stage the four last things—Death, Judgment, Heaven and Hell. Were some indeed predestined to eternal life and others to eternal damnation? There lingered on deep differences of interpretation; and when the religious awakening of the eighteenth century travelled across Europe, linking German Pietism with Methodism in these islands and extending to America, it was interpreted by the numerous evangelical clergy on the familiar Calvinist lines. But John and Charles Wesley were important exceptions, and in them the impulse of the revival was fused with a militant Arminianism, zealous to revive the ideals and practices of the apostolic Church. Their proclamation of the offer of universal salvation was incompatible with the harsher interpretations of Calvinism. Tension with the Calvinist wing of the revival was

A—2

thus always latent, and in the end exerted a decisive influence on the course of events. A brief reference to it is essential for a proper understanding of the character of the school which lay so near the centre of the movement, and adds interest to its story. All were united however in face of the prevalent rationalism which dispensed with the need for the supernatural in religion, and had made such headway as to drive the more earnest Bishops to exclamations of despair about the future of the Church.

When in the early spring of 1739 Wesley's younger Oxford associate the Rev. George Whitefield arrived in Bristol the startling popularity of his preaching and the irregularity of his proceedings led to his being refused permission to preach in the churches. He took to the fields, and began preaching to the colliers of Kingswood whose uncivilised behaviour had long been proverbial. The forest trees had disappeared, and primitive coal mines were dotted about in rough open country, whence the coal was transported down to the river Avon by means of packhorses. Many hundreds of families were scattered about in wretched hovels. Whitefield's preaching was attended with unprecedented success, but he did not stay many weeks in Bristol. He was, as he thought, on the point of leaving to return to his missionary work in the newly founded colony of Georgia. He wrote to Wesley, who had been his mentor in the Holy Club in Oxford and was then in London, urging him to come to Bristol and continue the work begun there. Wesley consented, and for the first time preached in the open air in Bristol and Kingswood. The district thus took its place with London as a focal point in the origins of Methodism.

Before Whitefield left, however, he had visited Wales and been impressed by the numerous schools he had seen there established by the Rev. Griffith Jones. Back in Kingswood he had begun to collect funds for the erection of a school for the children of the converted colliers, and had laid a foundation stone in the forest. On his departure immediately afterwards he handed the project over to Wesley, though he also continued to collect funds for it. Various references to the difficulties encountered by Wesley in the final acquisition of a site, and to the part played by their youthful associate John Cennick whose name came to be linked with the school are to be found in the Journals and correspondence of both Whitefield and Wesley. The story has an interest of its own, but to follow it here would take us off at a tangent, and the reader who desires to know more of these matters will find them discussed in Appendix I.

Much more was to happen before Wesley returned to Kingswood to build there the new model boarding school with which this history is concerned.

Between 1739 and 1741 the Wesleys were largely occupied with the affairs of their newly established societies in London, and in Bristol and Kingswood, and with disentangling themselves from too close an alliance with the extravagances of their Moravian friends. In 1742 and 1743 there followed rapidly one upon another the decisive steps which laid the foundations of later Methodism. Class meetings were organised. The London/Bristol axis was extended to Newcastle. Pivoted on these three centres the great itinerancy began, followed everywhere by the systematic organisation of societies. It was all, as the Wesleys believed and insisted, within the framework of the Church of England. The first Conference, comprising John and Charles Wesley, four other regular clergymen of the Church of England, and four lay preachers, met in London in 1744; and the second in Bristol in 1745, when the country was in a state of commotion over the threatening incursion of the Young Pretender, and anxiety was felt on every hand lest Protestants should suffer as they had done in France. Encouraged by success on a scale which they themselves hardly understood, the Wesleys redoubled their efforts to interpret the movement in terms of orthodoxy and adherence to the established Church. They set their eyes on an ambitious goal—"the reform of the nation, and in particular of the Church". It was a dream of spiritual revival within the Church of England which sometimes in the mid-seventeen forties seemed to be on the brink of realization.

Among those on whose support the Wesleys could rely was the Countess of Huntingdon. She was already deeply involved in the ferment of the times, and her influence was spreading through society in many directions. In the early forties both John and Charles Wesley were in lively consultation with her, visiting her home at Donnington Park. By 1743 in writing to Charles she would send "my love to the Kingswood flock". Thereafter through the middle forties and onwards her zeal equalled theirs. Her sister-in-law, Lady Margaret Hastings, married Wesley's old friend the Rev. Benjamin Ingham, and together they maintained a centre of evangelical activity in Yorkshire, as did the Countess herself in Leicestershire. In 1746 the Earl died, and the Countess was free to play a more personal part in the movement. Thus she may be seen in the early summer weather setting off from Bath in her carriage on an evangelical tour of Wales, accompanied by various leaders of the revival. Some twenty years later she would herself establish a college at Trevecka in Brecknockshire where young men might be trained for the ministry. But this was in the future. In the 1740's her support of the Wesleys was unstinted. Whether she took any part in sponsoring the new school at Kingswood Wesley does not tell us, but it would be strange if she did not. Certainly no story of the early days of Kingswood School would be complete which failed to take account of the part she played in this formative period, or of her frequent presence in Bristol in the first eventful years.

In Wales a somewhat earlier and interlocking religious revival associated with the name of Howell Harris had many links with the movement in England. In recent years much fresh light has been thrown on the scene by the publication of a small part of the immense correspondence accumulated by him at Trevecka. The comings and goings of the principal parties—the Wesleys and Lady Huntingdon among them—are there vividly depicted with a sometimes disconcerting novelty. It was through this movement that the Wesleys became acquainted with several influential families in Wales. As we shall see, from this milieu would come not only some of the boys at the new boarding school at Kingswood, but also two of its first six masters.

By the middle forties the revival was thus gaining momentum and attracting support in many quarters. At its head was the clear-cut and dominant figure of John Wesley, leading a dedicated life of early rising, prayer, fasting and constant communion, and inculcating in all who worked with him his sense of the continuity of the movement with Christian piety down the ages, and especially with the practices of the primitive Christians. In 1743 he had found time to finish the preparation of a tract entitled *Instructions for Children,* and added a preface addressed "To all Parents and Schoolmasters". This he distributed as widely as possible with the warmest commendation. "I have laid before you," he wrote, "in the following tract the true principles of the Christian education of children." It was not surprising, therefore, that as the excitement of the Forty-Five died down he judged the time opportune to provide his now numerous friends and supporters with a school at which their children might be educated "according to the accuracy of the Christian model".

II

"MY DESIGN WAS . . ."

THOUGH MANY of the records of the early days have been lost, we can with the aid of Wesley's Journal and correspondence trace much of the story. Moreover in later life he prepared *A Plain Account of Kingswood School*. "I judged it needful", he wrote, "to enlarge a little upon the nature of that institution; to lay down the grounds of those rules, and the reasons for what is peculiar in our methods."

He relates how "one or two tracts" upon education fell into his hands which led him to consider the methods pursued in the public schools. A few years later, he tells us, he had an opportunity of enquiring concerning some of the most celebrated schools in Holland and Germany.*

Then follows a list of the defects which he found to be universal. First is the objection that the schools were mostly placed in great towns, and that the children when they went abroad were likely to see sights which would divert them, and mingle with other children whose example would neither forward them in learning nor religion. Allied with this was the second objection, the promiscuous admission of all sorts of children, when as frequently happened the parents themselves have no more religion than their ungodly offspring. Third, the masters had no more religion than their scholars—consequently they were little concerned whether their scholars were Papists or Protestants, Turks or Christians. They looked upon this as no part of their business. Fourthly, the authors read were not well chosen—if they were, would Eutropius or Lucius Florus have any place among them? There were excellent Greek and Roman authors who excelled

---

* Wesley's reference to "one or two tracts" is an over-simplification of the numerous influences which moulded his thinking. His horizons were not limited to this country, and on the continent the theme of an education guarded from the world's corrupting ways had been widespread for more than a century. Its influence on Wesley's thinking is of much interest—See Appendix II.

as much in strength of understanding as in purity and elegance of style. Finally the masters put authors into the hands of their scholars that "with all the beauty of language, all the sweetness of expression instil into their minds both obscenity and profaneness". He boldly quoted examples of this obscenity.*

Wesley's dissatisfaction with the schools of his day was based upon his experience as a boy "in that great school wherein I had been educated (i.e. the Charterhouse)", and his knowledge of "such others as were in the highest repute, particularly those in and near London". He had been a Gown boy at Charterhouse for over six years (1714–20), when Dr. Walker was headmaster, and had acquitted himself with credit. The big boys did, he tells us, deprive the little boys of their meat, but he seems to have been happy enough, and retained a lifelong affection for the school, revisiting it from time to time.

It seems more than possible that Westminster was the main target of his criticisms. It had during the latter half of the seventeenth century acquired great prestige under its famous headmaster, Richard Busby, and was in the earlier half of the eighteenth century still in the very front rank, its reputation at least equal with Eton. John Wesley was through his brothers closely connected with Westminster. Both were educated there; his elder brother Samuel had become an usher, and it was with him at his house in Dean's yard that he lodged during the vacations from Charterhouse. He was thus well posted about what really went on at Westminster, and an illuminating piece of evidence, which seems to relate to conditions around 1690, has recently come to light which is only too consistent with the charges levelled by Wesley at the public schools.† The theme of the indictment is lack of supervision : too few masters, big boys tyrannising over younger ones, making them fetch what their elders' "greedy stomachs craved"; if they resisted,

---

* "Virgil's Alexis, the lewd Epigrams of Martial, and the shameless Satires of Juvenal, (even the sixth), so earnestly recommending sodomy as well as adultery!
　　　Nonne putas melius, quod tecum pusio dormit?
. . . and to this day we retain for the edification of our children
　　　Tonantem et fornicantem Jovem!"

† John Carleton, *Westminster School*, new edition 1965. The account quoted is described by the author, the present Headmaster, as by far the fullest and frankest description of an English public school of the period.

beating them with ropes' ends and sometimes with sticks and cudgels; boys seen both by day and by night out of the college and without their gowns, dressed up with swords, laced cravats and cravat strings, handing about young women in the streets and fields; and "some of them have lain out of college whole nights, and come in again early in the morning, having always command of the door". Lock and key were not able to confine them "without some particular eye to watch them besides". Perhaps things were not always as bad as they seem to have been around 1690; but Lord Chesterfield, writing to his son in 1750, remarked casually that Westminster School was undoubtedly the seat of illiberal manners and brutal behaviour. If, as we shall soon see in what follows, Wesley's regime seems altogether too restrictive, at least the faults of which he complained, especially the placing of schools in large towns and almost total lack of supervision out of school, were not imaginary. His criticisms were directed, he said, to the schools in or near London. They may have applied in some degree to St. Paul's and Merchant Taylors', but these two were, of course, day schools, and the scope for misbehaviour more limited.*

The passage, in which is described in Wesley's own words the foundation of the school, must be quoted in full:

After long inquiring, but inquiring in vain, for a school free from these palpable blemishes, at last a thought came into my mind, of setting up a school myself. The first point was, to find a proper situation; not too far from a great town; which I saw would be highly inconvenient for a large family; nor yet too near, and much less in it; which would have been attended by greater evils. After mature consideration, I chose a spot in the middle of Kingswood, three miles from Bristol. It was quite private, remote from all high roads, on the side of a small hill sloping to the west, sheltered from the east and north, and affording room for large gardens. I built the house capable of containing fifty children, besides Masters and servants; reserving one room, and a little study for my own use.

---

* Besides those mentioned above, four others made up the famous "nine". They would be more prominent later than they were in the earlier half of the eighteenth century. At Winchester, sadly in need of reform, the number of commoners fell to 18 in 1751. Harrow had begun to grow, but had dropped back, and it would not be until the second half of the century that it would overtake Winchester. The rise to fame of Rugby, and the revival of Shrewsbury belong rather to the second than to the earlier half of the eighteenth century (Vivian Ogilvie, *The English Public School*, 1957).

I then set myself to procure Masters. And in this respect I had such an advantage as few besides have, in being acquainted with every part of the nation. And yet I found it no easy thing to procure such as I desired; for I was not satisfied that they had learning sufficient for their several departments, unless they had likewise the fear of God, producing an unblameable conversation. I saw none would answer my intention, but men who were truly devoted to God; who sought nothing on earth, neither pleasure, nor ease, nor profit, nor the praise of men; but simply to glorify God, with their bodies and spirits, in the best manner they were capable of.

I next considered how to procure proper scholars; not any that came to hand, but, if possible, such as had some thoughts of God, and some desire of saving their souls; and such whose parents desired they should not be almost, but altogether Christians. This was proposed to them before their children came; and, to prevent future misunderstandings, they were desired attentively to read, and seriously to consider, the rules of the school; being assured they would be punctually observed without any favour or affection. One of these rules was that "no child shall be admitted after he is twelve years old". The ground of this rule was, a child could not well before that age be rooted either in bad habits or ill principles. But, notwithstanding the strictness of the rules, I had soon as many scholars as I desired; nay, considerably more; for I was afraid of having too many at once, knowing how difficult it was to govern a large number; children being so apt, when many of them are together, to hinder and corrupt one another.

Having procured proper Masters, and a sufficient number of children, most of whom were as well inclined as could be expected, our first point was, to answer the design of Christian education, by forming their minds, through the help of God, to wisdom and holiness, by instilling the principles of true religion, speculative and practical, and training them up in the ancient way, that they might be rational, scriptural Christians.

In April 1746, Wesley recorded that he preached at Kingswood ". . . and laid the foundation stone of the New House". His text was from Isaiah, the verses which begin—

> For brass I will bring gold,

and end on a note of triumphant prophecy—

> A little one shall become a thousand
> and the small one a strong nation.

Two years later the fifth Conference was held in Bristol, some fourteen persons being present. Part of its purpose was "to settle all things relating to the school which is now to be begun at Kingswood". On June 5th the programme for the new school was discussed at length.*

Q. By what name should this foundation be called? And the answer is

A. Kingswood School.

What in particular is to be taught there? How many classes? What is taught in the first class? . . . It is all there set out, the answers approximating closely to the *Short Account* and which must have been already in draft in Wesley's hands.

Q. What work do they do?

A. In fair days and particularly in summer they may work in the garden or grounds. In rainy days they may work at any handicraft work; and some of them will learn music.

Q. You leave no time to play?

A. He who plays when he is a child will play when he is a man.

Q. Do they go to school every day?

A. Every day except Sunday. We have no holy-days so-called.

To another question Wesley replied that he "designed to train up children . . . in every branch of useful learning till they are fit as to all acquired qualifications for the work of the ministry"; and he sketched out a five-year course for those who had "gone through the school". In fact, however, he "suspended" this course of advanced studies. Perhaps there were difficulties about provision of tuition, or perhaps he decided on reflection that it would amount to a step towards separation from the established church. At all events no more is heard of it in the earlier years, and as the details were first published in 1768, it will be more convenient to postpone consideration of it at this stage of the story.

The *Short Account of the School in Kingswood* containing the rules settled at the Conference of 1748 is a document of the greatest interest, and is here given in full. The manuscript alterations shown are in Wesley's handwriting. It differs in several significant particulars from the version of 1768, which alone appears in the various editions of Wesley's works, and has too often been used in accounts of the early days of the school. The *Short Account* is now a rare pamphlet, but was reproduced in facsimile in 1963. It should not be confused with the much later *Plain Account* quoted above.

* *Bennet Minutes,* Wesley Historical Society, Publication No. 1, p.54.

A SHORT

ACCOUNT

OF THE

SCHOOL

IN

KINGSWOOD,

Near *BRISTOL.*

BRISTOL:

Printed by *FELIX FARLEY.*

M.DCC.XLIX.

A SHORT
ACCOUNT
OF THE
SCHOOL in KINGSWOOD.

1. OUR Defign is, With GOD's Affiftance, to train up Children, in every Branch of ufeful Learning.

2. We teach None but Boarders. Thefe are taken in, being between the Years of Six and Twelve, in order to be taught READING, WRITING, ARITHMETICK, ENGLISH, FRENCH, LATIN, GREEK, HEBREW; HISTORY, GEOGRAPHY, CHRONOLOGY; RHETORICK, LOGICK, ETHICKS; GEOMETRY, ALGEBRA, PHYSICKS; MUSICK.

2. The School is to contain Eight Claffes:

In the Firft Clafs the Children read the *Hornbook, Inftructions for Children,* and *Leffons for Children;* and begin learning to write.

In the Second Clafs they read *The Manners of the Antient Chriftians,* go on in Writing, learn the *Short* ENGLISH GRAMMAR, the *Short* LATIN GRAMMAR, read *Prælectiones Pueriles:* Tranflate them into *Englifh,* and the *Inftructions for Children* into *Latin:* Part of which they tranfcribe and repeat.

In

In the Third Claſs they read Dr. CAVE's *Primitive Chriſtianity*, go on in Writing, perfect themſelves in the *Engliſh* and *Latin* Grammar; Read *Corderii Colloquia Selecta* and *Hiſtoriæ Selectæ*: Tranſlate *Hiſtoriæ Selectæ* into *Engliſh*, and *Leſſons for Children* into *Latin*: Part of which they tranſcribe and repeat.

In the Fourth Claſs they read *The Pilgrim's Progreſs*, perfect themſelves in Writing; learn DILWORTH's *Arithmetick*: Read CASTALIO's KEMPIS and CORNELIUS NEPOS: Tranſlate *Caſtalio* into *Engliſh*, and *Manners of the Antient Chriſtians* into *Latin*: Tranſcribe and repeat Select Portions of *Moral and Sacred Poems*.

In the Fifth Claſs they read *The Life of Mr.* HALIBURTON, perfect themſelves in Arithmetick; read Select *Dialogues* of ERASMUS, PHOEDRUS and SALLUST: Tranſlate *Eraſmus* into *Engliſh*, and *Primitive Chriſtianity* into *Latin*: Tranſcribe and repeat Select Portions of *Moral and Sacred Poems*.

In the Sixth Claſs they read *The Life of Mr.* DE RENTY, and KENNET's *Roman Antiquities*: They learn RANDAL's *Geography*: Read CÆSAR, Select Parts of TERENCE and VELLEIUS PATERCULUS: Tranſlate *Eraſmus* into *Engliſh*, and *The Life of Mr.* HALIBURTON into *Latin*: Tranſcribe and repeat Select Portions of *Sacred Hymns and Poems*.

In the Seventh Claſs they read Mr. LAW's *Chriſtian Perfection*, MARSHAL's *Myſtery of Sanctification*, and A. Bp. POTTER's *Greek Antiquities*: They learn BENGELII *Introductio ad Chronologiam*, with MARSHAL's *Chronological Tables*: Read TULLY's *Offices*, and VIRGIL's *Æneid*: Tranſlate BENGELIUS into *Engliſh*, and Mr. LAW into *Latin*: Learn (thoſe who have a Turn for it) to make Verſes, and The *Short Greek Grammar*:

Read

Read the Epiſtles of St. JOHN: Tranſcribe and repeat Select Portions of MILTON.

In the Eighth Claſs they read Mr. LAW's *Serious Call*, and LEWIS's *Hebrew Antiquities:* They learn to make Themes and to declaim: Learn VOSSIUS's *Rhetorick:* Read TULLY's *Tuſculan Queſtions*, and *Selecta ex* OVIDIO, VIRGILIO, HORATIO, JUVENALE, PERSIO, MARTIALE: Perfect themſelves in the *Greek* Grammar; Read the *Goſpels* and Six Books of HOMER's *Iliad:* Tranſlate TULLY into *Engliſh*, and Mr. LAW into *Latin:* Learn the *Short Hebrew Grammar*, and read *Geneſis:* Tranſcribe and repeat *Selecta ex* VIRGILIO, HORATIO, JUVENALE.

4. It is our particular Deſire, That all who are Educated here, may be brought up in the Fear of GOD: And at the utmoſt Diſtance as from Vice in general, ſo in particular from Idleneſs and Effeminacy. The Children therefore of *tender* Parents, ſo call'd, (who are indeed offering up their Sons and their Daughters unto Devils) have no Buſineſs here; for the Rules will not be broken, in favour of any Perſon whatſoever. Nor is any Child receiv'd unleſs his Parents agree, 1. That he ſhall obſerve all the Rules of the Houſe, and 2. That they will not take him from School, no, not a Day, till they take him for good and all.

5. The General Rules of the Houſe are theſe:

Firſt, The Children riſe at Four, Winter and Summer, and ſpend the Time till Five in private: Partly in Reading, partly in Singing, partly in Self-examination or Meditation (if capable of it) and partly in Prayer. They at firſt uſe a ſhort Form (which is varied continually) and then pray in their own Words.

Secondly, At Five they attend the Publick Service. From Six they work till Breakfaſt. For as we have no Play-Days (the School being taught every Day in the Year but *Sunday*) ſo neither do

we

we allow any Time for Play on any Day. He
that plays when he is a Child, will play when he
is a Man.

On Fair Days they work, according to their
Strength in the Garden; on Rainy Days in the
Houſe. Some of them alſo learn Muſick: And
ſome of the larger will be employed in *Philoſophi-
cal Experiments*. But particular Care is taken that
they never work alone, but always in the Preſence
of a Maſter.

We have Six Maſters in all; One for teaching
French, Two, for Reading and Writing, and
Three for the Antient Languages.

Thirdly, The School begins at Seven, in which
Languages are taught 'till Nine, and then Writing, &c. 'till Eleven. At Eleven the Children
walk or work. At Twelve they dine, and then
work or ſing 'till One. They diet thus:

Breakfaſt, Milk-porridge and Water-gruel, by
Turns:

Supper, Bread and Butter, and Milk by Turns:

Dinner, *Sunday*, Cold Roaſt Beef:

Monday, Haſh'd Meat and Apple-dumplins:

Tueſday, Boil'd Mutton.

Wedneſday, Vegetables and Dumplins:

Thurſday, Boil'd Mutton or Beef:

Friday, Vegetables and Dumplins. And ſo in
Lent:

Saturday, Bacon and Greens, Apple-dumplins.

They drink Water at Meals, nothing between
Meals. On *Friday*, ~~if healthy,~~ they faſt 'till Three
in the Afternoon. Experience ſhews, this is ſo
far from impairing Health, that it greatly conduces
to it.

Fourthly, From One to Four Languages are
taught, And then Writing, &c. 'till Five. At
Five begins the Hour of Private Prayer. From
Six they walk or work 'till Supper. A little before

fore Seven the Publick Service begins. At Eight they go to Bed, the youngeſt firſt.

Fifthly, They lodge all in one Room, in which a Lamp burns all Night. Every Child lies by himſelf. A Maſter lies at each End of the Room. All their Beds have Mattreſſes on them, not Feather-beds.

Sixthly, On *Sunday*, At Six they dreſs and breakfaſt: At Seven, learn Hymns or Poems: At Eight attend the Publick Service: At Nine go to the Pariſh Church; At One dine and ſing: At Two attend the Publick Service, and at Four are privately inſtructed.

6. The Method obſerved in the School is this:

The Firſt Claſs.

Morn. 7. Read. 10. Write 'till Eleven.
Aftern. 1. Read. 4. Write 'till Five.

The Second Claſs.

M. 7. Read *The Manners of the Antient Chri-
       ſtians:*
  8. Learn the *Engliſh* Grammar: When that
      is ended, the *Latin* Grammar.
 10. Learn to Write.
A. 1. Learn to conſtrue and parſe *Prælectiones
      Pueriles:*
  4. Tranſlate into *Engliſh* and *Latin* alter-
      nately.

The Third Claſs.

M. 7. Read *Primitive Chriſtianity:*
  8. Repeat *Engliſh* and *Latin* Grammar al-
      ternately:
  9. Learn *Corderius*, and when that is ended,
      Hiſtoriæ Selectæ.
 10. Write.
A. 1. Learn *Corderius* and *Hiſtoriæ Selectæ.*
  4. Tranſlate.   The

The Fourth Clafs.

M. 7. Read *The Pilgrim's Progrefs:*
8. Repeat the Grammar:
9. Learn *Caftalio's Kempis,* and when that is ended, *Cornelius Nepos.*
10. Write and learn Arithmetick:
A. 1. Learn *Kempis* and *Cornelius Nepos.*
4. Tranflate.

The Fifth Clafs.

M. 7. Read Mr. *Halyburton's Life.*
8. Repeat the Grammars:
9. Learn *Erafmus;* afterwards *Phædrus;* then *Salluft:*
10. Learn Arithmetick:
A. 1. Learn *Erafmus, Phædrus, Salluft:*
4. Tranflate.

The Sixth Clafs.

M. 7. Read Mr. *de Renty's Life:*
8. Repeat the Grammars:
9. Learn *Cæfar;* afterwards *Terence;* then *Velleius Paterculus:*
10. Learn Geography:
A. 1. Learn *Cæfar; Terence; Paterculus:*
3. Read *Roman Antiquities:*
4. Tranflate.

The Seventh Clafs.

M. 7. Read Mr. *Law's Chriftian Perfeftion:*
8. { *M. W. F.* Learn the *Greek* Grammar; and read the *Greek* Teftament: *Tu. Th. Sat.* Learn *Tully;* afterwards *Virgil:*
10. Learn Chronology:
A. 1. Learn *Latin* and *Greek* alternately, as in the Morning:
3. Read *Grecian Antiquities:*
4. Tranflate and make Verfes alternately.

The

The Eighth Clafs.

M. 7. Read Mr. *Law*'s *Serious Call:*

8. { *M. Th.* Latin.
   { *Tu. Frid.* Greek.
   { *W. S. Hebrew:* And fo at One in the
   {   Afternoons:

10. Learn Rhetorick:

A. 3. Read *Hebrew Antiquities:*

4. *Mond. Thurf.* Tranflate.
   Tuefd. Frid. Make Verfes:
   Wed. Make a Theme:
   Sat. Write a Declamation.

All the other Claffes fpend *Saturday* Afternoon in Arithmetick, and in tranfcribing what they learn on *Sunday*, and repeat on *Monday* Morning.

The Price for the Board and teaching of a Child (including his Books, Pens, Ink and Paper) is Fourteen Pounds a Year, while he is in the School: After he has gone thro' the School, Twenty, and he is then to find his own Books.

F I N I S.

Wesley's attitude to play and his ban on holidays have never ceased to excite comment from all who have had occasion to discuss the story of his school. But it is well to recall that he was not by any means alone in taking this view, and could claim the support of Locke, as well as the example of pious precedents on the continent.* It will also help to keep the whole in perspective if we bear in mind that it was common practice in Wesley's day to go to the other extreme. It was part of the indictment of Westminster already quoted that

"there are so many play daies beg'd and granted, that in some weekes the boys are from schoole full halfe the weeke, and now and then more than halfe . . . exposing them to idleness and all manner of vice."

Charles Wesley shared to the full his brother's aversion from play-days and supplied a metrical version:†

Let heathenish boys
In their pastimes rejoice,
And be foolishly happy at play:
Overstocked if they are,
We have nothing to spare,
Not a moment to trifle away.

Among those at that Conference of 1748 was one who was himself present only by invitation—Howell Harris, the leader of the revival in Wales. He jotted down notes in his *Journal*, and when he comes to the fourth of June there is the entry.

To the Foundery again to the Conference where I heard the whole affair of the school or Academy they are going to set up at Kingswood. Settled their diet, £1.10.0 for each scholar, 6 masters, 2 maids. The rules of the family, viz., at 4 private prayer, reading and singing private. At 5, public prayers. 6 breakfast. 7 to work—gather sticks or stones, or learn some trade, buttermaking, shoemaking, pick silk or wool &c. 8 to 10 English. 10 to 12 write. 12 to 1 work or walk, but always with their masters, then dinner. From 2 to 5 to their books, then to 6 work. No play, and to sleep from 8 to 4 the youngest,

* See Appendix II.
† The verses were published in *Hymns for Children*, 1763.

and the rest from 9 to 4. The school to consist of 7 classes before
they study the sciences after they go through Latin, Greek, Hebrew
and French. Named the authors for each class.*

It does not tally in every detail with what we know from other
sources, but it is a pretty good summary for one who was apparently hearing about it all for the first time. He passed on to
other topics, but when he came to the end of his notes for that
day he thought again of Wesley at his Conference—"seeing his
temptation, so many bowing to him, wholly submitting to him,
preachers, people, great and small." Howell Harris felt moved
to pray for him.

*Howell Harris's Visits to London, edited Tom Beynon, 1960, p.189.

III

THE SCHOOL IN WESLEY'S LIFETIME

(i) "The sons of our principal friends"

ON MIDSUMMER DAY, 1748, Wesley opened the school—

Friday the 24th, the day we appointed for opening the school at Kingswood, I preached there on "Train up a child in the way he should go; and when he is old he will not depart from it". My brother and I administered the Lord's Supper to many who came from afar. We then agreed on the general rules of the school, which we published presently after.*

Wesley's published sermon on the text he chose reflects faithfully his mother's views on the education of children. Many years before in 1732, he had elicited from her a detailed account of the methods she had employed in educating her family at Epworth.

Charles Wesley composed a hymn for the occasion, which for many years appeared in the *Collection of Hymns for the People called Methodists.*†

> Come, Father, Son and Holy Ghost,
> > To whom we for our children cry;
> The good desired and wanted most,
> > Out of thy richest grace supply;
> The sacred discipline be given,
> > To train and bring them up for heaven.

Another verse contained the lines—

> Unite the pair so long disjoined,
> Knowledge and vital piety.

* Wesley really tells us surprisingly little about the great occasion. Who were the "many who came from afar"? Were they parents from London bringing their boys?

We happen to know that Mr. Gwynne of Garth and his daughter Sally, soon to marry Charles Wesley, had arrived in Bristol a few days earlier, and on 25 June Charles Wesley carried them to see his Christian friends, "my principal ones especially at Kingswood". References to his preaching at Kingswood occur frequently in his journal for the period.

† The complete hymn, with two other similar hymns, may be found in the old hymn book, *A Collection of Hymns for the use of the People called Methodists*, 1780, Nos 473, 474, and 475.

John Wesley was at Kingswood at the most a day or two after the opening ceremony, for on June 27 he was at Stroud, and on the 29th at Evesham. Later in the summer he would be at Newcastle upon Tyne, and in September back among Lady Huntingdon's circle in London, whence he passed through Kingswood on on his way to Bristol and Cornwall. He intended the room he reserved to himself at Kingswood for an occasional lodging on his travels, and it is clear that he took his own absence for granted. He was under no illusions about some at least of the difficulties he might expect. He had written in February to his friend Mrs. Jones of Fonmon Castle in Wales:

At my return from Ireland, if not before, I believe the school in Kingswood will be opened. If your son comes there you will probably hear complaints, for the discipline will be exact . . .

The buildings of Wesley's day have long since disappeared, for the site was sold a hundred years later when the school moved from the outskirts of Bristol to its present site on the hills overlooking Bath. But the curious visitor who today makes the pilgrimage will not be altogether disappointed. The boundary walls are still there, and the buildings of the Kingswood Training and Classifying Schools do to some extent follow the layout of Wesley's school.*

With the help of the print of 1790 it is not difficult to picture Kingswood as Wesley built it. The New House was a solid rectangular block, with the dining hall on the ground floor; rooms for the staff, and the rooms reserved for Wesley himself on the first floor, and the one large dormitory above. Wesley may perhaps have had the block known as Gownboys at Charterhouse in mind. His buildings at Kingswood lacked, of course, the magnificence of those at Charterhouse, with their inwrought ceiling, but the accommodation for Wesley's fifty boys may not have been altogether different from that which housed him among the forty Gown boys of the Charterhouse.†

* The old site may readily be found from the Black Horse Inn on the main road through Kingswood, by proceeding along Black Horse Road and turning to the right into Kennard Road.

† The comparison was worked out in some detail by the Rev. E. W. Thompson when giving an address at Charterhouse in June 1937 (Epworth Press, 1937).

It was placed immediately adjoining the building of 1739/40, which served as chapel for the Kingswood society and housed also the day-schools for the colliers' children. The entrance of the chapel can just be discerned behind the trees on the left hand side of the picture.

Wesley would never reveal the source whence came the funds for the building. Dr. Coke and Mr. Moore in their *Life of Wesley*, published in the year after his death, insert the following paragraph into their brief but authoritative and accurate account of the school:

A circumstance respecting the erection of this edifice deserves to be remembered. Mr. Wesley was mentioning to a Lady, with whom he was in company in the neighbourhood of Bristol, his desire and design of erecting a *Christian School*, such as would not disgrace the apostolic age. The lady was so pleased with his views, that she immediately went to her scrutoire, and brought him five hundred pounds in bank-notes, desiring him to accept of them, and to enter upon his plan immediately. He did so. Afterwards, being in company with the same Lady, she enquired how the building went on; and whether he stood in need of further assistance. He informed her that he had laid out all the money he had received, and that he was three hundred pounds in debt; at the same time apologising, and entreating her not to consider it a concern of hers. But she immediately retired and brought him the sum he wanted.

The identity of the lady has remained a mystery. William Myles, in his invaluable *Chronological History of the people called Methodists*, quoted the above paragraph, and added "It would give me pleasure if I could record this lady's name; but though I cannot, I hope it is enrolled in the Lamb's Book of Life; and that her example will be followed by those who have it in their power to do good unto all men". Mr. Moore and Mr. Benson, "two of our senior preachers", had told him they heard Mr. Wesley relate the above anecdote. "I had often heard it", he says, "from sundry persons while labouring on the Bristol circuit, from 1800 to 1802."*

---

* Myles, 4th edition, 1813. Wesley's contemporaries clearly did not know who the lady was; but Jonathan Crowther in the 3rd edition of his *Portraiture of Methodism*, published in 1816, blandly inserted the name of Lady Maxwell, one of Wesley's friends and supporters who lived in Edinburgh. In his well-known and widely read *Life of Wesley*, published in 1820, Southey followed Crowther, inserting a long paragraph about Lady Maxwell; though

There were to be six masters for fifty boys. This can surely only mean that the masters were themselves to continue their studies whilst at the school and find there an environment in which they might follow a semi-monastic rule. Four of the six were in fact drawn from that little group of young men who had become Wesley's lay helpers, and some of them had been attending the Conferences of the preceding years. Their spiritual welfare had been very much in his mind. It had been minuted that assistants should regard themselves as learners rather than as teachers, "as young students in the university for whom a method of study is expedient in the highest degree". The method advised both echoed the rules of the Holy Club at Oxford in the thirties and foreshadowed the regime to be inaugurated at Kingswood—to rise always at four in the morning, to spend an hour every morning and every evening in meditation and prayer and in reading "some close practical book of divinity". Wesley would see to it that there was no lack of the right books at the school.

Dr. John Jones was appointed senior master "for the languages", and must be regarded as the first headmaster, so far as anyone can be so regarded in Wesley's day. He was a comparatively recent recruit to the movement. Born in Cardiganshire in 1721, he matriculated at Trinity College, Oxford in 1736, and appears as an adherent of Howell Harris in 1742, when he was seeking ordination. He graduated M.A. 1742, and B.Med. 1745, and again sought ordination in 1746. A striking letter to Howell Harris has survived*—

"Finding that the Bishop will not ordain me", he wrote, "nor assign me any reason for not doing it I intend as soon as possible to wait on the Archbishop, and lay my case before him . . . O to what a low state is this poor Church fallen, when her Bishops are enemies

---

he betrayed some uneasiness about the dating, mentioning that the school was founded "long before she became a member". Actually the dating rules her out decisively, for she would have been about six years old when the school was opened (*Life of Darcy, Lady Maxwell,* by the Rev. John Lancaster, 2nd edition, 1826, note to page 6).

More recently it has been suggested (see J. S. Simon, *Advance of Methodism,* 1925, page 92) that the lady was the wife of Colonel Gumley, who at a much later date made over the lease of her house in Chesterfield Street to Charles Wesley. But this seems to be no more than a conjecture by a Methodist antiquary, George Stampe of Grimsby, and no evidence is offered to support the suggestion.

Selected Trevecka Letters 1742–7, edited Gomer M. Roberts, 1956, p.190.

JOHN WESLEY
from the portrait by Nathaniel Hone, 1766
in the National Portrait Gallery

CHARLES WESLEY
by Henry Hudson
c. 1749

LADY HUNTINGDON
from the portrait by an
unknown artist in the
National Portrait Gallery

from the heart-roots to the life of religion and refuse to ordain candidates for no other reason, but because they suspect them to be Christians."

He failed to secure ordination, notwithstanding a testimonium signed by four neighbouring clergymen; and finding himself not altogether happy among Howell Harris' adherents, shortly afterwards joined Wesley in London. "John Jones (late a zealous Calvinist) preached for the first time at the Foundery", wrote Wesley on November 30, 1746. His accession to the movement was an event of considerable importance to the Wesleys. His name at once begins to appear first in the lists— "He (Wesley) settled John Jones next to him and his brother", wrote Howell Harris of the Conference of 1748, "then Mr. Maxfield, and the rest to look on themselves as students or pupils in the university."* His name stands first in the list of masters of Kingswood School in 1748. We shall of course meet him again.

Thomas Richards, whose name is placed next after that of John Jones "for the languages" came like him from Cardiganshire, and had been two years his senior at Trinity College, Oxford. He had thus matriculated in time to have been influenced by the Holy Club, before the Wesleys sailed for Georgia. He had been with Wesley from the start, being one of the "three young men who desired to serve me and labour when and where I should direct". He may be glimpsed here and there in the records, preaching, acting as a trustee of the earliest properties—"late of Trinity College, Oxford, gentleman"—endeavouring to reconcile Cennick with Wesley in Bristol, attending the first Conference in 1744, and being invited to Bath by Lady Huntingdon in 1745, where his preaching was attended with great power. He would not, however, remain long at Kingswood.

With John Jones as a man of learning must be ranked Walter Sellon.† "I know of none fitter for training up the young men in learning", Charles Wesley would be writing a year or two later,

---

* *Howell Harris's Visits to London*, edited Tom Beynon, 1960, p.188.

† His name is indeed placed by Myles in his *Chronological History* above that of John Jones in a list of five masters "for the classics" 1748–60, and he thus came to be regarded as the first headmaster. (e.g. Tyerman's *Life and Times of the Rev. John Wesley*, 1871, and *History of Kingswood School*, 1898). But this does not agree with Wesley's listing, and there seems no valid reason for according him priority over John Jones.

C

"than yourself or John Jones." Sellon was the grandson of a Huguenot minister who had fled to England on the revocation of the Edict of Nantes in 1685.* Born in 1715, he had not up to the year 1745 been introduced to Wesley. He told Wesley that he had formerly condemned him as an innovator, and had pitied those who followed him. But having heard him preach, and having read his sermon on Scriptural Christianity preached before the University of Oxford in 1744, his opinions concerning him and his followers were entirely changed.† After some two years at the school he would become one of the young clergymen associated with the Countess of Huntingdon, and curate of two churches near her home at Ashby, Breedon-on-the-Hill and Smisby. Like John Jones, Sellon enjoyed the confidential friendship of both the Wesleys, and would stand faithfully by them in their contentions both with those who wished to secede from the Church, and with the Calvinists.

These three young men were supported by others of lesser attainments but ample piety. Richard Moss had been converted by Wesley after a difficult early life, and had become one of his preachers. He acted also on occasion as Wesley's travelling companion, both before and after his appointment to Kingswood. Two of his letters describing attempts made by the press gang to seize him, and their forbearance when boldly confronted by him in his capacity as a Methodist preacher, were printed by Wesley in his *Journal* in 1745. He attended the Conference that year; and, like Richards, was invited by Lady Huntingdon to Bath. "Mr. Moss", says her biographer, "resided for some time with her Ladyship, who had a very sincere affection for him, and showed him many acts of kindness." He was later ordained with her help.

William Spencer was another of the young men converted in the early days of the movement. "Billy Spencer was with us from the beginning", wrote Charles Wesley some years later. In 1744

* Sellon's grandfather was a member of a notable family. He was the brother of Jean de Sellon, who was the maternal great-grandfather of Cavour, and paternal grandfather of Count Jean Jacque de Sellon, to whom Switzerland is indebted for the abolition of the death penalty. For an account of the family see Thomas Jay Williams, *Priscilla Lydia Sellon,* S.P.C.K. 1950.

† Tyerman's life of Fletcher of Madeley, *Wesley's Designated Successor,* 1882, pp.100 and 152-3, Sellon was later (1770-1792) Vicar of Ledsham, Yorkshire.

he is mentioned as a member of the family at Wesley's head-quarters at the Foundery in London.* With John Jones he was to prove one of the most stable elements in the early staff, and within a month or two we shall see him writing to Wesley about the spiritual progress of the school. Abraham Grou was the French master, but about him we have no information other than the reference by Wesley which follows shortly.

Besides the masters there was the housekeeper. Wesley's converts had included women of piety and ability, and scope was found for some of them as "sisters" in the centres in London and in Newcastle. Now at Kingswood one Mary Davey, a widow, was appointed housekeeper. It was evidently a position of consequence. There were four maidservants, and one R— T—, described by Wesley as "our man". All was no doubt very neat and plain. Wesley had been insisting on an almost Quaker-like simplicity of attire among the Methodists, and Kingswood was to set an example to all.

Within two or three months there were twenty-eight pupils in the school. School work seems to have begun on June 28, which is elsewhere recorded as the date on which the school "opened". The The hard core of the curriculum was provided by emphasis on Latin Grammar and texts. "Latin I look upon as absolutely necessary to a gentleman", Locke had written, and Wesley equally took it for granted. A comparison with the steps taken by Dr. Samuel Johnson some ten years earlier, when he had started a school near Lichfield, is instructive. Johnson had set himself to ascertain the practice of Charterhouse and Westminster before drawing up his own plan "of a method more rational than those commonly practised". In his list of authors we recognise many that appeared at Kingswood. When the formation of nouns and verbs had been "perfectly mastered" there followed Corderius, Erasmus, Eutropius, and Cornelius Nepos. Wesley's scheme was not dissimilar. The general plan of education, wrote John Hampson who was a boy at Kingswood somewhat later, was well calculated to give the pupils a good share of classical learning. "He permitted no translation whatever; and his grammars, which are very concise, are in English. The order in which the

* See a mention in a letter to Joseph Cownley, May 1764: W.H.S. Vol. XXVIII, p.150 and Vol.XIV, p.27 Whether or not Cennick and Spencer were ever masters at the colliers' school, as has often been stated, is open to question—see Appendix I.

higher books were read was much the same as in other schools."
Arithmetic, Geography and Chronology make an appearance as
the boys move up the school. In the seventh and eighth classes Greek
appears, with the Greek Testament and six books of the Iliad.

Little books specially prepared for the school at once began to
flow from Felix Farley's printing press at Bristol. First came a
Short Latin Grammar of 37 pages,* and a *Short English Grammar*
of 12 pages. They were soon followed by a whole series bearing
the dedication

In Usum Juventutis Christianae
Edidit Ecclesiae Anglicanae Presbyter

showing that Wesley had himself undertaken the preparation of
the text-books needed for his school. Most of them were reprinted
from time to time and kept on sale until the early years of the
nineteenth century. There was a kind of Latin exercise entitled
Corderii Colloquia Selecta—conversations arranged according to
their difficulty to the beginner in Latin, the subjects being moral
or religious. There were extracts from history in five books, moral
advice varied with anecdote; and there were carefully edited
editions of Sallust (110 pages) a Cornelius Nepos, and a volume of
excerpts from Ovid, Virgil, Horace, Juvenal, Persius and Martial;
and so on.†

Wesley's plan differed from that in other schools chiefly by
the choice of his tract *Instructions for Children* as the material for
exercises in translation to and from Latin; by the inclusion,
usually as an early morning lesson, of historical works descriptive
of the ways of the early Christians, *The Manners of the Ancient
Christians*; and by the prominence given to two accounts of
dedicated lives by which he had himself been deeply influenced—
The Life and Death of Mr. Thomas Haliburton, and the *Life of
Monsieur de Renty.*

To the latter especially Wesley attached the greatest importance. Gaston de Renty had played a leading part in founding
a religious order, the Company of the Blessed Sacrament, in
seventeenth-century France. He had turned his castle into a hostel
for victims of scurvy and dedicated his entire fortune to charity.

---

* Myles says it was "written" by John Jones, and certainly we hear later of
Wesley "perfecting" the Latin grammar for a second edition.

† The volumes will be found listed in Richard Green, *Wesley Bibliography,*
1896.

His life had been written by a Jesuit, Père de Saint-Jure, and Wesley had made a careful abbreviated version which he never ceased to commend.*

There was, too, a special Kingswood edition of Thomas à Kempis' *De Christo Imitando,* an abridgement of 143 pages. It is a beautiful little book and copies are seldom seen.

It is not easy to drop back into the mid-eighteenth century, and an effort of the imagination is needed to recapture those early days in the school at Kingswood. We must picture John Jones, Walter Sellon and their colleagues calling the boys as near four in the morning as might be, and, as soon as they were dressed setting them to their prayers. The masters had to see that the school made a proper appearance at the public service at five o'clock in the chapel adjoining the school, where would be gathered some of Wesley's earliest converts from the colliery population round about. These five o'clock morning services were a great feature of early Methodism, in winter as well as in summer, and we may think of the congregation making their way through the dark mornings with the help of many lanterns. The service over, there was work in the garden, or indoors, till breakfast. We must try to picture the simple meals at the long tables set college-fashion in the dining room. Then the school begins, at seven. There would be little groups gathered round the several masters, for there do seem to have been six masters and twenty-eight scholars in those early days. More school work in the afternoon; and again in the evening the religious exercises, at five the hour of private prayer and singing, then supper, and the public service in the chapel at seven.

On Sundays there was the public service in the chapel at eight, and at nine they went to the parish church. There was no parish church close at hand in those early years. Part of the forest lay in the out-parish of St. Philip and St. Jacob, a long way off in Bristol; part lay in the parish of Bitton, down by the river half-way to Bath. The school was close to the parish boundary, actually just within the parish of Bitton. But it seems that in the early days it looked to St. Philip and St. Jacob, for the records

---

* For the importance of De Renty see H. Daniel-Rops, *The Church in the Seventeenth Century,* p.9 off, 110–111, and for his influence on Wesley *The Church in the Eighteenth Century,* p. 174. Would Wesley, he asks, found something like the Company of the Blessed Sacrament?

show that some of the boarders were buried there. We must therefore imagine the boys making their way down Two-Mile-Hill and back again. On either side of the road would have lain the remnants of the forest, by this time reduced to scrub or waste. All has of course long since been obliterated by urban development, but something of the old-world flavour still lingers not far off at Crew's Hole and Conham, by the side of the Avon. The journey must surely have been something of an adventure, for the colliers of Kingswood had by no means all been converted to quiet ways by the Wesleys. The record of rioting continues down the years; thus in 1749, the school's first year, many of the colliers ranged about the country-side armed with cudgels and hay knives destroying the newly erected turnpike gates. Four years later many hundreds of colliers rioted for a week or more, extorting money from travellers and intimidating the neighbourhood. The school seems however to have escaped molestation. The Bristol to which they went had been vividly described by Pope a few years earlier—the first view of the twenty-odd pyramids of the glass-houses smoking over the city, the old walls, the gates, and the hundreds of ships, many of them engaged in the slave trade, their masts as thick as they could stand by one another. The scene reminded him of the Thames at Deptford. The city was given over to trade, and lacked the gaiety and politeness for which Bath was already famed. Whether the boys walked down to church, or went by conveyance of some kind we do not know. They had to be back again by one o'clock, for then "they dine and sing".

If the routine was in other ways subdued, it did not lack hymn-singing. In the services in the chapel the boys must have become familiar with the little collections containing Charles Wesley's hymns that would later echo round the world: "Christ, whose glory fills the skies", "O, for a thousand tongues to sing", "Love divine, all loves excelling", and many others. There were hymns for Christmas—"Hark how all the welkin rings", "Let earth and heaven combine"; hymns for Easter—"Christ the Lord is risen today"; hymns for the sacraments—"Victim divine, Thy grace we claim". Charles Wesley was often there in person to give out his own hymns, two lines at a time, as was then the custom. "I rode over to our children in Kingswood", he noted on October 22, 1748, " and was much comforted by their simplicity and love."

In the spring of 1749 he married Sarah Gwynne, who was noted for her lovely singing voice, and they made their home in Stokes Croft in Bristol till 1771. His *Journal* makes frequent mention of his preaching and administering the sacrament at Kingswood.

There were, too, hymns specially written for children. "I am writing an hymn-book for the scholars", wrote Charles Wesley to a parent a little later. We cannot be sure, but it could well be that a little collection of hymns and prayers, undated but believed to have been compiled by Charles Wesley at about this time, was that written by him for use at Kingswood.* If so it affords an interesting glimpse into what went on in those hours set aside for singing and prayer. The little booklet, the earliest entitled *Hymns for Children*, contains nine hymns. The first is "Gentle Jesus, meek and mild", the second "Lamb of God, I fain would be", the third "Come, let us join the hosts above"; five of them had been printed in *Hymns and Sacred Poems*, 1742. It contains, too, prayers to help children with their morning and evening devotions. Perhaps Charles Wesley felt that the younger children needed more help than they had so far been given— "As soon as ever you are awake in the morning, dear child, strive as much as you can, to keep all worldly thoughts out of your mind. . . ." They were to pray for God's blessing, not only for their relations, but also for their "Governors". If we are right in thinking the book was for Kingswood, it would be the masters who would be the "Governors".

Always there was the effort so to conduct the school that the pupils would acquit themselves well when next the Founder should call in on his travels, and "enquire particularly" into their progress in both religion and learning. At first all went well, and the boys were not slow to respond to the atmosphere of piety in which they found themselves. It is not surprising, for they came from the homes of Wesley's friends and supporters. Much was expected of children in such families, and Wesley did not hesitate to put clearly before them in his *Instructions for Children* the full force of his convictions about the terrors of the Lord. The appeal for response was often powerfully and effectively put in the services at Kingswood.

* The *Hymns for Children* is undated, and authorship has been questioned. For an interesting note see article *Charles Wesley's Hymns for Children* by Dr. Frank Baker, W.H.S., Vol. XXXI, p.81.

Nothing would please the parents better than the kind of news they began to receive from the school. By August 1748 one of the masters, William Spencer, was writing to Wesley to give him "a particular account of the work of God that continues among the little ones". It was sent, he said, at the desire of Richard Moss, whose soul had been for some time exceedingly sorrowful on account of the ill behaviour of some of the children, especially "R. J.". This is the son of that Mrs. Jones to whom Wesley had been writing before the school opened about the exact discpline to be expected there. Moss had been expounding the eighth chapter of St. Mark to them. As he spoke he had found "the spirit of God was with the Word". Some of the boys were pricked to the heart, and cried out "What shall I do to be saved?". Moss had called Walter Sellon, Grou and Spencer, and they had joined in singing and prayer till eight o'clock. In such strain the letter continued, ending with a postscript—

"The family give their duty to you. We all love one another, and each esteems the other better than himself."

In November the housekeeper, Mary Davey, was writing too in ecstatic strain—

"The spirit of this family is a resemblance of the household above. As far as I can discern they are given up to God, and pursue but the one great end. If anyone is afraid that this school will eclipse and darken all others . . . I believe it is not a groundless fear."

Many years later Wesley would print these letters with others of a similar edifying character in his *Arminian Magazine*.*

It was not only the children at Kingswood who were caught up in the excitement. Much else was happening at this time to encourage the Wesleys. Whitefield had returned that summer from some four years in America, and differences between the leaders were held in check. His preaching was as popular as ever

---

* *Arminian Magazine,* 1778, p.533. The letter is of interest as giving us the names of a few boys otherwise unknown to us. They include Gabriel Wayne, whose convictions were soon "trifled away". He was no doubt the son of that Mr. Wayne who lived near by at Conham, and was partner with Sir Abraham Elton in extensive copper and brass works at Crew's Hole and Hanham. Charles Wesley was a frequent visitor at the Waynes' house. W.H.S., Vol. VI, pp.138–9.

and reinforced the systematic organization of societies by Wesley.
Both Whitefield and Wesley were prevailed upon to preach to
titled and influential audiences gathered by Lady Huntingdon in
her house in Chelsea. The scene is vividly described in a fragment
of Wesley's *Journal* covering a fortnight in September 1748;
many were deeply moved, and Lady Huntingdon was in tears.*
The coincidence in timing of the early piety at Kingswood with
the high-watermark—or perhaps we should say the first of several
high-watermarks—of the impact of Methodism on society at
large helps to explain much at Kingswood. It was fulfilling
Wesley's expectations. Lady Huntingdon would in the following
summer take a house in Clifton, a short drive in her carriage
from Kingswood. Some of the masters were, as we have seen,
already well known to her, and she would soon be easing the
path to ordination for several of them. She was, too, now on terms
of the warmest friendship with Charles Wesley, and when a year
or two later his young wife fell a victim to smallpox faithfully
attended her twice a day through her illness.

John Wesley was himself at Kingswood on February 21, 1749,
and made the school his headquarters for several weeks whilst
he nursed a project for publishing "a complete library for those
that fear God". He had some thought, he told his banker friend
Blackwell, of printing on a finer paper, and with a larger letter,
all that was most valuable in the English tongue in three score
or four score volumes. The Christian Library, as it was known,
became an important pioneer effort in making books available to
a wider public. It began with *The Epistles of the Apostolic Fathers*,
and the preface was dated from Kingswood at this time.

He collected, too, some of his preachers at the school. "My
design", he wrote, "was to have as many of our preachers here as
could possibly be spared; and to read lectures to them every day,
as I did to my pupils in Oxford . . . I had seventeen of them in
all." There were moments which were to Wesley and his brother
Charles a foretaste of fulfilment:

"I spent half an hour with my brother at Kingswood," wrote
Charles in his *Journal,* "which is now very much like a college.
Twenty one boarders are there, and a dozen students, his sons and

---

* *Journal of John Wesley,* Standard edition, edited Curnock, 1909–16,
Vol. VIII, p.158.

pupils in the gospel. I believe he is now laying the foundation of many generations."

Henceforth in that eventful year of 1749 Wesley had but little time to supervise affairs at Kingswood. On April 3, he set out for his third extended visit to Ireland, accompanied on this occasion by Grace Murray, whom he had appointed housekeeper at the Orphan House at Newcastle. She was a young widow. Her little boy Jackie Murray was among the early pupils at Kingswood. Wesley had been in Newcastle in the late summer of 1748, and there, by her "inexpressible tenderness" when nursing him whilst he was ill, she had engaged his affections. At the end of March 1749 she was at Kingswood, and it was perhaps then that she brought her little son there, before setting out with Wesley for a missionary tour in Ireland.* Wesley noted in his diary how she was "in every capacity an helpmeet for me". Among her many excellent qualities was the fact that if he married her she would "desire nothing more than she had before . . . And would cheerfully consent, that our children (if any) should be wholly brought up at Kingswood . . .". Before they had left Ireland their affection so deepened that they entered into a contract of marriage.

They returned late in July, and on the 24th after a stormy crossing landed at Bristol Quay. On Tuesday the 25th there is the entry in Wesley's *Journal*—

"I rode over to Kingswood and enquired particularly into the state of the school there. I was concerned to find that several of the Rules had been habitually neglected. I judged it necessary therefore to lessen the family—suffering none to remain therein who were not clearly satisfied with them and determined to observe them all."

What this serious entry meant we shall see in a moment, but first let us follow Wesley himself a little further in this time of crisis for his school. He stayed almost a week and on August 1 spent a solemn hour with the children at Kingswood, and "having settled all things there" returned to London. A little later he set out for the North. In the September of that year, had it not been for the intervention of his brother Charles he might well have married Grace Murray. The story has often been told, and is no

---

* Charles Wesley mentions her presence at the end of March, and speaks of her with Mary Davey, the housekeeper at Kingswood, as "our beloved sisters".

part of the history of Kingswood School. But it was for Wesley one of the great crises of his life, and the timing of it so relevant to the story of early Kingswood that reference to it helps us to picture those early months in the life of the school. By mid-October it was all over; Grace Murray was married to another, John Bennet, and Wesley all but heart-broken. By November he was back at Kingswood, writing part of the sermons he had promised to publish that winter.

"I was concerned to find", he had written in July, "that several of the Rules had been habitually neglected." We do not know exactly what had happened. But the whole scheme as Wesley had conceived it had, of course, placed an incredible burden on the human beings who made up his Christian family at Kingswood. For one thing, their singlemindedness had been distracted by thoughts of matrimony. Impossible as it must have seemed but a year before, both Charles Wesley and John Jones were now married, for the latter had in February married Elizabeth Mann, herself a leader of one of the women's classes in London; and John Jones's colleague, Thomas Richards, and Mary Davey, the housekeeper, would be married ere long. This was natural enough; but besides all this, gossip about John Wesley's own relationship with Grace Murray had thrown all the societies into a ferment. Was it any wonder that already a less austere spirit had begun to pervade the school?

What too, had been happening at the school in those last months whilst Wesley was in the North? By great good fortune a little packet of letters was preserved by Mrs. Robert Jones of Fonmon Castle which throws a revealing light on events that year. She was a widow, a friend of the Wesleys and sent her son to be one of the first boys at Kingswood.* We have already seen how

---

* Her husband Robert Jones came of a Cromwellian family of consequence in Glamorganshire, with an ancient seat at Fonmon Castle, some dozen miles west of Cardiff. Both he and his wife had become adherents of the Welsh evangelist Howell Harris, and in 1741 Charles Wesley had called on them. "Mr. Jones received me very courteously", he wrote in his Journal, ". . . (we) found we were contemporaries at the same college." His early death in 1742 was a blow to the Wesleys, but his widow remained their friend, and continued to consult them about her son, named Robert after his father.
  Fonmon Castle is today the home of Sir Hugo Boothby, Bt., descended on the maternal side from the Jones family of the seventeenth and eighteenth centuries. The papers here quoted are deposited in the County archives of Glamorganshire in Cardiff.

Wesley had warned her about the exact discipline to be expected there. There are first three letters from Charles Wesley, one which carries the date October 30, 1749. The meaning is clear enough.

"My dear Sister,—Let not your heart be troubled. Before this reaches you, you will probably see our poor fugitive; seduced by that wicked boy Williams. If I might advise, you will deal very tenderly with him; and if he is sensible of his fault, *bring* rather than send him back. The ringleaders my brother will never more receive into the school, but for Robin I will be bond myself, and he shall not be corrected at all if you can have confidence in him that he will be mischievous no more. What you can do with him at home I see not. Inevitable ruin will be the effect of absolute liberty. But I trust his father's prayers, and yours, and the Church's shall yet prevail for him."

and again,

"Bring my ward hither to me and he shall not have an angry word. My love and blessing and prayers attend him. He will yet make amends."

and again,

"My dear Sister,—My brother consents to try them for a little longer—Jackie Williams for a week only. If he behaves wickedly in any respect at the week's end Mr Jones is to send him home. If he keeps his promises we shall have saved a soul from Death. But however he behaves he is not to converse at all with the other boys.

"If Robin will not be led he must be driven; I mean whipt through Westminster or some other great school. But I hope he will yet know his true interest."

Charles Wesley had evidently carried a large measure of responsibility for the school while his brother had been away. By November John Wesley was back at Kingswood, and himself writing to Mrs. Jones at Fonmon Castle.

"My dear Sister—On Saturday my brother and I were both determined that none of these children should come to the school any more. But the masters interceded so earnestly for them that we were at length induced so far to change our purpose as to take them on trial from week to week. If they behave well they may remain with us. If not we must put them quite away, that they may not corrupt the rest. I have ordered that they shall not be corrected at all for what is past; nor will it ever be mentioned if they give no fresh occasion.

I do not think it will be right for your son to come again unless he is thoroughly sensible of his fault. In that case I should hope for a lasting change. May God be your comfort and support. I am, Your very affectionate brother and servant."

Besides Wesley's letter there is one to Mrs. Jones from one of the masters, Walter Sellon, which gives precious glimpses of life at the school. It was written the day before Wesley's.

"I received your kind letter wrote, I find, before the late unhappy affair happened. I doubt not you have had grief enough since. By what I have felt I can in some measure feel what a parent must feel. But I have still hope that even this shall work together for good, I in some measure see it already. All Master Bobby's companions are returned to us except T. Roades, who by his mother's advice was the first that had any notion of going away in such a manner. After consulting last Sunday what should be done with them it was resolved that as it was not known what was the will of God in bringing them here again that they should be tried from week to week, and if they committed any daring crime they should be immediately sent home. Mr. John Wesley accordingly met all the children together, told them his resolution, and the three delinquents were given up to my care never to leave me day or night. And I hope I shall be able by God's assistance to give a good account of them yet. That they may not be disheartened and continually remarked by the rest on account of this separation three more are joined with them who always out of school hours walk with me or sit with me in my own room. The same care is to be taken with regard to your son if he ever consents to come again. Mr. Wesley has given Mr. Spencer the same charge of him—always to have him under his eye with two or three more; so that I believe for the future all combinations will be cut off. J. Williams is indeed an artful boy, but I hope God will give us prudence to countervail all his art. It was in vain to hinder Bobby's and his correspondence by day when they lay in the same room by night . . . ."

Sellon could not but think it was a scheme of the devil's contriving to bring odium on the work of God. He enclosed a letter to Master Bobby. Whether Robin Jones ever returned to Kingswood is uncertain, but there are further letters from Charles Wesley to his mother. On December 31, 1749 he is writing—

"My dear Friend—I am sorry we had not more time together at Bristol and must therefore write my thoughts about your poor wild boy, for whom no one can be more concerned than me except yourself. Now is the Crisis. The next step is irrevocable. And it appears to me as well as my brother and Mr. Lloyd* and our truest most disinterested friends that as soon as he is let loose in a great school his ruin is inevitable. His temporal ruin, I mean; for as to his soul, there is not the smallest chance for that (if I may so speak) in the modern way of education. You will ask what else can you do with him— I know the objections to Mr. Meriton are not groundless. In some respects he is not such as we would wish him" (The Rev. John Meriton had been associated with the Wesleys, and although he did not meet with their full approbation they advised Mrs. Jones to place Robin in his care.) "Yet as he has such authority over the youth can you do better than have him to his care, suppose another half year, in which time he may be subdued and tamed as that you may trust him with less hazard to others' care."

He writes again on January 29, 1749/50

"I am most concerned for poor thoughtless Robin. What will you do with him? I ask; but cannot advise. Williams is going away. Mrs. Hardwick is come, a blessing to our family and a mother. We feel the good effects already. I am writing an hymn book for the scholars."

Robin Jones did not follow in father's footsteps, but his subsequent career is no part of the story of Kingswood, and here we must leave him. His mother continued a faithful friend of the Wesleys into old age. A portrait of her son as a young man, by Sir Joshua Reynolds, hangs in the hall of Fonmon Castle, together with a family group by Hogarth.†

Whitefield wrote to Benjamin Franklin a letter in which we can surely catch an echo of what was being said in defence of the pious regime at Kingswood. The subject is the new "academy" with which Benjamin Franklin was concerned in Philadelphia.‡ The date is February 1750; Whitefield had been at Kingswood a

---

* Samuel Lloyd, a banker in London, cousin of Mrs. Charles Wesley.

† Felix Farley's *Bristol Journal* later reported his marriage to an heiress, the rise of his family, and an adventure on Hounslow Heath fatal to a highwayman.

‡ Which was to become the University of Philadelphia.

few days earlier. The plan that Franklin had sent, says Whitefield, is certainly well calculated to promote polite literature; but religion is mentioned too late, and too soon passed over—

".... As we are all creatures of a day, as our whole life is but one small point between two eternities, it is reasonable to suppose that the grand end of every Christian institution for forming tender minds should be to convince them of their natural depravity, of the means of recovering out of it, and of the necessity of preparing for the enjoyment of the Supreme Being in a future state. Arts and sciences may be built on this, and serve to embellish the super-structure, but without this there cannot be any good foundation."

The main thing, he says, will be to get proper masters, who will constantly care for the welfare of the youth committed to them. There might, too, he thinks, be a "well approved Christian orator who should visit and take pains with every class, and teach them early how to speak, and read, and pronounce well". This would be of great service, whether the youth be intended "for the pulpit, the bar, or any other profession whatsoever". Here too we can detect something of the intentions at Kingswood : as at the other classical schools of the day, which prepared for Oxford and Cambridge, and at some of the Dissenting Academies too, ordination was a prominent objective, but other professions had their place also.

It may come as a surprise to the reader to learn that girls as well as boys were taken, but such was in fact the case. They were boarded, Wesley tells us, in the old house, as distinct from the boys boarded in the new. It is clear that they had to abide by the rules, for a copy of the *Short Account of Kingswood School* exists amended to provide for girls, at a fee of £10 a year as against the £14 for boys. "Girls are taken in betwixt 6 & 12 to teach them reading, writing and sewing, and if it be desired English Grammar, Arithmetic, and all sorts of needlework". Music is heavily crossed out. Among those who entrusted their children to Wesley's care at Kingswood was the well-known clergyman, the Rev. William Grimshaw of Haworth, who had embarked on evangelical activities in his parish and the surrounding district. Grimshaw sent to Kingswood not only his unruly son, but his thirteen-year-old daughter Jane. Her case is well docu-

mented, for she died at the school in January 1750, and her
brother John sent her father a pathetic account of her illness and
devout ending, happy in the knowledge of her salvation. Her
death is mentioned too by Charles Wesley in his *Journal*—"a
daughter of our brother Grimshaw's was just departed in the
Lord".*

Of Jane Grimshaw's mistress Wesley had a very high opinion
indeed.

"When Molly Maddern taught a few children at Kingswood", he
wrote many years later, "I saw a truly Christian school. To make the
children Christians was her first care; afterwards they were taught
what women need to learn.† I saw another Christian school at
Leytonstone, under the care of Miss Bosanquet. I do not remember
I discovered any defect, either in the former or the latter; I observed
nothing done which I wished to be omitted, nothing omitted which
I wished to have done".‡

He was using Molly Maddern's success as a standard for
another school which had not quite answered his expectations.
What was the matter in this other school he could hardly say—
"good breeding I love, but how difficult it is to keep it quite clear
of affectation. . . ." But he could point to examples of Mrs.
Maddern's success. Mrs. Castleman was one of her scholars—
"she is genteel, yet she is a Christian".§ Perhaps there were also a
few girls who went by day to Kingswood, for in 1751 we find
Wesley writing to a friend to tell him that a certain Miss Lloyd
might board for £12 a year with a serious and prudent woman—
"and for forty shillings a year more be by day at one of the best

* For a full account see Frank Baker, *William Grimshaw* 1708–63, 1963
p.165ff. Grimshaw's son soon afterwards went home with his father and
caused him much distress.

† Her name is given in the Grimshaw narrative as Mrs. Francis, and it
is safe to identify her with the Molly Francis, the mention of whose name
in "an idle tale" told at Bristol or Kingswood in July 1749 at the time of
Wesley's visit upset Grace Murray; and further to assume that Molly Francis
later became Molly Maddern by marriage to John Maddern, one of the
masters at Kingswood from 1750 onwards.

‡ To Miss Bishop, about a school she maintained at Keynsham. *Letters
of John Wesley*, Standard edition, Telford, 1931, VII, p.62.

§ Her maiden name was Letitia Fisher, and her husband was a Bristol
surgeon. The Castlemans were good friends of the Wesleys, and John Wesley
often stayed with them when in Bristol in later life.

JAMES ROUQUET
master *c.* 1752–4
from an engraving by
Ames, 1777, in the
Bristol Reference Library

St George's Church,
Kingswood, erected by
Bishop Butler in 1756
(see pp. 52, 60) from a
watercolour by
H. O'Neill, 1823

JOHN HENDERSON
pupil *c*. 1760– (see pp. 85–6)
from the frontispiece to *Malvern
Hills with Minor Poems and Essays*
by Joseph Cottle, fourth edition
1829

JOSEPH BENSON
master 1766–8 (see pp.
64ff.) from an engraving
by Ridley in the
Methodist Archives

schools in Bristol." It may, or may not, be a reference to Kingswood.*

The records of the burials in the vestry of St. Philip and St. Jacob in Bristol show besides that of Jane Grimshaw what must have seemed to Wesley to have been the work of Satan himself—

> 1752 Apr Walter Sellon Mr. Westly's boarder
> Drowned in ye Rain water Siston

He was no doubt a little son of Walter Sellon, one of the first masters at the school. A big underground water "siston" is still known to exist close to the site of the pump at Old Kingswood.

The presence at the school of the children of Grimshaw of Haworth, of Walter Sellon's son, of Grace Murray's little son Jackie Murray, and the reference quoted above to Wesley's own thoughts of sending any children that he and Grace Murray might have had if they had married, help us to picture the early intentions of the founder regarding his school. They add meaning to the phrase that the school was intended for "the children of our principal friends". It was not only for the sons of the Joneses of Fonmon Castle who might otherwise have sent their children to the "great" or public schools, but also for the sons of the evangelically minded clergy and others associated with the movement.†

In March 1750, Wesley records that he "talked at large with the masters of Kingswood School concerning the children and the management". They all agreed that "one of the boys studiously laboured to corrupt the rest". Wesley would not suffer him to

---

* Letter to Samuel Lloyd, July 8, 1751, W. H. S. XXVI, p.63. What he recommends, he says, would be far safer than boarding at one of those schools which would soon root out the very notion of heart-religion; and be likewise considerably less expensive, entrance money and other perquisites being saved.

† John and Charles Wesley had too a nephew for whose education they accepted responsibility, and undated letters in the Methodist archives from Charles Wesley to the boy's mother Patty raise the question, did he too go to Kingswood? Little Westley Hall was born in 1742 and died in 1757 of smallpox. Would John write to John Jones about him, asks one of the letters. Charles Wesley in another refers to the mother's desire to see her son "than which nothing is more reasonable". Charles would do his best to bring the boy to meet her at Bath whenever she set the time, but he has to add that Mr. Jones allows no breaking up at Barthelmy-tide. The references seem to suggest the time when John Jones was in charge at Kingswood 1748–1751 or so, but Kingswood is nowhere actually mentioned, and some uncertainty remains.

stay any longer under the roof, but sent him home that very hour.* Trouble evidently continued, for Wesley records that on return in July from the Irish tour of 1750 he walked over to Kingswood and found the family lessened considerably.

> "I wonder", he wrote, "how I am withheld from dropping the whole design; so many difficulties have continually attended it: Yet if this counsel is of God, it shall stand; and all hindrances shall turn into blessings."

By September the numbers were down to eighteen, and Wesley determined to purge the house thoroughly. "Two more of the children (one of them exquisitely wicked) I sent home without delay." Mary Davey, Thomas Richards, Richard Moss and three of the maids were gone away already, Walter Sellon and Abraham Grou went "after", which apparently means that they left. Only two masters, John Jones and William Spencer remained, with Mrs. Hardwick, one maid and sixteen scholars.†

His determination not to fail at this time is marked by his own presence at the school. He reached Kingswood on the evening of September 24, and the next day selected passages of Milton for the eldest children to transcribe and repeat weekly. His Journal entries give us a glimpse of the Founder among his pupils—

> "Thur. 27—I went into the school, and heard half the children their lessons, and then selected passages of the *Moral and Sacred Poems*.
> Fri. 28—I heard the other half of the children.
> Sat. 29—I was with them from four to five in the morning. I spent most of the day in revising Kennet's *Antiquities* and marking what was worth reading in the school.
> Wed. Oct. 3—I revised, for the use of the children, Archbishop Potter's *Grecian Antiquities*; a dry dull heavy book.
> Thur. 4—I revised Mr. Lewis's *Hebrew Antiquities;* something more entertaining than the other, and abundantly more instructive.

---

* This was presumably another boy, not the Jackie Williams of the letters to Mrs. Jones, for there is a letter from Charles Wesley to her on May 9, 1750, telling her that Jackie Williams leaves at Midsummer.

† Wesley's friend, Vincent Perronet, was writing to Sellon in 1752—"My dear brother John Wesley wonders at the bad taste of those who seem not to be in raptures with Kingswood School. If there were no other objection but the want of good water upon the spot, this would be insuperable to all wise men, except himself and his brother Charles."

Sat. 6—I nearly finished the abridgement of Dr. Cave's *Primitive Christianity*, a book wrote with as much learning and as little judgement as any I remember to have read in my whole life; serving the ancient Christians just as Xenophon did Socrates —relating every weak thing they ever said or did.

Thur. 11—I prepared a short *History of England* for the use of the children, and on Friday and Saturday a short Roman History, as an introduction to the Latin historians."*

In February 1751 Wesley took his friends by surprise by an ill-starred marriage to a banker's widow, Mrs. Vazeille. Whilst recovering from a sprained ankle in her house in London he wrote a Hebrew Grammar for Kingswood. He resigned his Fellowship at Lincoln College, Oxford, spent the early summer of 1751 in the North, and by making his first visit to Scotland. In June he was back in Bristol, accompanied by his wife.

On Friday, June 21, 1751 he drew up an account of "the case of Kingswood School". After listing the household as it was when it began, he tells us that he had met with all sorts of discouragements—

Cavillers and prophets of evil were on every side. An hundred objections were made both to the whole design and every particular branch of it: Especially by those from whom I had reason to expect better things: Notwithstanding which, through God's help, I went on; wrote an English, a Latin, a Greek, a Hebrew, and a French Grammar, and printed "Praelectiones Pueriles", with many other books for the use of the school; and God gave a manifest blessing. Some of the wildest children were struck with deep conviction; all appeared to have good desires; and two or three began to taste the love of God.

He had been hampered by human frailty. The maids had divided into two parties. R— T— the serving man had studiously blown up the coals by constant whispering and tale-bearing; and the housekeeper did not supply the defects of the other servants, being chiefly "taken up with thoughts of another kind"†

---

* The reference does not necessarily imply publication; Wesley did publish a *Short Roman History,* but not until 1773.

† Mary Davey had married Thomas Richards, one of the masters, in 1749. Richards was for more than thirty years the indefatigable curate of St. Sepulchre's in London, just by Newgate prison. He died in 1798, aged 82. "Contented with little," said the *Gentleman's Magazine,* "he really dealt out his bread to the hungry and scarcely ever ate a meal but the sick and needy partook with him."

The Masters should have corrected these irregularities; but they added to them. T— R— was so rough and disobliging that the children were but little profited by him. A— G— was honest and diligent; but his person and manner made him contemptible to the children. R— M— was grave and weighty in his behaviour, and did much good, till W— S— set the children against him; and instead of restraining them from play, played with them himself. J— J— and W— S— were weighed down by the rest, who neither observed the Rules in the School nor out of it.

The continual breach of that Rule 'Never to let the children play but in the presence of a Master' occasioned their growing wilder and wilder, till all their religious impressions were worn off; and the sooner, as four or five of the larger boys were very uncommonly wicked.

He tells us how, after the changes in the previous September, he had hoped the time had come for God to revive his work:

. . . but we were not low enough yet. So first John Jones and then William Spencer grew weary; the Rules were neglected again; and in the following winter Mr. Page died, and five more scholars went away. What weakened the hands of the masters still more was the bitter evil speaking of some who continually endeavoured either to drive away the children that remained or to prevent others from coming.

There are now two masters, the housekeeper, a maid and eleven children. I believe all in the house are at length of one mind, and trust God will bless us more in the latter end than in the beginning.

We do not know whether John Jones was one of the two masters who remained, or whether he left when he "grew weary". It seems most likely that he left. "Do you know what is the matter with John Jones?" Wesley asked his friend Blackwell in July, "I suppose he will speak freely to you. He seems to be much troubled at something, and I doubt offended." Was it that he felt that his efforts at Kingswood had not been appreciated— perhaps that the whole understanding on which he had gone there had been forgotten by Wesley? We do not know. But in October there is the entry in Wesley's Journal "I had much comfort among the children at Kingswood, finding several of them that really feared God."

John Jones continued to live in Bristol, and is constantly mentioned in the correspondence of both Charles Wesley and of Lady Huntingdon. Whenever there was trouble it was to Dr. John Jones that they turned. Thus in October 1754 hearing of unrest among the preachers Lady Huntingdon tells Charles Wesley that she ordered her coach and went directly to Mr. and Mrs. Jones. "I wish he were in orders," she wrote a little later, "but no way appears open." His central role in the fifties and sixties, often deputising for one or other of the Wesleys in Bristol or in London, and apparently second only to themselves in the hierarchy, has received scant attention in the histories of Methodism.*

(ii) A fresh start?

At the time of the crisis or soon afterwards Wesley persuaded James Rouquet to come to Kingswood. A son of Huguenot refugees—his grandfather had been condemned to the galleys for his religion—Rouquet had fallen under the spell of Whitefield while a boy at Merchant Taylors, and had been at St. John's College Oxford. Whilst there "he received repeated invitations to preside over the school instituted by Mr. Wesley for the children of the Methodists . . . which he accepted through the purest motives, and in which situation he acquitted himself with singular success"† We know very little of his time at the school, and it comes as a surprise to find him inserting an advertisement in a Bristol newspaper in December 1752 in terms which seem to imply something like a fresh start at Kingswood on more orthodox lines.‡

---

* For further reference to his later life see pp.58–9.

† A. C. H. Seymour *Life and Times of Selina, Countess of Huntingdon,* 1840, Vol.II, p.53.

‡ Felix Farley's *Bristol Journal,* December 26, 1752, and three following weeks.

Dec. 26, 1752

WHEREAS it has been long complained of, that Children generally fpend feven, eight and ten Years in learning only two or three Languages; and that together with these, they learn fuch Vices as probably they never unlearn more:

This is to give Notice,

That in the Foreft of *King's-Wood*, near BRISTOL, in a good clear air a BOARDING-SCHOOL is now opened, wherein are taught, at 14*l. per Annum—Englifh, French, Latin, Greek, Hebrew, Hiftory, Geography, Chronology, Rhetoric, Logic, Ethics*; *Geometry, Phyfics*; together with *Writing* in all the ufeful Hands; *Arithmetic,* Vulgar, Decimal, and Inftrumental; *Merchants' Accompts* by Single and Double Entry; *Trigonometry,* Plain and Spherical; *Surveying* and *Mapping* of Land; *Gauging* in all its Parts; *Menfuration* of all Superficies, Solids, *&c.* at much less Expence of Time than ufual: Where particular Care is alfo taken of the Morals of the Children, that they may be train'd up at once to LEARNING and VIRTUE,

By JAMES ROUQUET,
(Late of St. *John*'s College, OXFORD)
And ASSISTANT.

N. B. No Child is received above the Age of twelve Years

We can but speculate on the circumstances which prompted or permitted this extraordinary move. Had Wesley's insistence on his rules all but emptied the school, and was he momentarily persuaded to let the twenty-two-year-old Rouquet make a fresh start? It seems unlikely. Were there perhaps contrary advices to be had in Bristol? It was a time when Charles Wesley and Dr. John Jones were on terms of close friendship with the Countess of Huntingdon, and when relations between John Wesley and his friends in Bristol were not always without strain.* Perhaps they believed that, by appointing Rouquet, Wesley had sanctioned a more normal regime at Kingswood, and helped Rouquet to fill the school.

At all events, and whether or not in response to Rouquet's advertisement, the school did survive, and by August of 1753 Wesley was writing in his Journal

* Cf. for example his letter to Charles Wesley of a slightly later date "So far are you from following advice of mine, even from asking it . . . And yet I can say without vanity that I am a better judge of the matter than either Lady Huntingdon, Sally, Jones, or any other." (*Letters,* Vol.III, p.112.)

I endeavoured once more to bring Kingswood School into order. Surely the importance of this design is apparent, even from the difficulties that attend it. I have spent more money, and time, and care on this than almost any design I ever had; and still it exercises all the patience I have. But it is worth all the labour.

Perhaps this time it was Rouquet's well-meant efforts that were being overhauled. The absence of any reference by name to Rouquet or his colleague John Maddern is in curious contrast to Wesley's overt criticism of the earlier masters. The school must have been full, for we know that one of Wesley's young preachers, Peter Jaco, then twenty-two years old, was unable to obtain admittance. "In the year 1753", he wrote to Wesley, "you proposed my going out for Bristol in April 1754 : but to my great disappointment I found the school full, and a letter from you desiring me to come immediately to London." The incident is interesting ; for it shows that though Wesley had "suspended" the academical course at the school, he was sending to it the occasional promising student who might later become an itinerant preacher.

Rouquet's mastership at Kingswood does not seem to have lasted more than some three years, for in 1754 he was ordained to the curacy of Sandhurst near Gloucester, and soon became a leading personality among a group of "awakened" clergy whose influence in Bristol was very marked in the second half of the century.* He was followed by John Parkinson, of whom we know nothing save that Wesley seems to imply that his scholarship did not match that of other masters, but that his character was above reproach.†

If we know little of what was happening at the school at this time, we do know that for the Wesleys the fifties were a time of great difficulties. Methodism was as yet but little more securely established than was Kingswood School. It was not then clear how much further the movement could count on continued support from clergy within the Establishment, and the fifty or sixty lay preachers or "helpers" to whom Wesley was forced to turn to maintain the itineracy were volunteers liable to human

* for some further reference to Rouquet see pp.52–3.
† See p.51 and p.65.

frailty and prone to go their own way. One by one were evolved the means to preserve discipline and unity of spirit among them. The appointment of "Assistants" to the several circuits with powers to superintend the "Helpers" dates from 1749, and the first mention of a Quarterly Meeting is also of this date. In 1752 it was settled that travelling preachers were to have a fixed allowance of £12 a year. In the following year were drawn up the "Rules of a Helper", which played a vital part in the subsequent story; the preachers were to be diligent; not "to affect the gentleman"; not to be ashamed of fetching wood or drawing water, and there was special stress on believing evil of no one, and speaking evil of no one. The rules were reinforced by close scrutiny at Conference of the character and teaching of each, when the final verdict was given "We are all well satisfied with each other". The unity of spirit thus developed enabled Wesley's preachers to hold together, despite the continuous stress to which their unity was subjected.

In 1753 and the following year Wesley's health all but failed and gave great cause for anxiety. In November he wrote his own epitaph—"who died of a consumption in the fifty-first year of his age"; and he spent some months in the early part of 1754 lodging with his wife near the Hot Well in Bristol, trusting that the water would make amends for the cold of his dwelling. "Nor have I", he wrote, "any place to ride but the river side, or over the downs where the wind is ready to carry me away". He began writing his *Notes on the New Testament*, and later on was able to drive over in the chaise to Kingswood where he administered the sacrament. Charles Wesley was hard put to it to avoid a break-away on the part of some of the preachers and wrote to Walter Sellon for support, as one who stood firmly by the Established Church.

At the Bristol Conference of 1756 there were read over the Rules of the Society and the Rules of Kingswood School. The necessity for keeping in the Church, and "using the clergy with all tenderness" was considered; and there was no dissenting voice. The Rules of the School were read over and considered one by one, and all were convinced that they were agreeable to Scripture and reason. It was decided that a short account of the design and present state of the school be read by every assistant in every Society, and that a subscription for it be begun in every place, and (if need be) a collection made every year. Whether any action was taken, and if so what, we do not know.*

The school was at this time a school for all who wished to send their boys thither, and were willing to pay the fees—£14, a usual boarding school fee of the time. It was still, as Coke and Moore correctly describe it in their *Life of Wesley*, intended for "the children of our principal friends". We catch a mention of it in a letter from Charles Wesley, wanting one Sheen—presumably a master at the school—to be told that there was a hue and cry in London because parents had not been informed of the safe arrival of their boys at school.†

Another glimpse of the school in the autumn of 1757 is occasioned by a fire.

In my return (from preaching at Bath and Escot), wrote Wesley, a man met me near Hanham, and told me the Schoolhouse at Kingswood was burned down. I felt not one moment's pain, knowing that God does all things well. When I came thither I received a fuller account. About eight on Monday evening, two or three boys went into the gallery, up two pairs of stairs. One of them heard a strange crackling in the room above. Opening the staircase door he was beat back by smoke on which he cried out "Fire! Murder! Fire!". Mr. Baynes hearing this, ran immediately down and brought a pail of water. But when he went into the room, he had not the presence of mind to go up to it, but threw the water upon the floor. Meantime one of the boys rung the bell; another called John Maddern from the next house, who ran up, as did James Burges quickly after, and found the room all in aflame. The deal partitions took fire immediately, which spread to the roof of the house. Plenty of water was now brought; but they could not come nigh the place where it was wanted, the room being so filled with flame and smoke that none could go into it. At last a long ladder which lay in the garden was reared up against the wall of the house. But it was then observed that one of the sides of it was broke in two, and the other quite rotten. However John How (a young man who lived next door) ran up it with an axe in his hand. But he then found the ladder was so short that as he stood on the top of it, he could but just lay one hand over the battlements. How he got over to the leads none can tell. But he did so and quickly broke through the roof, on

* It may be the need did not in fact arise until later. See below p.54.

† Charles Wesley's *Journal* II, p.266—"How could the masters be so stupid as not to send to parents word, that their children are safe arrive?"

which a vent being made, the smoke and flames issued as from a furnace. Those who were at the foot of the stairs with water, being able to go no further, then went through the smoke to the door of the leads and poured it down through the tiling. By this means the fire was quickly quenched, having only consumed a part of the partition, with a box of clothes, and a little damaged the roof, and the floor beneath.

Wesley commented "What can we say to these things, but that God had fixed the bounds which it could not pass?"

Little is known of the two masters here mentioned. Baynes was ordained in 1760 and later assisted Wesley at the chapels in London. Maddern had been one of Wesley's preachers in 1747, and had been at the school in Rouquet's time. He had married the mistress of the girl's school, of whom Wesley so much approved*

It seems probable that the Madderns left in 1757, for at this time Wesley resolved to entrust much of the management of the school to another woman of whose zeal and capacity for good works he had formed a very high opinion. Mrs. Sarah Ryan was a widow in her early thirties when appointed housekeeper in 1757. At her request he set down again "the rules of our family".†

"My dear Sister" (he wrote), "In the hurry of business I had not time to write down what you desired—the rules of the family. So I snatch a few minutes to do it now; and the more cheerfully, because I know you will observe them.

1. The family rises, part at four, part half an hour after.
2. They breakfast at seven, dine at twelve, and sup at six.
3. They spend the hour from five to six in the evening (after a little joint prayer) in private.
4. They pray together at nine, and then retire to their chambers; so that all are in bed before ten.
5. They observe all Fridays in the year as days of fasting, or abstinence."

Wesley's action in appointing a convert like Mrs. Ryan to such

---

* See note p.40 above.
† i.e. the abbreviated rules that concerned the housekeeper.

a post not unnaturally drove Mrs. Wesley to outbursts of fury, and aroused a storm of criticism. Sarah Ryan had indeed been unfortunate. She had "married" first a man who proved a bigamist, then a sailor who deserted her and was thought lost at sea, and finally an Italian who had treated her kindly. She had found refuge among the Methodists, but her life story was quite enough to enable Southey to pour scorn on Wesley's judgement. Tyerman in his *Life and Times of Wesley* felt obliged to follow suit. How was it possible, they ask, that he should appoint such a woman "with three husbands living" to be his housekeeper at Kingswood? But so far as the history of Kingswood is concerned the fact remains that Wesley upheld her, and that for some four years she remained as housekeeper at Kingswood, meeting a hundred persons every week in Methodist class or band, and also making excursions into the country societies round Bristol. In January 1758 there is a triumphant entry in Wesley's *Journal*—

I rode over to Kingswood and rejoiced over the School, which is at length what I have so long wished it to be—a blessing to all that are therein, and an honour to the whole body of Methodists.

Sarah Ryan's success as housekeeper had not however solved the problem of finding masters. John Parkinson died in June 1758—"Yesterday died of a long and painful illness at Kingswood School Mr. Parkinson, Master of the said School : a young gentleman of singular piety and learning who lived beloved by all and died universally lamented."* At the Conference that year Wesley asked "Shall we drop the school at Kingswood?", and the answer was "By no means, if a fit master can be found". What happened after Parkinson's death is not clear, perhaps a succession of young masters who soon sought ordination.† Again in November 1761 there is a reference in Wesley's *Journal* to the school in a flourishing state. In 1762 Sally Ryan returned to London, and in company with Miss Bosanquet maintained an orphanage at Leytonstone. Wesley admired her letters for their strong sense and piety, and published a selection of his to her and hers to him.

* Felix Farley's *Bristol Journal*, June 24, 1758.
† Myles gives us as masters for the languages the names of Jonas Eastwood (1758–60), later vicar of Whitechapel near Leeds, and of Thomas Greaves. Other masters appear but incidentally in the record until we reach firmer ground in the mid-sixties.

Meanwhile a new church, St. George's, had been erected on the hill between Bristol and the school. Wesley's work at Kingswood had been followed up by Bishop Butler, and a new parish had been carved out of that of St. Philip and St. Jacob. St. George's, a very neat though plain building, with a large square tower, was opened in 1756, the Mayor and Corporation attending in their coaches. Whether the boys from Kingswood thereupon began attending St. George's we, strangely, do not know; but presumably they did so, and certainly some of them were buried there. From 1759 onwards the vicar was the Rev. Richard Hart, a member of the small group of "awakened" Bristol clergy to whom reference has already been made. It was their practice to unite in making preaching excursions about the countryside. So far therefore from there being any antipathy between Wesley's school at Kingswood and the newly erected St. George's there must have been the warmest sympathy.*

It may help us to picture the Bristol of the day if we recall that James Rouquet, lately at Kingswood, and also an "awakened" clergyman was fast becoming a well known figure. Ordained in 1754, he nevertheless appeared in the following year in Wesley's list of "half-itinerants", attended his Conference in 1755, and made a brave effort to fill the double roll of clergyman and Methodist. His curacy in Sandhurst (near Gloucester) could not hold him, and following Wesley's example he began at once to draw "crowded auditories" in Bristol Newgate; to preach the "condemned sermon"; and to attend those executed on St. Michael's Hill. Undeterred by marriage into the aristocracy, he dedicated the whole of his short life (apart from a short period as vicar of West Harptree, under Mendip) to the prisons and hospitals of Bristol. He became chaplain of Newgate, lecturer of St. Nicholas, chaplain to St. Peter's Hospital and Colston's Almhouse Chapel, and curate of St. Werbergh's. He helped to move Bristol opinion towards changes in the highly unsavoury conditions in St. Peter's Hospital, and in the methods of disposal of paupers' bodies. His work grew; he succeeded in setting up an organization in Bristol for the release of small debtors, and the press published his

---

* The church of Bishop Butler's day was partly rebuilt in 1845, being felt to be "not very ecclesiastical". It was burned down in 1878, and rebuilt as it stands today. (It should not, of course, be confused with Holy Trinity in Kingswood itself, erected in 1821.)

accounts of monies received and spent; thus in 1775 alone his subscribers (they included Edmund Burke, Hannah More and other
well-known names) helped him to release seventy-two poor
debtors. He became indeed the central figure of Bristol charities,
was prominently involved in many controversies and was the
decisive witness in a clash between Wesley and Caleb Evans
over the war with the American colonies. With Wesley he remained all his life on terms of intimacy. To him Wesley con-
fided the details of his own unhappy marital affairs; in 1768
Wesley, in a will, named him as trustee of "all my manuscripts".
He remained a friend not only of both the Wesleys but of the
Countess of Huntingdon, preached at her chapel in Trowbridge
and at her Trevecka anniversary. He gave warm encouragement
too, to the youthful Rowland Hill, destined to become a leading
figure among the Evangelicals of the next generation. He died in
1776 of a "putrid fever"—no doubt typhus, then rife in the
prisons. He was aged 47, and was "attended to the grave by such
weeping multitudes as Bristol had scarce ever seen before". The
boys from Kingswood were, it would seem safe to assume, among
them. The activities of Rouquet and others in Bristol must have
been well-known to, and followed with deep interest by, the little
community at Kingswood; and one of them, Joseph Easterbrook,
at once followed him as chaplain at Newgate.*

(iii) The Preachers' Boys

With the accession of George III in 1760 there began a period
of expansion among the Methodists, and Wesley was thereby
encouraged to review the organization of Methodism. There were

* The interest and significance of the part played by Rouquet has been
obscured by the picturesque but confusing account given in the *Life of the
Countess of Huntingdon*, Vol.II, p.53 which is from a funeral sermon
preached by the Rev. Caleb Evans. The account given above is largely based
on notices in the Bristol newspapers.

now thirty-one circuits in the three kingdoms,* and in the early sixties there were more than a hundred preachers.

The suggestion of an annual collection for the school, first mentioned in 1756, was followed up by the issue of an appeal, which in the earliest published form that has come down to us, that of 1763, ran as follows:†

Q. What can be done to make the Methodists sensible of the excellency of Kingswood School?

A. 1. Let every assistant read the following account of it yearly in every Society.

2. Let every preacher earnestly exhort all parents that are able to send their children thither, and be at pains to answer all their objections, and refute all the lies they have heard about it.

1. The wisdom and love of God have now thrust out a large number of labourers into his harvest: men who desire nothing on earth but to promote the glory of God, to save their own souls, and those that hear them. And those to whom they minister spiritual things are willing to minister to them of their carnal things so that they have food to eat and raiment to put on, and are content therewith.

2. A competent provision is likewise made for the wives of married Preachers. These also lack nothing; having a weekly allowance, over and above, for the little children: so that neither they nor their husbands need to be careful about many things, but may wait upon the Lord without distraction.

3. Yet one considerable difficulty lies on those that have boys, when they grow too big to be under their mother's direction. Having no father to govern and instruct them, they are exposed to a

---

* The circuits were:

In England Twenty		In Ireland Seven
1. London	12. Lincolnshire	1. Dublin
2. Sussex	13. Sheffield	2. Waterford
3. Norwich	14. Leeds	3. Cork
4. Bedford	15. Birstall	4. Limerick
5. Wiltshire	16. Haworth	5. Castlebar
6. Bristol	17. York	6. Athlone
7. Devonshire	18. Yarm	7. The North
8. Cornwall	19. The Dales	In Wales Two
9. Staffordshire	20. Newcastle	1. Pembrokeshire
10. Chester	In Scotland Two	2. Brecknockshire
11. Whitehaven	1. Edinburgh	
	2. Aberdeen	

† The wording was revised from time to time. See Appendix IV.

thousand temptations. To remedy this, we have a School on purpose for them, wherein they have all the instruction they are capable of, together with all things needful for the body, clothes only excepted. And it may be, if God prosper this labour of love, they will have these too shortly.

4. In whatever view we look upon this, it is one of the noblest charities that can be conceived. How reasonable is the institution! Is it fit that the children of those who leave wife and all that is dear to save souls from death, should want what is needful either for soul or body? Ought not we to supply what the parent cannot, because of his labours in the Gospel? How excellent are the effects of this institution! The Preacher, eased of this weight, can the more cheerfully go on in his labour. And, perhaps, many of these children may, hereafter, fill up the place of those that shall rest from their labours.

5. It is not strange therefore, considering the excellence of this design, that Satan should have taken such pains to defeat it: particularly by lies of every kind, which were plentifully invented and handed about for several years, even by some of our Preachers.* But truth now prevails, and its adversaries are put to silence. It is well known that the children want nothing; that they scarce know what sickness means; that they are well instructed in whatever they are capable of learning; that they are carefully and tenderly governed; and that the behaviour of all in the house, elder and younger is as becometh the Gospel of Christ.

6. But the expense of such an undertaking is very large, so that although we have at present but thirteen or fourteen poor children, we are continually running behind, notwithstanding the yearly subscription made at London and Bristol. The best means we could think of at our Conference, to supply the deficiency, is, once a year, to desire the assistance of all those, in every place, who wish well to the work of God; who long to see sinners converted to God, and the kingdom of Christ set up on all the earth.

7. All of you, who are thus minded, have an opportunity now, of showing your love to the Gospel. Now promote as far as in you lies, one of the noblest charities in the world. Now forward, as you are able, one of the most excellent designs that ever was set on foot in this kingdom. Do what you can to comfort the parents, who give up their all for you, and to give their children cause to bless you. You

* See Appendix IV.

will be no poorer for what you do on such an occasion. God is a good paymaster. And, you know, in doing this, you lend unto the Lord: in due time He shall pay you again.

Q. But how can we keep it out of debt, which has never been done yet?

A. Let a collection be made for it the Sunday before or after Midsummer, in every preaching-house throughout England.

Sons of the preachers begin to appear in the records, and an old account book 1764–70 gives us the names of nine of them. The collection is first recorded in 1765, when it was £100 9s. 7d. Two years later it was £121 9s. 0d. This clearly disappointed Wesley, for the record of the Conference that year reads:

Q. This will by no means meet the demand. What can be done to procure a sufficient supply?

and the answer is

A. Let the Midsummer collection be taken in every place great and small.

Let a subscription be set on foot at Dublin, Newcastle, Leeds, Manchester and Liverpool.

In 1768 the response to the collection rose to £173. A year later the problem of preachers' families was again discussed—"if married preachers are sent the people look upon them with an evil eye, because they cannot bear the burden of their families". A definite system of allowances was arranged in 1770: a preacher was to receive besides the £12 a year he had for himself a similar sum for his wife, and £4 a year for each of his children, to be paid quarterly: the boys till they were eight years of age, fit to go to Kingswood School: the girls till they were fourteen, fit to go to business. There were at this time two and thirty wives of the preachers, besides those that kept themselves. But as "several of them" had children, the overplus was to be divided among them as the need required.

In 1770 it was asked at Conference "What poor children may be admitted now at Kingswood?" and the answer is John Poole's child and John Peacock's. By 1773 the form of the question had changed. It is asked not what poor children, but what preachers' sons are admitted; and the answer is Barry's, Greenwood's,

Poole's. Thereafter two or three sons of the preachers are admitted each year. "What can be done in order to pay for the clothes of the preachers' children?" it was asked in 1774. "If their parents can pay for them in the school, they should : if they cannot, all is well."

We have the names of some eighty boys who were at the school during the years 1764–69. Among them can be found the names of twenty or so whose fathers were at one time or another associated with Wesley as itinerant preachers in the early years of the movement. Thus Cornelius Bastable had been asked by Wesley in 1748 if he would leave all—relations, friends, business, home —and give himself up to the one work of calling sinners to repentance. He had said he was, and Wesley had told him to go home and fetch his horse. He had two sons at Kingswood in the early sixties. Joseph Cownley had been commissioned by Wesley in 1746, encountered much mob violence in Staffordshire and elsewhere, and was one of those involved in the rioting against the Methodists in Cork in 1749. His boy at Kingswood was later a surgeon in the Queen's Rangers. William Darney, a man of prodigious size and a broad Scots dialect founded many societies in Lancashire and the West Riding. His little son at the school needed but a brief entry : "Physic 2s. od., Doctor's bill £1 3s. 9d., six shoes mending 9½d., coffin, shroud etc. 19s. od." Others may without much difficulty be identified as sons of friends mentioned by Wesley in his *Journal* or correspondence, as for instance "good old Mr. Arundell", or William Clulow, who was Wesley's solicitor. In all we can thus trace from the principal Methodist sources some thirty of the eighty or so boys whose names are known to us.

The preachers' boys naturally paid no fees. The old account book shows too, sundry items of clothing, hats, breeches, for which no payment was recorded. For the others £14 was the normal fee, and one or two of the boys were permitted a little latitude in meeting their requirements. Thomas Maurice, for example, of whom we shall hear more on a later page, twice had 10s. for pocket money, three volumes of poets and books cost 6s. 6d., and a book of Horace 6s. A suit cost £2 15s. 8d. The boys came from all over the country, as the entries for travel expenses show— Newcastle, Birmingham, London, Sheffield and Dublin, wherever Wesley's friends were to be found.

E

(iv) Mounting tension in the Sixties

But we have been anticipating. The beginnings of a collection for the school and the first appearance of the preachers' sons were not the only accompaniments of the early years of George III. As the decade advanced and still more "multitudes of sinners were converted from the error of their ways", Wesley's difficulties increased. Methodism was passing through a series of crises. We cannot here discuss them in any detail, but it will help us to sense the excitement and uncertainty of the times, and to see the school in its context, if for a moment we take in wider horizons.

Let us start with Wesley. His activities had now begun to assume a definite pattern. Early in each year he would start off from his headquarters at the Foundery in London on one of his tours; to the North, it might be, or to Ireland. And it would last quite a long time, filling the columns of his *Journal* with many an incident. He would usually be back in London in May or June, holding a Conference there, or in some other centre as convenience might dictate. He would be off again in July or August, a shorter tour, perhaps Kent, or Cornwall, and quite often he would call at Kingswood for a few days in September. In the late autumn he would usually be back in London. Such a programme meant he had to rely very largely on others to supervise the large mother societies in London and in Bristol. In the West the presence of Charles Wesley eased the situation. In London the case was different, and when in the early sixties the societies there, with their many hundreds of members, were distracted by the aberrations of Thomas Maxfield, Wesley relied increasingly on his old friend and colleague, Dr. John Jones. He had indeed been, after John and Charles Wesley themselves, the right-hand man of the movement all through the years since he had left Kingswood. The Bishops had perhaps naturally refused him ordination, despite the efforts made by Lady Huntingdon on his behalf. In 1763, when affairs in London took a critical turn, Wesley thought to side-step the opposition of the English Bishops by recourse to a Bishop of the Greek Orthodox Church then in London, at whose hands John Jones was ordained. It was not an acceptable solution, and caused a furore, the repercussions of which have not yet quite died away.*

In his need Wesley turned also to the evangelical clergy, with whom, despite their Calvinism, he had much in common. Prompted perhaps by Rouquet, also earlier at Kingswood, he sought an understanding with some fifty of them, to whom he sent an appeal for unity. It brought little response, save an "exceedingly friendly letter" from Richard Hart, of St. George's, close at hand at Kingswood. The tone of that letter throws a gleam of light on the relationship between the school and its parish church at this time. For a while in the mid-sixties the Wesleys worked more closely with Lady Huntingdon and the clergy associated with her. Thus in 1766 Wesley was preaching in her newly opened chapel in the vineyards in Bath. (It still stands, now used by Presbyterians, not far along the London Road from the foot of Lansdown.) Wesley's preaching there was vividly, but acidly, described by Horace Walpole. But with every year that passed he became more ready to question the formulæ that had been accepted since the Reformation. Sitting alone in his coach on December 1, 1767 he reflected that a man might be saved notwithstanding that he had never heard of, or even denied, the doctrine of justification by faith. It is the point fixed by Lord Acton as marking Wesley's effective separation from the Church of England.† At the end of the decade he would publish anti-Calvinist minutes in line with his reflections in the coach. They closed the door to further co-operation with the predominantly Calvinistic clergy, and perhaps contributed

* Wesley defended his action in a letter to the press (*Letters*, Vol. IV, page 289), where he gives the Bishop's name as Erasmus. The Bishop had in 1762 published in London a work entitled *Lapis Offendiculi*, being a discussion in Latin of the causes of the separation of the Eastern and Western Churches in early times. A copy of this book was placed by Wesley in the library at Kingswood. The book, incidentally, gives the name of the Bishop in both a Greek form, *Gerasimos Aulonetes*, and a Latin form, *Erasmus Aulonita*. He is there described as Bishop of Arcadia in Crete. As the Bishop's credentials are still occasionally the subject of discussion (cf. Colin Williams, *Wesley's Theology Today*, 1960), and the book seems to have escaped notice, the point is not without interest.

John Jones continued as Wesley's right-hand man in London, and is so listed in 1765 and 1766. Later, when, as he himself explains, his health failed, he was re-ordained by the Bishop of London and spent his later years quietly at Harwich, in charge of the Free School there, and finally as Vicar of Harwich. He died there in 1785, aged 64. There is a memorial tablet in the church at Harwich. Some letters protesting his continued affection for the Wesleys are preserved at City Road.

† Acton, quoted Temperley, *Cambridge Modern History*, Vol. VI. p.85.

to the ultimate separation of the Wesleyan body from the Establishment.

Against such a background it may come as less of a surprise to the reader to learn that we are about to encounter a phase of mounting tension at the school, culminating in a series of scenes of religious excitement recorded at length by Wesley, and inevitably dwelt upon by Southey and many others as exemplifying Wesley's extravagances. The first hint comes with a record of smallpox at the school in 1763. Coming from preaching at Bath, Wesley and his companion saw a coffin being carried into St. George's with many children attending it. "When we came near we found that they were our own children, attending the corpse of one of their own schoolfellows, who had died of the smallpox; and God thereby touched their hearts in a manner they never knew before." Three days later Wesley held a solemn watchnight, and had an opportunity of speaking closely to the children. "One is dead," he records, "two recovered, seven are still ill, and the hearts of all are like melting wax."

Much more was to follow. At the Conference in 1765 the condition of the school was carefully reviewed. It was decided to appoint three or five trustees, and to require each Bristol preacher to spend an hour a week at least with the children. It was also decided to appoint James Hindmarsh and his wife as writing master and housekeeper. Hindmarsh had been one of Wesley's earlier helpers, had proved unstable, and had been re-instated.* In October Wesley recorded that the boys at the school were all in health, they behaved well, they learned well; but alas! (two or three excepted) there was no life in them.

His impatience was quickened by riding out to Leytonstone, where, as we have seen, Sarah Ryan was helping Mary Bosanquet run an orphanage.

"There I found one truly Christian family," he wrote, "that is, what Kingswood should be, if it had such governors".

Before long he was able to make changes at Kingswood. Thomas Greaves, who had been holding the fort for the last five years, was "just ordained", and early in 1766 Wesley sent instead Joseph Benson, a man of great ability of whom we shall have

* See *W.H.S.*, Vol. VII, p.66.

more to tell presently, but at this time very young, to join Hind-marsh and take charge of the classics. In March he rode over to Kingswood, and "having told my whole mind to the Masters and servants, spoke to the children in a far stronger manner than ever I did before. I will kill or cure; I will have one thing or the other, a Christian school or none at all". A little later he had the satis-faction of finding four of the children "rejoicing in the Lord".

In August he delivered the management of Kingswood House to stewards in whom he could depend. "So I have cast a heavy load off my shoulders", he wrote. "Blessed to God for able and faithful men, who will do his will without any temporal reward." In October he left Bristol with a firm hope that at Kingswood things would now be conducted to the glory of God and the honour of true religion.

Deeply involved as he was elsewhere, the school was never long out of his mind. "Look upon our little ones at Kingswood as often as you can," he wrote to his brother Charles in January 1768. "A word from you will be a quickening to them—O how many talents are we entrusted with!"

When therefore the revival of 1768 swept the local congregation off its feet, it was echoed in the school, and Hindmarsh was not the man to miss the opportunity to earn Wesley's approval. In April he was able to write to Wesley describing how the boys had responded to the strong sug-gestion to which they had been exposed, and how as he wrote the cries of some of them resounded from their several apart-ments. "The House rings with praise and prayer", wrote another correspondent. Wesley printed the letters in his *Journal,* for they seemed to reinforce his belief that a child of tender years could undergo a profound religious experience.

In October Wesley spent an hour with the children, much to his satisfaction. "There is reason to hope that the grace of God is still working among them", he noted. "Some are still alive to God: and all behave in such a manner that I have seen no other schoolboys like them."

At the Conference in Bristol in that year the question was asked:
Q. What can we do for the rising generation? Unless we take care of these, the present revival of religion will be Res Unius Aetatis: it will last only the age of a man. Who will labour therein . . .? and the

answer was, Preach expressly on this, especially at Midsummer, when you speak of Kingswood.

The Methodists responded and sent their children, for a year later Wesley recorded that the grievance was the number of children. There were near fifty, and the masters were burdened, and it was scarce possible to keep them in so exact a manner as a smaller number. ". . . However this still comes nearer a Christian school than any I know in the Kingdom."

The school was central to much of Wesley's thinking at this time, and part of his defence against those who assailed him on the ground that Methodism was tantamount to renunciation of reason. ". . . To put this matter beyond dispute", he wrote to a correspondent, "I appeal to something more than words. Can any man seriously think that I despise learning who has ever heard of the school at Kingswood? especially if he knows with how much care and expense and labour I have kept it on foot these twenty years? Let him but read the rules of Kingswood School, and he will urge this objection no more."*

He was able to write with pride in reply to a Swedish professor, John Liden of Lund, who was seeking an account of the organization of Methodism:

"They (i.e. the Methodists) have many schools for teaching reading, writing and arithmetic, but only one for teaching the higher parts of learning. This is kept in Kingswood near Bristol, and contains about forty scholars. These are all boarders, and might be abundantly more, but the house will not contain them. The Rules of Kingswood School give an account of the books read and the method therein."†

The year 1770 was again marked by extravagant scenes. Wesley was himself there explaining and "enforcing upon" the children the first principles of religion. They were taken by Hindmarsh to see the body of a neighbour, who had died two or three days before and Hindmarsh subsequently met them and gave them an exhortation suitable to the occasion, till they were constrained to cry aloud for mercy. The tension was maintained for thirteen days and another Methodist

---

* Part of a long reply to Dr. Thomas Rutherford, at one time Professor of Divinity at Cambridge. *Letters*, Vol. V, p. 359.

† *Letters*, Vol.V, p.154–6. In the same letter is a short list of those whom Wesley supposed to be the best preachers. It is of interest that it includes T. Simpson, who was later to be headmaster at Kingswood.

preacher, Thomas Rankin, seconded Hindmarsh's efforts. Wesley marvelled and inserted lengthy accounts in his Journal. Some of the children and three of the maids "found peace with God". All this time too, he tells us it was observed that there was an uncommon revival of the work of God in the societies round about, and the society at Kingswood increased within a few months to over three hundred members. The effect was transient. A further brief revival at the school followed three years later, in which a third Methodist preacher, Ralph Mather,* was concerned. When it had been going on for a week or so Wesley went over to Kingswood—

Hearing in the evening that they were got to prayer by themselves, I went down; but not being willing to disturb them, stood at the window. Two or three had gone in first, then more and more, till above thirty were gathered together. Such a sight I never saw before and since. Three or four stood and stared, as if affrighted. The rest were all on their knees pouring out their souls before God in a manner not easy to be described.†

This revival, like the others, soon died away, and left Wesley asking how long it would be his lot to weave Penelope's web.

The incidents, and the publicity Wesley gave them through his *Journal*, have inevitably come to occupy a prominent place in every account of early Kingswood. Southey observes that it was a wonder the boys were not driven mad by their instructors, and that the scenes were worthy of Bedlam. But a less extreme view is possible if we recall that in these late sixties many Methodist societies were caught up in a wave of emotion, and the boys were but echoing what was going on around them. Wesley too insisted vehemently on pastoral visiting, on family religion, and on his *Instructions for Children*. His preachers were told in no uncertain manner that they must instruct the children; not in a dull, dry, formal manner, but in earnest, with their might. He was awed and elated by results which bore so much resemblance to the life-changing conversions which were going on all around. The record shows that they were a passing phase in the life of the school.‡

But we must retrace our steps.

* Hindmarsh, Rankin and Mather were Methodist preachers: for a very fair description see A. H. Body, *John Wesley and Education*, 1936, pp. 119–30.
† *Journal*, Vol. V, entries for September 3–10, 1773.
‡ Wesley seems to have taken a different view in later life—see pp. 105–6 for his definition of religion in 1783.

(v) Joseph Benson

A very different light is thrown on the Kingswood of the late sixties by a series of letters from Wesley to Joseph Benson, which at the risk of some disproportion in the narrative must be set out here at length for their raciness and quality.

Benson, as we have seen, had been appointed a master at the school in 1766. Setting out from Cumberland to walk to London, he had sought out Wesley. At Ferry Bridge a gentleman had seen him reading the Greek Testament near the kitchen fire in the inn, and took him to London in the basket of his carriage. He arrived in the middle of February, and after a month with Wesley at his headquarters in London, went with him to Bristol. Wesley at once treated him as a person of consequence, which his subsequent career was fully to justify. Although only eighteen years of age he took over the teaching of classics at the school. By December he was writing to Wesley somewhat despondently. The school had not yet answered his expectations; the difficulties were great, and altogether such as to make their hands hang down; but with regard to learning the children did profit, and he could assure Wesley would now make more proficiency than ever, and with respect to order and good manners they would not be deficient. In January 1768 Wesley was writing to tell Benson he should have what money he wanted; not only sixty pounds, but sixty on that; and in November

"Dear Joseph,

. . . You have now twenty more volumes of the Philosophical Transactions. Dr. Burton's Latin and Greek Poems you have in the study. Malebranche and some other books are coming. Logic you cannot crack without a tutor: I must read it to Peter* and you, if we live to meet. It would not be amiss if I had a catalogue of the books at Kingswood; then I should know the better what to buy. As fast as I can meet with them at sales, I shall procure what are yet wanting. But beware you be not swallowed up in books: an ounce of love is worth a pound of knowledge.—I am, dear Joseph,

Your affectionate brother."

* Peter Price was a master at Kingswood 1765–68, and later a Methodist preacher.

". . . Logic you cannot crack without a tutor. I must read it to
Peter and you if we live to meet." The letter give us a precious
glimpse of a side of Wesley too often forgotten. Advice which has
become proverbial—"an ounce of love is worth a pound of knowledge"—is mingled with practical detail for Wesley was almost
as much concerned with Benson's own advance in learning as
with building up the library at Kingswood. Another friend has
ventured to advise Benson on his reading, but Wesley will have
none of it—"it is better to read these books than his". And again,
on this same theme—

"My dear Joseph,—You do not quite take my meaning yet. When I
recommend to any one a method or scheme of study, I do not barely
consider this or that book separately but in conjunction with the
rest. And what I recommend I know; I know both the style and
sentiments of each author, and how he will confirm or illustrate
what goes before and prepare for what comes after. Now, supposing
Mr. Stonehouse, Rouquet or any other to have ever so great
learning and judgement, yet he does not enter into my plan. He
does not comprehend my views nor keep his eye fixed on the same
point. Therefore I must insist upon it, the interposing other books
between these till you have read them through is not good
husbandry. It is not making your time and pains go so far as they
might go. If you want more books, let me recommend more, who best
understand my own scheme. And do not ramble, however learned
the persons may be that advise you to do so. This does indulge
curiosity, but does not minister to real improvement, as a stricter
method would do. No; you would gain more clearness and strength
of judgement by reading those Latin and Greek books (compared
with which most of the English are whipped syllabub) than by four-
score modern books. I have seen the proof, as none of your Bristol
friends have done or can do. Therefore I advise you again, keep to
your plan (though this implies continual self-denial) if you would
improve your understanding to the highest degree of which it is
capable.—I am, dear Joseph, Your affectionate brother."

Benson's strength was not equal to the burden, and Wesley seems
to have complained that the school had not been kept in exact
order. Benson thought of resigning his position.

"You forget John Jones, Mr. Sellon and Mr. Rouquet were far
better scholars than Mr. Parkinson; and T. Simpson, yea and P. Price

(when he was well) were very properly qualified.* But change of masters it is impossible to prevent unless we could bribe them with much money, which I neither can nor will. The case lies here: *A master may be weary on other accounts,* but he certainly will if he do not grow in grace. Again, the devil is more deeply concerned against this school than against any other in England.

If I cannot get proper masters for the languages, I shall let the school drop at the Conference. I will have another kind of school than that at Trevecca† or none at all. I would within this year but for want of two things—time and money. So we must creep till we can fly."

And again in another letter (now in the possession of the school)

"Your grand point is, Bring the boys into *exact order*, and that without delay. Do this at all hazards. I think we have found another master. In the meantime let John Whitehead learn all he can.‡ I doubt it cannot be helped. Those hot-heads at Oxford will constrain me to beat them. But first let Dr. Dixon speak."

The purport of the reference to the hotheads at Oxford and to Dr. Dixon will shortly appear.

In May 1769 Benson had what Wesley called a "clear providential call to Oxford"; but Wesley warned him—

"When I was at Oxford, I never was afraid of any but the almost Christians. If you give way to them and their prudence an hair's breadth, you will be removed from the hope of the gospel."

and as to Kingswood School—

"I have one string more: if that breaks, I shall let it drop. I have

* This incidental comment on the masters at the school is of much interest as giving Wesley's assessment of their capacity. T. Simpson had apparently already been a master, and would later be in charge—see pp.88ff.

† Lady Huntingdon's College, see below.

‡ A young itinerant then stationed in Bristol, later the well-known Dr. John Whitehead, one of Wesley's biographers. There was some thought of his being a probable successor to Benson at Kingswood (*Letters*, Vol.V, p.142). "But I do not wish you to meddle at all unless you propose to stay there" (*London Quarterly and Holborn Review*, Oct., 1946, p.324).

borne the burthen one-and-twenty years; I have done what I could: now let someone else do more."

In the autumn, Benson must have sent Wesley some account of trouble and said that he had had enough—

" 'This gives any one enough of Kingswood School'. 'Ah! simple Master Shallow!' as Shakespeare has it, should not *I* then have had enough of it long ago?"

Benson was under pressure to exchange his post at Kingswood for the headmastership of the Countess of Huntingdon's new college at Trevecka in Brecknockshire, and we must see what had been happening.* The Countess and her friends hoped to educate pious young men for the ministry. She was at this time again on excellent terms with Wesley, as well as with Whitefield. She had persuaded the Rev. John Fletcher, the saintly vicar of Madeley, whom later Wesley wished to designate as his own successor, to become the visiting President of her new college. A boy from Kingswood had gone to be Fletcher's assistant, and to teach the learned languages, though he did not long remain there.† In September 1769, in company with Wesley, the Countess visited Kingswood, and, presumably, in some sense on Wesley's recommendation, Benson was invited to take up the post at Trevecka. Wesley may have commended him to the Countess, but was clearly upset by talk of his leaving Kingswood. At any rate all was not going well—

---

* Trevecka (or Trevecca as in Wesley's references) lies a little more than a mile from Talgarth. Howell Harris had established there a religious settlement, and the buildings became quite extensive. A great part of the settlement still stands.

The building acquired by Lady Huntingdon and used by her as the college is some distance away. It is now a farmhouse, and may be recognised by a curious carving of Batavian angels over the entrance. (In the illustrations in the *Journal* Vol.V, p.334 the captions are confusing. It is the building in the lower picture which was the "college" of Wesley's day.)

† Tyerman in his *Life of Wesley* said that the boy from Kingswood was Joseph Easterbrook. In his later work about Fletcher of Madeley *Wesley's Designated Successor* he retracted this statement, and adduced evidence to show that it was John Henderson, not Easterbrook, who taught at Trevecka. Henderson was twelve years old when he went to Trevecka. For a further account of him see pp.85-6.

"Indeed Joseph, I am not well pleased at all . . . What, are you seeking to pick a quarrel with me? Well, if you require me to be serious, I *will* be serious . . . Honour and power have done you no good; I am sorry for you, but I know not how to help you. If you *will* go, you *must* go."

Benson thought he had good reason to be ruffled—*

"I knew you were not well reconciled to me when you left Bristol; and, farther, it occurred to my mind in what manner you had parted with most of the masters, who I find have generally gone away with offence . . .

"You think 'honour and power have done me no good'. I should think you mentioned *honour* by way of irony, and as for *power* I am puzzled to find where I have had any, unless you mean over a few children.

"But so it is, and so it has always been: you have had the misfortune to mistake your friends and enemies. Whoever has made it a point (in order to gain your favour) to contradict you in nothing, but professed implicitly to follow your direction and abide by your decision, especially if they added thereto the warmest expressions of regard for you and told you a tale of their being saved from sin and perfected in love, they never failed to gain your favour in a high degree, and what is worse, have often used it to a bad purpose, by filling your ear with insinuations against others. And such have generally gained credit with you . . . On the other hand, whoever, from a conviction that all men are fallible and that implicit obedience is due to God alone, could not in conscience acquiesce in your bare *ipse dixit,* but have believed it their duty to call in question some things you have advanced . . . such persons have in general stood low in your esteem and had the misfortune and discouragement to find you set light by their services and put a misconstruction on their whole conduct . . ."

He quotes Wesley's "If you *will* go, you *must* go"; and asks

"Is this all the answer I must have, when after stating the case, and showing you the necessity, I asked your advice in an affair of such importance? These are all the thanks I must receive for putting myself to so many inconveniences to serve you? After exhausting my spirits from morning to night in a school where you are sensible I should have had an assistant, especially for these twelve months last, to the prejudice of my spiritual proficiency, to

* Letter in Methodist Archives in City Road, London.

say nothing (for they are not worth mentioning) of temporal inconveniences? And why should I not take you at your word? No, I have too much love for the children, too much regard for their parents, and (whether you will believe it or no) too much sense of duty to God and respect for yourself, to leave things in such confusion."

Wesley replied on December 3—

"You must not expect that I should answer particularly a letter of a sheet long. I have only time to take notice briefly of two or three of the mistakes it contains.
1. I have been told an hundred times, 'You love those that flatter you and hate all that deal plainly and honestly with you' . . . But nothing under heaven can be more false. What man did I ever love like T. Walsh? What woman do I now regard like Miss Bosanquet? And what human creatures have dealt so plainly and honestly with me? . . .
2. The first spring of the reproach cast on Kingswood School was not any mismanagement there. It was the hatred of good which is in the devil and his children. Therefore even Mr. Parkinson never did or could escape it. Therefore a fresh flood of it has been poured out even since you was there.
3. This *you* had reason to expect, and therefore ought not to have been surprised, much less discouraged at it. . . .
4. 'Is this all the thanks I receive for serving you?' Nay, I think the thanks are due to *me*. When I first sent you to Kingswood, it was to serve *you* at least as much as myself. Nay, it was not to serve myself at all. For what is the school to *me*? It has been and may be of use to many. But it is no more to *me* than to *you* or Lady Huntingdon.
There are other mistakes in your letter (which is all wrote in a spirit of discontent), but I have no time to point them out. You told me you would stay at the school till March. Till then you should be as much at Kingswood as you can."

Benson did delay his departure, and Wesley wrote on December 26, 1769—

"Dear Joseph,—Every man of sense who reads the rules of the school may easily conclude that a school so conducted by men of piety and understanding will exceed any other school or academy in Great Britain or Ireland. In this sentiment you can never be altered. And if it was not so conducted since *you* was there, Why was it not, you had power enough. You have all the power which *I* have. You may do just what you please. Dirue, edifica; muta quadrata rotundis. And I will second you to the uttermost. . . ."

and again on January 27, 1770—

"Dear Joseph,—All is well. We have no need to 'dispute about a dead horse.' If the school at Trevecca is the best that ever was since the world began, I am glad of it, and wish it may be better still. But do not run away with any of my young men from Kingswood: that I should blame you for. I have wrote already to T. Simpson, and will write again. Do all the good you can in every place."

In the spring of that year Benson went to Trevecka, and for some time things went on "excellently well".

In October, Wesley was writing to him again with news of Kingswood. A Mr. Keard from Aberdeen, and a Mr. Wootton, a new writing master, were there, Benson evidently had a prospective pupil for Kingswood—"But does Mr. J—— know the price? —sixteen pounds a year. Does he know the rules of the school? Again: of what age are the children? I will take none that is above twelve years old".* And after reference to the differences developing between Benson and the Countess—

"Child," said my father to me when I was young, "you think to carry everything by dint of argument. But you will find by-and-by how very little is ever done in the world by clear reason." Very little indeed! It is true of almost all men, except so far as we are taught of God,—

> Against experience we believe
> We argue against demonstration;
> Pleased while our reason we deceive,
> And set our judgement by our passion.

Passion and prejudice govern the world, only under the name of reason. It is our part, by religion and reason joined, to counteract them all we can. . . .

It was unfortunate for Benson's headmastership at Trevecka that the tension between Wesley and the Calvinistic party, always latent, developed at just this time into the major crisis to which we have already referred and which proved to be a permanent

---

* *Letters*, Vol.V, page 202 reads "nine years old" in error. The ms. in the Methodist Archives at City Road reads "twelve years old".

parting of the ways. Benson was no Calvinist, and had to leave abruptly.

When he had left Trevecka, Wesley wrote that he was welcome to stay at Kingswood until he was better provided for. He sought to take his degree at Oxford, but as we shall soon see his troubles were not yet at an end. Meanwhile we may perhaps digress so far as to give his own picture of the Wesley he had known so well.

"I was constantly with him for a week. I had an opportunity of examining narrowly his spirit and conduct; and, I assure you, I am more than ever persuaded, he is a *none such*. I know not his fellow, first for abilities, natural and acquired; and, secondly, for his incomparable diligence in the application of these abilities to the best of employments. His lively fancy, tenacious memory, clear understanding, ready elocution, manly courage, indefatigable industry, really amaze me. I admire, but wish in vain to imitate, his diligent improvement of every moment of time; his wonderful exactness, even in little things; the order and regularity wherewith he does and treats everything he takes in hand; together with his quick dispatch of business, and calm, cheerful serenity of soul."*

(vi) The University of Oxford

We have seen how strongly marked was the religious tension at Kingswood in 1768–73, and we have seen in Wesley's correspondence with Benson something of the inner working of the school. It remains now to take account of a third event, or series of events, which also occurred in 1768–69 and had important consequences for the school, and for its relationship with the universities. In that year, six undergraduates were expelled from Oxford, on account of their Methodism. Since its foundation in 1748 Wesley had thought of Kingswood as a school preparatory to Oxford and Cambridge and, for those who sought it, ordination by the well-trodden path. He would now have to alter course.

It is therefore relevant to recount in some detail what happened at Oxford in 1768. Pious young men sponsored by the Countess of Huntingdon and intended by her for the ministry had been admitted for the most part to St. Edmund Hall. The Principal of the Hall, Dr. Dixon, was sympathetically disposed to those who

* Quoted by Tyerman from the *Methodist Magazine*, 1825, p.386.

were called "Methodists". The young gentlemen behaved well, he said, they did nothing contrary to the doctrine or discipline of the Church of England. His attitude was not however shared by his Tutor, Mr. Higson; and when Lady Huntingdon wrote about yet another young man high words ensued between Principal and Tutor. Dixon was so angry that he treated Higson "with abusive language", and in short threatened to dismiss him from his Tutor's post in the Hall. Higson thereupon drew up a formal complaint against seven students already in residence, who had not only been meeting in the town for prayer and Bible study, but had "behaved indecently by neglecting to attend his lectures, or misbehaving in them". Higson appealed to the Vice-Chancellor, and a Court of Enquiry was granted.*

The little chapel of St. Edmund Hall was crowded for the occasion with noisy gownsmen, and Queen's Lane was full of those unable to get in when the procession of red-robed Doctors arrived from the University Church. The accused students were charged inter alia with being connected with reputed Methodists —Mr. Venn, Mr. Newton, Mr. Fletcher† ; with being frequenters of an "illegal conventicle" (i.e. a drawing room in the town); and with being men destitute of learning. They were set to translate on the spot crabbed Latin from the University Statutes, and passages from the Greek Testament. Two did so, the others stumbled, and Higson claimed his point proved. Dr. Dixon defended them. He never remembered seven youths whose lives were so exemplary; but six of the seven were found guilty, and sentenced to be expelled from the university. Protagonists on either side took up the challenge, and blast and counter-blast followed. Among the most pointed of the comments was White-field's oft-quoted observation. "It is to be hoped", he told the Vice-Chancellor, "that as some have been expelled for extempore praying, we shall hear of some few others of a contrary stamp, being expelled for extempore swearing, which by all impartial judges must undoubtedly be acknowledged to be the greater crime of the two."

* See Higson's MS. defence of his actions preserved among St. Edmund Hall papers in the Bodleian Library, Oxford.

† i.e. Evangelical clergymen, since revered as leaders of the Evangelical party in the Church of England: not, be it noted, Mr. Wesley. It was Lady Huntingdon's wing of the movement that was the principal target of the proceedings. For a vivid account see G. R. Balleine, *History of the Evangelical Party in the Church of England,* 1908.

Among the six was one who had been at Kingswood, Erasmus Middleton. Much of the attack was concentrated on him, and his offences were detailed; among other things, that he had been a teacher in a school belonging to Mr. Wesley. Defending himself he owned that he had known Mr. Wesley, and that about three years before he had been a scholar in Mr. Wesley's school near Bristol, but he steadfastly asserted that he conformed entirely to the Church of England. It was of no avail; he was expelled with the others. He was however subsequently ordained, and became a well-known Evangelical, curate for a while at St. Margaret's, Westminster, and author of a large four volume work entitled *Biographica Evangelica*.

Little more than a year later the proposed matriculation from St. Edmund Hall of another pupil from Kingswood, one Stephen Seager, caused renewed commotion in the university. Dr. Dixon consulted the Vice-Chancellor, who sent for Seager and elicited the fact that he had indeed—at the age of near twenty-one—been at the school at Kingswood near Bristol, where he had read Sallust, Caesar's Commentaries, part of Terence and Virgil, and was then reading the Greek Testament. The Vice-Chancellor consulted the Hebdomadal meeting, with the result that enquiries were set on foot into Seager's religious principles. It transpired that he had in Birmingham, and before going to Kingswood, been closely connected with the Methodists, and had told his companions of his intention of going to or near Bristol to be instructed in an academy there, in such a manner as would qualify him to go to Oxford, and become a preacher. The Hebdomadal Board was unanimous that the whole affair should be laid before Convocation, and the sentiments of the House be taken whether it would be expedient for the Vice-Chancellor to matriculate Mr. Seager.*It was inevitable that the verdict should go against him, but Seager composed and printed a letter to the Vice-Chancellor.

"Reverend Sir", it began, "though I perceive it is in vain to flatter myself with hopes of being admitted a member of this University, being unfortunately represented as having connexion with the Methodists, a sort of people which I see the University is disposed to reject without distinction . . ."

* A copy of the notice summoning Convocation (June 1769) survives among the St. Edmund Hall papers in the Bodleian, quoted J. S. Reynolds, *The Evangelicals at Oxford 1735–1871*, 1953.

F

He went on to cast aspersions on the accuracy of the account of himself supplied to the authorities—phrases invented, he presumed, to make him appear as ridiculous as possible—and to assert his adherence to the Articles of the Church. He disclaimed too, the Calvinistic notions respecting absolute predestination and final perseverance attributed to the young men expelled, and averred that if he were indeed ordained without having been to Oxford his behaviour would be such as would be no just cause of offence.

Wesley heard about the case, no doubt from Joseph Benson, for there are references to it in a letter to him of August 7, 1769:

"I have wrote to Dr. Dixon. He appears to be a very sensible as well as a serious man.

The case of Mr. Seager is extremely odd. But nothing comes by chance. The hand of God is in all this. Perhaps whether he will or no, he will make Kingswood a university as well as a school."

Benson himself was soon in trouble with Higson's successor at St. Edmund Hall. As we have seen, on leaving Trevecka he went to Oxford to complete his studies. On finding that the works which the gentlemen under his tutor read were Cornelius Nepos and the Greek Testament, he made bold to intimate that these works, and most of the Greek and Latin classics, were very familiar to him. He was excused attending, though as none of the other gentlemen were capable of reading any others, his tutor could not conveniently give him lectures in any other. Worse was to follow. In conversation with his tutor he was induced to relate in the most full and undisguised manner some particulars of his history, especially his connections with Mr. Wesley and Lady Huntingdon. The prejudice of his tutor was excited; and the upshot was that his tutor peremptorily refused to sign his testimonial for orders, or even consider him any longer in the character of a pupil. Benson obtained nevertheless testimonials from four beneficed clergymen, and a title to a large and populous parish near Bristol, and presented his testimonials to the Bishop of Worcester. The Bishop refused to ordain him, assigning as a reason his want of an academical degree. He thereupon joined Wesley's band of itinerants. He was to become a pillar of early Methodism and a great man in his own right.

Wesley's reaction to the rebuff at Oxford was to revive his project for an academical course at Kingswood. The reader may recall that before the school was opened Wesley had produced a draft scheme of reading extending over four or five years for those who had "gone through the school", but that he had suspended it, and that no mention of it was to be found in the *Short Account* of 1749. He now for the first time put it into print, and the *Short Account* of 1768 sets it out in full.* The range is, as might be expected, considerable. Besides revision of classical authors and Wesley's favourite commentaries and writers on ecclesiastical history, we find Euclid, and Newton's *Principia*, Plato, Locke, and Malebranche, and much else. "Whoever goes carefully through this course", Wesley added, "will be a better scholar than nine in ten of the graduates at Oxford or Cambridge." How far the dream was ever realised is a matter for conjecture; certainly at Kingswood in 1768 onwards there existed little more than the opportunity for study for the ardent student. And, of course, the books. Many of them are still in the library at the school.†

Wesley defended his course of action in paragraphs clearly penned in white heat at this time, though not published till 1781.‡ He is speaking of the advanced course at Kingswood, and is led on to speak of the universities. His words must be quoted at length, for they describe in memorable language the universities of the day.

"It is true," he wrote, "I have for many years suspended the execution of this part of my design. I was indeed thoroughly convinced ever since I read Milton's admirable *Treatise on Education,* that it was highly expedient for every youth to begin and finish his education at the same place. I was convinced nothing could be more irrational and absurd, than to break this off in the middle, and to begin it again at a different place, and in quite a different method. The many and great inconveniences of this, I knew by sad experience.

* See Appendix III. The rules of 1749 were reprinted with slight but significant alterations; three masters, not six, and on Sundays the boys no longer "go to the Parish Church".
† See Appendix III.
‡ See page 89. The quotation here is from *Plain Account of Kingswood School,* paras 16–22: reprinted *Works of John Wesley,* edited Jackson, 1829–31, Vol.XIII, pp.255–67. The phrase "the late remarkable occurrence" and the reference to Seager on page 76 clearly date these paragraphs to 1768–69.

Yet I had so strong a prejudice in favour of our own Universities, that of Oxford in particular, that I could hardly think of any one's finishing his education without spending some years there. I therefore encouraged all I had any influence over, to enter at Oxford or Cambridge; both of which I preferred in many respects, to any University I had seen abroad. Add to this, that several of the young persons at Kingswood had themselves a desire of going to the University. I cannot say I am yet quite clear of that prejudice. I love the very sight of Oxford: I love the manner of life; I love and esteem many of its institutions. But my prejudice in its favour is considerably abated: I do not admire it as I once did. And whether I did or not, I am now constrained to make a virtue of necessity. The late remarkable occurrence of the six young students expelled from the University, and the still more remarkable one of Mr. Seager, refused the liberty of entering into it, (by what rule of prudence, I cannot tell, any more than of law or equity), have forced me to see, that neither I, nor any of my friends, must expect either favour or justice there. I am obliged to Dr. Nowell,* and the other Gentlemen who exerted themselves on either of those transactions, for not holding me longer in suspense, but dealing so frankly and openly. And, blessed be God, I can do all the business which I have in hand without them. Honour or preferment I do not want, any more than a feather in my cap; and I trust most of these who are educated at our school are, and will be, of the same mind. And, as to the knowledge of the tongues, and of arts and sciences, with whatever is termed academical learning; if those who have a tolerable capacity for them do not advance more here in three years, than the generality of students at Oxford or Cambridge do in seven, I will bear the blame for ever.

It may be objected, 'But they cannot have many advantages here which they have at the University. There the professors are men of eminent learning; and so are also many of the Tutors. There they have public exercises of various kinds; and many others in their several Colleges. Above all, they have there such choice of company as is not to be found elsewhere in all the kingdom'.

This is most true. But may I be permitted to ask, (and let calm, sensible men give the answer,) What is the real, intrinsic worth of all these advantages? As to the Professors, how learned soever they are, (and some of them I verily believe yield to none in Europe,) what benefit do nine in ten of the young Gentlemen reap from their learning? Truly, they do them neither harm nor good;

---

* Dr. Thomas Nowell had published a lengthy tract vindicating the action of the authorities.

for they know just nothing about them. They read now and then an ingenious lecture, perhaps three or four times a year. They read it in the public schools: But who hears? Often vel duo vel nemo. And if two hundred out of two or three thousand students hear how much are they edified? What do they learn, or what are they likely to learn, which they may not learn as well or better at home? For about fourteen years, except while I served my father's Cure, I resided in the University. During much of this time, I heard many of those lectures with all the attention I was master of. And I would ask any person of understanding, considering the manner wherein most of those lectures are read, and the manner wherein they are attended, what would be the loss if they were not read at all? I had almost said, what would be the loss if there were no Professorships in the University? '*What*! Why Dr. ——— would lose three hundred a year!' That is a truth: it cannot be denied.

'But the Tutors', you say, 'in the several Colleges, supply what is wanting in the Professors.' A few of them do: and they are worthy of all honour; they are some of the most useful persons in the nation. They are not only men of eminent learning, but of piety and diligence. But are there not many of another sort, who are utterly unqualified for the work they have undertaken? who are far from being masters even of Latin or Greek? who do not understand the very elements of the sciences? who know no more of logic or metaphysics than of Arabic, or even of that odd thing, religion? Perhaps, if a person who knew this were to examine therein the famous gentleman of Edmund Hall, who made such a pother with the young men for their want of learning, he might be found as very an ignoramus as Mr. Middleton.*

And even with regard to many of those Tutors that have learning, how little are their pupils the better for it? Do they use all diligence to instil into them all the knowledge which they have themselves? Do they lecture them constantly? every day, either in the languages or sciences? Do they instruct them regularly and thoroughly, in logic, ethics, geometry, physics, and metaphysics? Are there not some, who, instead of once a day, do not lecture them once a week? perhaps not once a month, if once a quarter? Are not these precious instructors of youth? Indeed, when I consider many of the Tutors who were my contemporaries (and I doubt they are not much mended since,) I cannot believe the want of such instructors to be an irreparable loss.

'Well, but they lose also the advantage of the public exercises, as well as of those in their several Colleges.' Alas, what are these

---

* See page 73 above.

exercises? Excuse me if I speak with all simplicity. I never found them any other than an idle, useless interruption of my useful studies. Pray, of what use are the stated disputations for degrees? Are they not mere grimace? trifling beyond expression? And how little preferable to these are most of the disputations in our several Colleges! What worthy subjects are usually appointed for the scholars to dispute upon! And just suitable to the importance of the subject is the management of it. What are the usual examinations for the degree of a Bachelor or Master of Arts? Are they not so horridly, shockingly superficial as none could believe if he did not hear them? What is that, which should be the most solemn exercise we perform, for a Master of Arts' degree? The reading six lectures in the schools; three in natural, and three in moral, philosophy. Reading them to whom? To the walls: it being counted an affront for any one that has ears to hear them. This is literally true: You know it is. But what an execrable insult upon common sense! These are the public exercises: and is it a loss to have nothing to do with them? to spend all our time in what directly tends to improve us in the most useful knowledge?

'However, there is no such choice of company elsewhere as there is at Oxford or Cambridge.' That is most true; for the moment a young man sets his foot in one or the other, he is surrounded with company of all kinds,—except that which would do him good; with loungers and triflers of every sort (*nequid gravius dicam*); with men who no more concern themselves with learning than with religion;

> who waste away
> In gentle inactivity the day,

to say the best of them; for it is to be feared they are not always so innocently employed. It cannot be denied, there is too much choice of this kind of company in every College. There are likewise gentlemen of a better kind. But what chance is there, that a raw young man should find them? seeing the former will everywhere obtrude themselves upon him, while the latter naturally stand at a distance. Company, therefore, is usually so far from being an advantage to those who enter at either University, that it is the grand nuisance, as well as disgrace, of both; the pit that swallows unwary youths by thousands. I bless God we have no such choice of company at Kingswood; nor ever will, till my head is laid. There is no trifler, no lounger, no drone there; much less any drunkard, sabbath-breaker, or common swearer. Whoever accounts this a disadvantage, may find a remedy at any College in Oxford or Cambridge.

'Be this as it may, there are other advantages of which no other place can boast. There are exhibitions, scholarships, studentships, fellowships, canonries; to say nothing of headships, and professorships, which are not only accompanied with present honour and large emoluments, but open the way to the highest preferments, both in Church and State.'

All this is indisputably true: I know not who can deny one word of it. Therefore, if any of these advantages, if honour, if money, if preferment in Church or State, be the point at which a young man aims, let him by all means go to the University. But there are still a few, even young men, in the world, who do not aim at any of these. They do not desire, they do not seek, either honour, or money, or preferment. They leave Collegians to dispute, and bite, and scratch, and scramble for these things. They believe there is another world; nay, and they imagine it will last for ever. Supposing this, they point all their designs and all their endeavours towards it. Accordingly, they pursue learning itself, only with reference to this. They regard it merely with a view to eternity; purely with a view to know and teach more perfectly, the truth which God has revealed to man, 'the truth which is after godliness', and which they conceive men cannot be ignorant of without hazarding their eternal salvation. This is the only advantage which they seek; and this they can enjoy in as high a degree, in the school or academy at Kingswood, as at any College in the universe.

'But whatever learning they have, if they acquired it there they cannot be ordained' (you mean, episcopally ordained: and indeed that ordination we prefer to any other, where it can be had;) 'for the Bishops have all agreed together not to ordain any Methodist.' O that they would all agree together not to ordain any drunkard, any sabbath-breaker, any common swearer, any that makes the name of religion stink in the nostrils of infidels, any that knows no more of the grounds of religion than he does of Greek or Hebrew! But I doubt that fact. I cannot easily believe that all the Bishops have made such an agreement. Could I be sure they had, I should think it my duty to return them my sincerest thanks. Pity they had not done it ten years ago, and I should not have lost some of my dearest friends. However, I am extremely obliged, if they have agreed to prevent my losing any more the same way; if they have blocked up the door through which several others were likely to run away from me."

Wesley was plainly very sore in 1769–70. The paragraphs throw a revealing light on his state of mind at this critical period in the story of Methodism.

(vii) Across the Atlantic

If in these years the doors of the universities were at least partially closed, other forces were at work which would greatly increase the hold of Methodism on the country as a whole. The industrial revolution was getting into its stride, population was steadily increasing in the North and North-West, and there came a shift in the geographical balance of power which was later to be a chief cause of the demand for political change and parliamentary redistribution. In these areas Methodism grew apace, and the seventies and eighties saw the Connexion with its ever more numerous itinerant preachers go from strength to strength. Their boys were sent to Kingswood.

Nor was this growth or the influence of Kingswood confined to these islands. Already before the end of the sixties there can be detected the first Methodist societies on the far side of the Atlantic, and a "pressing call" from those in Maryland and New York came before Wesley's Conference in Bristol in 1768. A year later Wesley called for volunteers and two of the preachers responded—Richard Boardman and Joseph Pilmoor. To these two men it fell to play a part that entitles them to be ranked among the founding fathers of Methodism in America. Pilmoor had been converted in his sixteenth year under the preaching of Wesley, and Wesley had sent him to Kingswood, where he had spent four years in the late fifties studying English literature, Latin, Hebrew and Greek. Though Boardman was his senior, Pilmoor proved the more aggressive, effective and physically durable.[*] His work achieved striking success in the early seventies and included the purchase of a half finished meeting house which became St. George's, Philadelphia. When two years later Francis Asbury and Richard Wright also arrived from England, it was at St. George's that they were welcomed. After the arrival of Thomas Rankin with overriding authority from England, Pilmoor returned to England (1774), and the leadership of the American Methodists passed to others. Pilmoor had however, always felt his Methodism to be comprehended within the established Church, and his relations with the Anglican evangelical clergy in Philadelphia were such that after some further years of service with

_____

[*] *History of American Methodism,* edited Emory Stevens Bucke, New York, 1964, Vol.I, pp.82ff.

Wesley he returned to Philadelphia in 1784 and became associate Rector of St. Paul's, and later Rector of the united churches of Trinity, St. Thomas, and All Souls.*

The outbreak of the war of American Independence in 1776 by no means extinguished Methodism in America, and its links with Wesley remained unbroken though subjected to severe strain. When all was over the societies that were to become the Methodist Episcopal Church were firmly established with Francis Asbury as their leading figure. Already in 1779 Asbury was discussing the need for "a Kingswood School in America",† and when in 1784 Dr. Thomas Coke arrived as Wesley's emissary to confer with Asbury concerning the future of Methodism in America, the establishment of such a school was among the very first subjects discussed.‡ How far school, how far college? There were differences of opinion. Three objectives finally emerged; first, to nurture the preachers' sons, and keep them from temptation whilst their fathers were riding the circuit; second, to take in poor orphans; and third, to receive the children of "our competent friends", who could pay for their sons' education in an atmosphere where religion and learning might go hand in hand. Land was bought at Abingdon, not far from Baltimore, and a substantial brick building in the Georgian style was erected "where the waterfront forms one of the most beautiful views in the United States". There were to be three masters, and the first President was named by Wesley. He was an Anglican clergyman named Heath, who had been master of a grammar school at Kidderminster. "The college", Coke wrote to tell him, "is erected on the plan of our school at Kingswood. I believe that we shall have one hundred scholars, but we intend to begin with fifty, and three masters. The headmaster's salary will be £60 sterling and lodging in the college, board, washing and so forth, for himself and family . . . ." Wesley evidently had high hopes of Mr. Heath—there are several letters about him and to him—and gave him detailed advice. "The best and shortest method which can be taken to make children critical scholars is Latin, Greek and

* "Joseph Pilmoor, Anglican Evangelical", article in *Historical Magazine of The Protestant Episcopal Church of America*, Vol. XVI, 1947.
† Asbury's *Journal*, November 30, 1779.
‡ *Extracts of the Journals of the Rev. Dr. Coke's Five Visits to America*, 1793, p.16. See also *Methodist Beginnings in Higher Education*, John O. Gross, 1959, where will be found an extended account of these efforts to establish a college.

Hebrew." Among the names proposed for the college was New Kingswood, but it was finally called Cokesbury, after Thomas Coke and Francis Asbury—a choice of name which did not at all commend itself to Wesley.

The *Plan for erecting a College* was printed in full in the first *Discipline of the Methodist Episcopal Church*, in terms which follow broadly the Kingswood model. The rules about play and the banning of holidays were endorsed and defended by the founders of Cokesbury. The recreations that were to take the place of play are given with a detail which we do not happen to be able to parallel from the Kingswood records—gardening, walking, riding and bathing, without doors; and the carpenter's, joiner's, and cabinet-maker's or turner's business, within doors. Agriculture was to be studied in connection with Virgil's *Georgics*, so that the students could delightfully unite the theory and practice together. "We do not entertain the most distant thought of turning these employments into drudgery, but into pleasing recreations for the mind and body." The General Rules proposed for Methodist seminaries of learning continued for many years to be printed in the annual minutes of the Methodist Episcopal Church in America. In one respect indeed they went further than anything that appears in Wesley's rules for Kingswood. "Idleness", read the rule, "may be punished with confinement, according to the discretion of the master. A convenient room shall be set aside as a place of confinement."

The departures from the traditional educational programme were, surprisingly, justified by the founders of Cokesbury by appeal to two of the greatest thinkers of the age, Locke and Rousseau, who were said to have the same sentiments. The reference to Locke is intelligible, for we have noticed his influence on Wesley. But Rousseau is another matter, for Wesley had dismissed his *Emile, ou de l'Education des Enfants* in language of vigorous condemnation when he had read it in 1770.*

Cokesbury College was opened in 1787 with twenty-five students, and despite financial and other difficulties—Mr. Heath soon left—grew in importance and influence among the early Methodists in America. In 1792 there were seventy-two students enrolled; but in December 1795 a disastrous fire completely destroyed it, and Asbury confessed himself unwilling to face again

---

* *Journal*, Vol.V, p.352.

the many difficulties which had attended the enterprise. Dr. Thomas Coke however set to work to make a fresh start in Baltimore, and acquired buildings there; but, this too, after a promising start was completely burnt out a year later. Kingswood and Cokesbury can therefore only in a very general sense be said to be ancestral to the numerous Methodist universities and liberal arts colleges that have succeeded them on the far side of the Atlantic.

(viii) Eighteenth-century eccentrics

It is time to return to the school. The memoirs of Thomas Maurice contain illuminating details of how he came to be sent to Kingswood (1767-69).* His education had been begun at Christ's Hospital and continued at a school in Ealing, where he learnt chiefly classics and botany. His widowed mother had, however, become an ardent admirer of "the celebrated preachers Wesley and Madan". Maurice was himself induced to commit to memory the best of the hymns of Watts and other sacred lyrists. These were for Sunday; on Monday he returned to the study of Ovid and of botany. But "the legends of Ovid were not so chaste, nor his gods so pure" as to entitle them to approbation in his mother's circle. She was without much difficulty persuaded to send him to Kingswood. He calls the school "the fountain head of inspiration—the Helicon of Methodist muses".

"Mr. John Wesley himself," he continues, "make no doubt, with the best intentions possible, strongly recommended my mother to place me among the candidates for holy renown in his own seminary. then recently instituted near Bristol . . . The resolution of banishing me to that dreary spot was singular enough, but the mode of conveying me thither was still more so; for though I had never been on the outside of a horse in my life; never had, like other boys bestridden even a jackass, and had only sometimes indulged myself in taking a journey round the room mounted on a cane . . . I was to commence a journey of above 120 miles on horseback."

He was to accompany a preacher bound thither, and the horse was to be none other than Wesley's own, a horse of the pony kind that had no more vice than his master. Nothing could then

* *Memoirs of the Author of a History of Indian Antiquities, 1819.*

depress Maurice's eager anticipation of contemplating the delightful landscapes and the magnificent villas which he was to pass in performing the enchanting journey. They were to visit the lofty castle of Windsor, and the romantic rock of Clifton. The morning came, the steed arrived, and they contemplated each other with mutual satisfaction.

"I was sportive and playful, bounding on and off his back with wonderful agility, and he seemed to prick up his ears, and shake his full flowing mane with delight. Hypocrisy was never better acted than by this caitiff horse; for as soon as he got into motion, with me seated on his back, and felt the whip which I made no scruple to apply . . . he set off at full speed with his astonished rider on the public road towards Bath; the preacher, equally astonished, galloping close behind, and making fruitless efforts to stop the infuriated animal . . ."

The inevitable happened; he was carried home almost insensible, and the whole catastrophe was imputed to the machinations of Satan. However, within the month he and his younger brother were transported by a safe conveyance to Bristol, whence they were conveyed to "the Athens of Methodist literature"—

"I have no fault whatever to find", he tells us, rather surprisingly, "with the general method of conducting this secluded school . . . The only complaint I have to make is against those unfeeling friends who permitted *me* to be sent to such a barbarous place for mental improvement . . . The presiding classical master (i.e. Joseph Benson) was by no means deficient in learning, in talents and in zeal to promote the improvement of the pupils."

The habit of early rising, and the strict discipline observed were, he thought, good and salutary but he was critical of "the long prayers, the occasional fastings, and restraint from the usual sports of school boys". What follows is of interest in showing what occasional concessions to "tender parents" were sometimes permitted:

"Myself and my brother, being placed there particularly under the guardian protection of the two Mr. Wesleys, had I believe, more than usual indulgence shown to us: but bleak and terrific was the prospect of the barren desert that surrounded us; and the only human beings we beheld, or could converse with, without the walls of this holy Bastille, were the sooty delvers of the coalpits, that ex-

tended for miles on every side of it. Two miserable years were passed
in the bosom of this howling wilderness, the solitude of which was
alleviated only by occasional visits to Bristol, where my mother
resided as a boarder in a house of a lady of the Methodist persuasion
in Queen Square."

Release was to come unexpectedly. The coach that carried his
mother to London once a year to receive the dividends due to
her at the Bank and the India Office was overturned near Reading; and the effects of the contusion and violent fever that
followed were such that, to the consternation of her friends and
her sons, she was inveigled into a clandestine marriage with an
Irish fortune hunter. The new husband summoned the boys
to an inn at Bristol; they then took "leave of Kingswood's dreary
bounds for ever". Only by drastic measures taken by the young
hero himself was his mother set free, and saved from signing
away her family's fortune. Maurice was thus enabled to continue
his education, which he did by joining some fifty boys who had
followed Dr. Samuel Parr to Stanmore in a secession from
Harrow.* In this excellent school Maurice found himself more
at home than at Kingswood, went on to Oxford, became a vain-
glorious poet and author of a history of Indian Antiquities.

Another who merits more than a passing word was that youthful genius whom we have glimpsed teaching Latin and Greek
at Trevecka. Born in 1757, John Henderson was the son of one
of Wesley's itinerant preachers. "The young Henderson was born,
as it were, a thinking being . . . The questions he asked, as soon
as he was able to speak, astonished all who heard him."†

He was sent, as early as possible, to Kingswood. At the age
of eight he was teaching Latin in the school; at twelve, as we
have seen, he went to teach at Trevecka. Returning from
Trevecka he seems to have taught in his father's school, where one
Joseph Cottle was among his pupils. Cottle was later to undertake
the publication of *Lyrical Ballads* for Wordsworth and Coleridge.
The accounts of Henderson's precocity and learning are such as
to strain credulity, and it would be tedious to list his reputed
accomplishments. But a chance encounter in a coach with

---

* For this school see Warren Derry, *Dr. Parr, A portrait of the Whig Dr.
Johnson,* 1966.
† *Sermon occasioned by the death of the celebrated Mr. J. Henderson, B.A.,
of Pembroke College, Oxford,* by the Rev. Wm. Agutter, M.A.

the learned Dr. Tucker, Dean of Gloucester, resulted in the suggestion to Henderson's father that his son should go to one of the universities, and the suggestion was supported by a gift of two hundred pounds. He was accordingly entered at Pembroke College, Oxford. There his eccentricities did not prevent his making many friends. It is even asserted that many of the Heads of Colleges habitually attended his evening parties—"an honour unknown before ever to have been conferred on any undergraduate". In all companies, we are told, he led the conversation, and although perpetually surrounded by admirers remained unspoiled. He attracted Dr. Johnson's notice, and such was the latter's admiration that "in whatever company he entered on his annual visits to Oxford he stipulated for the introduction of his young friend John Henderson". But Henderson did not live to become another Dr. Johnson. He died while still young, and was buried at St. George's, Kingswood. He left nothing of note behind him ; a maidservant at his father's house had used his manuscript one winter to light the fires, an incident of which Henderson could not bring himself to speak. To Joseph Cottle, Henderson's memory was precious—had he not sat up with him till three in the morning listening to the wonderful discourse on the day before his last departure for Oxford? He wrote an account of his friend's life and printed it with his own verses, and Henderson's portrait as a frontispiece.* Wesley, as was perhaps natural, took a more severe view. He spoke briefly of Henderson as "one who, with as great talents as most young men in England", had lived two and thirty years, "and done just nothing".

It is a misfortune that the records do not enable us to trace the careers of more of the boys of those early decades. Amongst the seventy-five or so boys whose names are known to us in the decade eight are to be found in the *Dictionary of National Biography*. Some no doubt took orders. Joseph Easterbrook had at about this time gone to Madeley to help Fletcher with a school there, was ordained and became Vicar of the Temple Church in Bristol in 1779. He made it an important centre of evangelical work in Bristol, and carried on the work in the Bristol Newgate.

* See *Malvern Hills with minor poems and essays,* by Joseph Cottle, fourth edition, 1829. An account of Henderson appeared in the Monthly Review 1789, and another in the Arminian Magazine 1793. Tyerman devotes some pages to him in his life of Fletcher, *Wesley's Designated Successor.*

"He is a pattern to all Bristol", wrote Wesley in 1790, "and indeed to all England; having, beside his other incessant labours, preached in every house in his parish." He died in 1791 and is buried under the leaning tower of Temple Church, not far from Temple Meads.

Simon Lloyd, of Bala, was at Kingswood in 1770, became one of the evangelical group at Oxford in the seventies, was ordained, and later became a leader in the Welsh Calvinistic Methodist movement. Peter Le Lievre, the son of one of Wesley's nieces who had married a French Protestant refugee, was educated at Kingswood, took orders in the Church, taught for a while at the school, and later became Vicar of Lutterworth. Others of the boys no doubt became schoolmasters; we know that later on there was a strong demand for boys from Kingswood to act as schoolmasters, and it may well have existed in the latter decades of the eighteenth century.

(ix) Mr. and Mrs. Simpson

When Joseph Benson left in 1770, Wesley had been writing to Thomas Simpson. Perhaps Simpson was not well enough to come at once, for in the autumn of 1771 we find two letters from Wesley to Isaac Twycross, evidently in charge at Kingswood, and once again there had been trouble of some kind.

"Dear Isaac, Surely it is a mistake . . . For was there not a cause for all and more that I did according to the account you yourself have given me? The rules were not observed! Are they being observed now? Do *you* rise at four? Do you observe the other rules? I hope Mr. Albert, who is coming in a few days will observe them for conscience sake."

and again, on December 28,

"I perceive you do not take the matter right. When James Hindmarsh went away I told the Trustees 'I will not have any schoolmaster burdened with temporal things any more. Do *you* lay out the money and keep the accounts.' They ought to have done this before, without it. It naturally belongs to them to see that the things round the house be kept in order."

Of Twycross we know little save that like other early masters he took orders. However, Simpson was now clearly ready to take over. We have already seen him mentioned as among the best preachers, and there is a letter to him.

"Dear Tommy,—I make no doubt at all but God will give you strength according to your day.

I found John Glascock in want of everything; I sent him to Kingswood, that he might want nothing. But, since he is neither thankful to God nor man, send him back again as soon as you please.

Whenever we can find a young man that can and will conscientiously observe the rules of the house you shall have him directly. Is the young man of Coleford such a one? If so, take him without delay."

The reference to a likely young man shows that Wesley was taking every opportunity of recruiting young men such as Jaco and Benson who would pursue the advanced course of studies set out in the *Short Account* of 1768. Indeed there were those who thought the school might be more usefully employed as a theological college for the itinerant preachers, and in 1775 Joseph Benson worked out detailed proposals and submitted them to Fletcher of Madeley, for his advice.*

The staff was strengthened in 1773 by the appointment of Cornelius Bayley, who had been a master in the Grammar School at Whitchurch, Salop. Whilst at Kingswood he published a Hebrew Grammar. He asked Wesley to read it, only to receive a snub. "It is the glory of the Methodists to have few authors", said Wesley, for he had himself written a Hebrew Grammar. But Bayley was ambitious, and the title page advertised the whole to be digested in so easy a manner that a child of seven years old may arrive at a competent knowledge of the Hebrew Scriptures with very little assistance. Wesley must have relented, for he appears as an original subscriber for four copies.

The school prospered in the seventies under Simpson and Bayley, and the references in Wesley's *Journal* and correspondence are mainly concerned with finding room for applicants. "Boarders at Kingswood pay twenty pounds a year. There is no entrance money or further expense of any kind." Wesley's words might be those of a headmaster of today. He added that the masters were men of sense, learning and piety.† The

* The correspondence is too lengthy to quote here. It is printed as Appendix XXIX of Wesley's *Journal*.

† Letter to Miss Roe, September 16, 1776.

Simpson regime was not perfect—there are rumblings now
and again, and Wesley went over to Kingswood and put things
right.* At the time of the great panic in March 1778 when France
threw her weight into the scales with the American Colonies
against Britain, Wesley spent an hour with the children at Kingswood. Many he found "truly desirous to save their souls", but
another entry shows that several of them "have trifled their
convictions away". On into the eighties the school continued
"quite full",† "exceeding full"‡. It was a case of "making room
for the little boy".§

When therefore in 1778 Wesley embarked on his monthly
Arminian Magazine, it was proper that space should be found
for references to Kingswood School. Simpson's was among the
early portraits published, and accounts of the revivals at Kingswood that we have already noticed appeared among other edifying material. But he went further and in 1781 serial articles appeared entitled *A Plain Account of Kingswood School.*

The *Plain Account* is an invaluable addition to what we know
from other sources, and the reader will recall that we have drawn
upon it in describing both the opening of the school in 1748 and
Wesley's reaction to the rebuff from the universities in 1768-69.
As we have seen, internal evidence dates the writing of much,
if not the whole, of the *Plain Account* to the period 1768-69
rather than to the date of its publication in 1781. Wesley must
have had it by him unpublished, and found it useful when
material was needed for the Magazine, which he edited himself.
No doubt times had changed, and the reasons which had prevailed against publication no longer applied.‖

It was a defence of the school. He would have supposed, he
said, that the bare publication of the rules of the school would
have been sufficient, but he found that what was as clear to him
as the sun at noon day was not so clear to everyone. He judged it
needful therefore to enlarge a little on the nature of that institution, and to explain "what is peculiar in our method".

---

* *Journal,* September 3, 1773, and again March, 1774.
† Letter to John Bredin, October 1781.
‡ Letter to William Bland, July 1783.
§ Letter to Mathew Mayer, December, 1783.
‖ *Works* Vol. XIII, pp. 255-67.

G

The reader will know by now what to expect in Wesley's description of the school. He insists once again on the reasonableness of the "uncommon rule" that the parents shall not take the child away, "no, not for a day, till they take him for good and all". The reasonableness of this uncommon rule is shown by constant experience: For children may unlearn as much in one week, as they have learned in several; nay, and contract a prejudice to exact discipline, which never can be removed. The early rising he knows by constant observation, and by long experience, to be of admirable use, either for preserving a good, or improving a bad, constitution. It is of peculiar service in almost all nervous complaints, both in preventing and in removing them. Particular care is taken that they never work alone, but always in the presence of a master. This circumstance he adopted from the great school at Jena in Germany.* It lays much labour upon the masters; but the advantage is worth all the labour. It prevents abundance of evil; (and it is far better to prevent evils, than to punish them) not only rudeness and ill manners, but many sins that children would easily teach each other.

Their food is simple as possible; two days in a week it is wholly vegetable. At eight they go to bed, the youngest first. They all lodge in one room (every child having a bed to himself) in which a lamp burns all night. A master lies in the same room. The propriety of these circumstances is so manifest that it needs not be enlarged upon. "All the beds have mattresses on them, not feather-beds; both because they are more healthy, and because we would keep them at the utmost distance from softness and effeminacy."

This glowing prose had scarcely gone to the printer before Wesley had fresh cause for complaint. On September 7, 1781, there is the entry—

"I went over to Kingswood, and made a particular enquiry into the management of the school. I found some of the rules had not been observed at all, particularly that of rising in the morning. Surely Satan has a peculiar spite at this school! What trouble has it cost

---

* Wesley presumably means the celebrated school at Halle. He passed through Jena on his way thither. See Appendix II.

me for above these thirty years! I can plan, but who will execute? I know not; God help me!"

It was unfortunate for Simpson's later reputation that a young man sent by Wesley to the school in 1782 was later to become the well-known Dr. Adam Clarke. For Adam Clarke in his youth* did not take kindly to the school, and his memoirs contain vigorous strictures on the regime. They afford nevertheless a shaft of light on the school at just the moment when, as we know from Wesley's outbursts quoted above, Simpson's management was failing.

Adam Clarke was the precocious son of a schoolmaster at Killowen, and had been noticed by one of Wesley's itinerants, John Bredin, on the Coleraine and Londonderry circuit. Bredin had lent him books, and supposing him to be called to the ministry, wrote to Wesley. Wesley offered to take him for a time at Kingswood, where he might increase his knowledge of the classics, and have the opportunity of exercising his ministerial talents in the various societies in the neighbourhood. In August 1782 he set out from Ireland, narrowly escaping the attentions of the press-gang, whose search of the vessel is vividly related in his memoirs. He arrived in Liverpool, and friends procured for him an outside place on the fly. This was one of the first stage coaches, which carried six insides, and as many outsides as could stick on, together with an enormous boot and basket, which made it "little inferior to a wagon in size, and not a great deal superior in speed". His admission that he was a Methodist aroused hilarity among his travelling companions, but he carried all off well by exchange of quotations from Horace. In Birmingham friends asked him what he proposed by going to Kingswood School. Adam, who had been led to consider it in the light of a university, only much better conducted, referred them to some of the late magazines, where such an account was given as quite justified all his expectations. This, of course, was Wesley's panegyric in the Arminian Magazine, which had appeared in 1781. "Some of us", said his friends, "know the place well; and know you will not meet in it what you have been led to expect." He spent the night

* His age at the time is uncertain: it is variously given as 18 to 22. The account which follows, and in quotations used, are from the Life of Adam Clarke, 1833.

at the inn, as the coach left at three in the morning. He reached the Lamb Inn at Broadmead, Bristol, at eight o'clock that night, subsisting on a penny loaf and a halfpennyworth of apples.

The next morning he walked to Kingswood and arrived when preaching in the chapel was about to commence. But Simpson had heard nothing from Wesley to warn him of Adam's arrival and high expectations; the school was full, every bed was occupied. Adam had to await Wesley's arrival from Cornwall and to submit to quasi-isolation, for the headmaster's wife was afraid he might have brought an infection with him from Ireland. He never forgot or forgave the unhappy impression made upon him by her dominant personality. He likened her to a Bengal Tiger. "She was probably very clever, all stood in awe of her. For my own part, I feared her worse than I feared Satan himself."

His account, with its illuminating detail mingled with all the trivialities that upset him, makes quaint reading. There is much that rings true enough. Here we must be content with extracts—

The school at that time consisted of the sons of itinerant preachers, and parlour boarders. The latter were taken in, because the public collections were not sufficient to support the institution.

As a religious seminary, and under the direction of one of the greatest men in the world, Mr. J. Wesley, (though his multitudinous avocations prevented him from paying much attention to it), the school had a great character, both over Europe and America, among religious people. Independently of several young gentlemen, the sons of opulent Methodists, there were at that time in it several from the West Indies, Norway, Sweden and Denmark.

The following was the domestic establishment:

Mr. Thomas Simpson, M.A., was head master. Mrs. Simpson, housekeeper. Miss Simpson, assistant. The Rev. Cornelius Bayley, afterwards Dr. Bayley, of Manchester, was English teacher, who had I believe at that time only £12 per annum and his board for his labour. Mr. Vincent de Boudry was occasional French teacher; and Mr. C. R. Bond was a sort of half boarder, and assistant English teacher.

Mr. S. was a man of learning and piety; much of a gentleman, but too easy for his situation. Mr. Bayley was a man of the strictest morals and exemplary piety. Mr. De Boudry was a man of plain sense and true godliness. Mr. Bond was a young man of little experience, and shallow in talents, but affectionate: whose highest ambition seemed to be, to reach the exalted place and character of a clergyman.

The scholars were none of them remarkable for piety or learning. The young gentlemen that were introduced had spoilt the discipline of the school; very few of its Rules and Regulations were observed; and in no respect answered the end of its institution . . .

. . . it was the worst school I had ever seen, and though the teachers were men of adequate learning, yet as the school was perfectly disorganised, and in several respects each did what was right in his own eyes, and there was no efficient plan pursued, they mocked at religion, and trampled under foot all the laws. The little children of the preachers suffered great indignities; and it is to be feared their treatment there gave many of them a rooted enmity against piety and religion for life. The parlour boarders had every kind of respect paid to them, and the others were shamefully neglected. Had this most gross mismanagement been known to the Methodist preachers, they would have suffered their sons to die in ignorance, rather than have sent them to a place where there was scarcely any care taken either of their bodies or souls. I found to my great discomfort, all the hints thrown out by Mr. B. and my Birmingham friends more than realized. . . .

But to return to the remainder of my short stay in Kingswood. For the sake of exercise, I often worked in the garden. Observing one day a small plot which had been awkwardly turned over by one of the boys, I took the spade and began to dress it: in breaking one of the clods, I knocked a half-guinea out of it. I took it up and immediately said to myself, this is not mine; it belongs not to any of my family, for they have never been here; I will take the first opportunity to give it to Mr. Simpson. Shortly after, I perceived him walking in the garden. I went to him, told him the circumstance, and presented the half-guinea to him; he took it, looked at it, and said 'It may be mine, as several hundred pounds pass through my hands in the course of the year, for the expenses of this school; but I do not recollect that I ever lost any money since I came here. Probably one of the gentlemen has; keep it, and in the meantime I will enquire.' I said 'sir, it is not mine, take you the money, if you meet the right owner, well; if not, throw it in the funds of the school'.

Out of the half-guinea, the finding of which he could only regard as providential, Clarke gave Mr. Bayley six shillings as his subscription for the Hebrew Grammar; "by which work I acquired", says Clarke, "a satisfactory knowledge of that language which ultimately led me to read over the Hebrew Bible, and make those short notes which formed the basis of the Commentary since published! Had I not got that Grammar I probably should never have turned my mind to Hebrew learning; and most certainly had never written a Commentary on Divine Revelation!"

When Wesley appeared, Adam Clarke was brought out of his prison house, as he calls it, and

. . . I had a bed assigned to me in the large room with the rest of the boys, (for about forty lay in the same chamber, each in a separate cot, with a flock bed), and had permission to dine with the family . . . It was soon observed at table that I drank no person's health. The truth is, I had ever considered it an absurd and senseless custom, and could not bring my mind to it. At this table, every person when he drank was obliged to run the following gauntlet. He must drink the health of Mr. Simpson—Mrs. Simpson—Miss Simpson—Mr. Bayley—Mr. De Boudry—all the foreign gentlemen —then all the parlor boarders, down one side of the long table, and up the other, one by one, and all the visitors who might happen to be there—after which it was lawful for him to drink his glass of beer.

On Mrs. Simpson's insisting upon my going through this routine and drinking all healths, I told her I had a scruple of conscience, and could not submit to it till better informed; and hoped she would not insist on it. She answered. 'You certainly shall: you shall not drink at table unless you drink the healths of the company as the others do. Mr. Wesley drinks healths; Mr. Fletcher does the same; but you will not do it, because of course you have more wisdom and piety than they have'. To this I could not reply. I was in Rome, and it would have been absurd in me to have attempted to contend with the Pope.

But Simpson had taken care to see Wesley first, and the upshot was that Adam Clarke was sent almost at once to fill a vacancy for a preacher in the Trowbridge circuit.

He left on the morning of September 26, 1782, and walked to Bath, where he heard Wesley preach. He concludes

I left Kingswood without a sigh or a groan. It had been to me a place of unworthy treatment, not to say torment: but this had lasted only one month and two days; thirty-one days too much, if

God had not been pleased to order it otherwise. But the impressions made upon my mind by the bad usage received there, have never been erased: a sight of the place has ever filled me with distressing sensations; and the bare recollection of the name never fails to bring with it associations both unpleasant and painful. Those who were instruments of my tribulation are gone to another tribunal; and against them I never made any complaint.

Adam Clarke's account is indeed invaluable, but we must now return to the story of the school as known to us from other sources. Wesley had, as we have seen, found cause for complaint before Adam Clarke's arrival there. That Cornelius Bayley had long been dissatisfied we know from a letter of his to Wesley in 1776. He had spoken of the want of peace and harmony "which has ever been the destruction of the school", and had been driven to desperation by the dissension and tale-bearing on the part of the housekeeper. He had been on the point of resignation—"it is with a broken heart I write, to think I should leave the school of a person I love and honour above all men . . . if I could have had peace and unanimity though double the salary of your school had been offered me it would not have drawn me away from it." Bayley had however stayed, and we find him still there in 1780, just ordained, yet unwilling to leave without proposing a proper person in his place—"and certain I am the good of the school greatly depends on a proper colleague with Mr. Simpson." Wesley was at Kingswood in March 1782, and again in March 1783. In the May of that year he married Bayley in Buxton,* and no doubt again discussed the state of affairs at the school.

At the Conference that year Wesley took action—

My design in building the house at Kingswood was, to have therein a Christian family; every member whereof, children excepted, should be alive to God, and a pattern of all holiness.

* For Bayley's subsequent career see W.H.S., Vol.XXXIV p.153ff. He settled in Manchester, officiating for a while at the Oldham Street Chapel. Manchester was growing fast, and Bayley became responsible for the building of St. James's, of which he became incumbent. The congregation there was supposed to be the most numerous of any of the churches, and he became one of the chief instruments of pioneering Sunday schools in Manchester and its neighbourhood. Whilst still at Kingswood he had been admitted at Trinity College Cambridge as a "Ten-Year Man", and was awarded a Cambridge D.D. in 1800.

Here it was that I proposed to educate a few children according to the accuracy of the Christian model. And almost as soon as we began, God gave us a token for good; four of the children receiving a clear sense of pardon.

But at present the school does not anywise answer the design of the institution, either with regard to religion or learning.

The children are not religious. They have not the power, and hardly the form, of religion. Neither do they improve in learning better than at other schools: No, nor yet so well.

Insomuch that some of our friends have been obliged to remove their children to other schools.

And no wonder that they improve so little either in religion or learning; for the rules of the school are not observed at all.

All in the house ought to rise, take their three meals, and go to bed, at a fixed hour. But they do not.

The children ought never to be alone, but always in the presence of a Master. This is totally neglected; in consequence of which they run up and down the wood, and mix, yea, fight, with the colliers' children.

They ought never to play. But they do, every day; yea, in the school.

Three maids are sufficient. Now there are four; and but one, at most, truly pious.

How may these evils be remedied, and the school reduced to its original plan? It must be mended, or ended; for no school is better than the present school.

Can any be a Master that does not rise at five, observe all the rules, and see that others observe them?

There should be three Masters, and an Usher, chiefly to be with the children out of school.

The Head Master should have nothing to do with temporal things.

Wesley's strictures were hard on Simpson's reputation. Myles in his account puts it more simply; "Mr. Wesley found it necessary at this time to change the master at Kingswood School, on account of a total want of discipline . . . He would have them, instead of play to learn husbandry or some mechanic art".

"But how can Mr. Simpson be provided for?" asked the members of the Conference. "He desires to become an itinerant preacher", was the reply. He had formerly, we know, been a good preacher; in Wesley's view, one of the best. But clearly he changed

THOMAS SIMPSON
1770–83 (see pp. 87ff.)
from an engraving in the
Arminian Magazine

THOMAS McGEARY
1783–94 (see pp. 98ff.)
from an engraving in the
Arminian Magazine

KINGSWOOD SCHOOL IN 1790
The engraving by James Heath (see p. 100) was respectfully inscribed to the
Revd. Mr. Wesley, M.A. by his Dutiful Servant, Thos. McGeary.
In Gloriam Dei Opt. Max. in Usum Ecclesiae & Reipublicae

WOODHOUSE GROVE SCHOOL (see pp. 118ff.)
from an engraving in *Woodhouse Grove School* by J. T. Slugg

OLD KINGSWOOD
from an engraving of the early nineteenth century

his mind, for in fact he set up a school in Keynsham, where his son later became vicar.*

It was decided that either the school should cease, or the rules of it be particularly observed.

The finding of new masters occasioned the writing of a letter by Wesley in his most succinct style to Thomas Welch, who had written offering his services as writing master.†

Bristol, August 15, 1783

"Dear Thomas,—You seem to be the man I want. As to salary, you will have £30 a year; board, &c will be thirty more. But do not come for money. (1) Do not come at all unless purely to raise a Christian school. (2) Anybody behaving ill I will turn away immediately. (3) I expect you to be in the school eight hours a day. (4) In all things I expect you to be circumspect. But you will judge better by considering the printed Rules. The sooner you come the better.—I am, Your affectionate brother."

Welch, however, was advised to stay in Coventry, and Wesley was not at all pleased—"You use me very ill. I have turned away three masters on your account." Welch later regretted that he had not accepted the position.

Wesley must have felt it incumbent on him further to defend his rules, and in 1783 published *A Thought on the Manner of Educating Children.* If the critics were right who thought that it was a mistake to press religion on children whether they will or no, "how much mischief has been done, is now doing, at Kingswood, where (if this hypothesis be true) we are continually ruining fifty children at a time!" Wesley had his defence ready—"Many of the men . . . who were educated at Kingswood are holy in heart and life, and trust they shall praise God to all eternity that they ever saw the school". The document is of much interest, but it will be convenient here first to follow further the story of the school.

---

* Wesley visited this school in October 1787 and commented favourably on the spirit and behaviour of the children.

† *Letters,* Vol. VII, p. 188.

(x) Success at Last

The new headmaster was Thomas McGeary, M.A. He was, we are told, only twenty-two on appointment, and was to remain at the school until 1794, and to give every satisfaction.

Wesley visited the school every few months during the last decade of his life. He should be thought of with his cassock, his black silk stockings, his large silver buckles, and his old lumbering carriage with a bookcase inside it. No one who saw him, even casually, in his old age, says Southey, could have forgotten his venerable appearance. "His face was remarkably fine: his complexion fresh to the last week of his life: his eyes quite keen and active. When you met him in the street of a crowded city, he attracted notice, not only by his band and cassock and his long hair, white and bright as silver, but by his face and manner, both indicating that all his minutes were numbered, and that not one was to be lost."

Kingswood now met with his warm approval—

"I talked at large with our masters at Kingswood School", he wrote in March 1784, "who are now just such as I wished for. At length the rules of the house are punctually observed, and the children are all in good order."

In September he preached in Bristol, hastened to Kingswood, and preached under the shade of that double row of trees which he had planted about forty years before. Later that month he records a conversation in Bristol with John McGeary "one of our American preachers just come to England"—perhaps the headmaster's brother, for later the same day Wesley is at the school. He was there for some little time, for on October 2 many of the children were much affected, and Wesley observed "an uncommon awe resting upon them all".

The school was clearly in demand, for in the following year Conference resolved not to receive any preachers' sons under nine years of age. In March 1786 all was in excellent order. In July he was there again—

"I walked over to Kingswood school, now one of the pleasantest spots in England. I found all things just according to my desire, the rules being well observed, and the whole behaviour of the children showing that they were now managed with the wisdom that cometh from above."

It is a great pity that we do not know more about McGeary, and every glimpse of him is precious. Two letters addressed to him by Wesley are treasured in the library at the school—

London, September 25, 1786.

"Tommy, Tommy! You put me in mind of my father. Once and again he has laid his hand upon my breast, and said, "Down, proud Heart!" I did not like it then: But I knew afterwards, it was wholesome for me. But how it is, that you thus kick and wince at Censure? Did you never read the Rules of our Society! O Tommy you are a poor Methodist! Had I been of your mind I should have turned back long ago. I perceive your spirit has been hurt. The fact of pride has come against you. But God is able to heal you. I am
                                    Your Affectionate Brother . . ."

There was difficulty in finding another master—

London, February 15, 1787.
"Dear Tommy,
    It is a wonderful strange thing, that in all the three kingdoms, we cannot find such a school master as we would, I have sent to every part of England, and to every Assistant I wrote to; but none can give me any information. We are expecting every day to hear from one and another; but still, we hear nothing. There is only one point more, That *I* should be weary and say 'Let it go as it will: I will trouble myself about it no more'. Then there is an end of Kingswood School, and the labour of near forty years is lost! But I trust that will not be the case yet; for God heareth the Prayer! I am, with love to S. McGeary. . . ."

In March 1787, Wesley found the school in a better state than he expected, considering the want of a second master, and in September spent an evening at the school "and was much pleased with the management of it".

A year later everything at Kingswood was still "in excellent order". In September of 1788 Wesley was writing—

"The school is now in just such a state as I wish. Mr. McGeary has three pious and able assistants, out of those that were brought up in it; and I doubt not it will supply a sufficiency of masters for the time to come."

A year later it earned high praise indeed—

"I went over to Kingswood; sweet recess! where everything is now just as I wish. But
> Man was not born in shades to lie
> Let us work now; we shall rest by and by."

In January 1790, Wesley is writing to McGeary the last letter that has come down to us—

"Dear Tommy—There is no danger of my thinking your writing troublesome . . .
You must be absent from the School at some times, that you may be present more effectually. But I desire you will take a little tour next month if the weather will allow. The spending a week or two now and then in the open air is the best physic in the world for you. Perfect love is not ill-behaved or ill-natured. Peace be with all your spirits!—I am, dear Tommy, yours most affectionately,
Mr. Bradily, a pious young man from Antigua, earnestly desires to be a boarder at Kingswood. I do not object."

It is to McGeary that we owe the engraving of the school in 1790, which shows Wesley walking in the garden with a companion; perhaps McGeary himself, or more probably Joseph Bradford, who often acted as Wesley's travelling companion. Wesley's features are remarkably clear, and must plainly be a careful likeness. His last visit to Bristol was in July and August 1790, and it was perhaps at this time that the engraving was made. It is a good engraving, the work of James Heath, who in 1791 became an Associate Engraver to the Royal Academy, and in 1794 was appointed Engraver to the King. A copy is to be found in the British Museum among the topographical prints and drawings formerly in the library of George III, now in the Map Room. This and other copies bear wording which states that the engraving is respectfully inscribed to the Rev. Mr. Wesley by his dutiful servant Thomas McGeary, and shows that it could be obtained at the "preaching houses in town and country". McGeary's inscription refers to the school as "erected" in 1741. It is strange that he should say this. The New House was "erected" in 1748. Nor, so far as we know did any part of the older buildings date from 1741. The engraving was clearly at one time widely distributed, but is now scarce.*

The New House, already over forty years old, is proudly displayed. On the left, just visible through the avenue of trees, can be discerned the original building of 1739 which served as chapel for the local society, as well as for the school. The nature of the smaller building in the centre of the picture is not certain; perhaps stables or domestic offices, but it is known that later on, in 1822, the schoolroom on approximately this site was converted into a laundry when a larger schoolroom was built. It seems possible that the building was indeed the schoolroom, built at some early date but never separately mentioned. If so, it would explain what is otherwise a mystery—where school work was done in the early days. It does not seem likely that the original schoolroom or chapel of 1739 long served a dual purpose, as has sometimes been supposed, for in other cases Wesley thought such a practice was attended with many inconveniences.

The gardens are a prominent feature. What part Wesley played in their design we do not know, but he made a point of visiting gardens, and would speak of the exquisite beauty and symmetry of those he saw on his short visit to Holland in 1786.† In the garden are some of the boys, in the presence of a master who improves his mind by reading a book.

The boys, it will be noticed, no longer wear a miniature version of their fathers' attire, but loose light coloured garments open at the neck. The change may be attributed to the influence of Rousseau.‡ The idea had begun to dawn that children were not, and ought not to be, miniature reflections of their elders, and in the second half of the eighteenth century there was a real im-

---

* It has been reproduced in colour in recent years, and copies can be obtained through the school.

† A little note of instructions about a garden survives which, though it may not relate to Kingswood, illustrates Wesley's attitude (*Letters,* Vol.I, p.xvi).
"I desire 1. That the gate may be hung. 2. That the hinge of the garden door may be mended. 3. That the door may be kept locked. 4. That the garden may be made and kept as neat as the adjoining garden. 5. That gooseberries and currants may be planted down the middle walk and strawberries under them. 6. That the rest of the ground may be sown with whatever it will bear. 7. That a part of it be planted with raspberries and part with flowers. J.W."

‡ See James Laver, article in *Tatler,* November 9, 1962.

provement in children's clothes. Boys anticipated the grown-up clothes of a later age, for they were put into trousers at a period when every gentleman wore knee-breeches. In the Kingswood print some wear trousers, some breeches.

Indeed to judge by a bill-book of 1789–94 the regime sounds surprisingly liberal. Boys could have newspapers and magazines, some drew cash, another paid for tickets for Hansford's astronomy lecture. Boys could wear different clothes; one boy, Paul Grut, had six muslin cravats made for him, could buy stockings in Wells and shoe a horse there, and wear a Kersey-Royal waistcoat. He entered at 11 and before he left at 15 he had bought dissecting instruments. The fees had gone up to £16 a year, sometimes £20, as specified for those taking the academical course; it was £22 2s. 0d. if tea were included.

Wesley died in London in 1791 at the age of 88, and the Bristol newspapers carried quaint obituary notices. The school went into mourning for its great Founder. We see them through the eyes of the bill-book joining in the universal tribute, in their black suits, black stockings, black shoes and buckles, "love ribbons" in their hats. The modish Paul Grut has abandoned his smart waistcoat for a new and expensive mourning suit; the two Trumans, the brewer's sons, have new suits, considerably less in cost; another, a £20 boarder, makes do with new breeches; the preachers' sons with their best suits.

In his will Wesley left his books, furniture, "and whatever else belongs to me in the three houses at Kingswood" in trust to Thomas Coke, Alexander Mather and Henry Moore to be employed in teaching and maintaining the children of the poor travelling preachers.

Meanwhile the school was quietly changing its character. From being a school intended for "the sons of or principal friends", with whom were associated a few of the preachers' sons, it was becoming primarily a school for the latter. In 1788, Conference resolved that the number of preachers' sons be raised to forty, and the number of paying boarders reduced to ten as soon as possible. What caused Wesley to decide in the eighties to make or permit such a fundamental change in the character of the school? It may of course have been simply the increasing pressure from the preachers, coupled with the good repute of the school under McGeary's management.* But there is surely another possible explanation. May it not be that McGeary persuaded Wesley that the school of his dreams where religion and learning were to flourish together was more likely to be realised by building up the little group who came from the homes of the preachers than by admitting more of the sons of the "opulent" Methodists whom we have seen Wesley busily recruiting in the seventies, and that he accordingly took steps to encourage the preachers to send their boys to the school?

The race of preachers whose boys now increasingly filled the school must be thought of as for ever on their horses, in blue coats, black waistcoats and breeches, white linen stocks and three-cornered hats; their wardrobes and their libraries in their saddle-bags; and their allowance would be raised in 1800 to £16 a year each. It is recorded that they loved study, that they improved themselves in various branches of learning, and that since they did not in general remove oftener than once in two years from one circuit to another they became more known to the people at large, and were less persecuted. But the Bishops and the parish clergy were for the most part hostile to the movement and fearful for the Establishment: many refused Holy Communion to members of Wesley's Societies. Met in Conference in the years after Wesley's death, the preachers were greatly troubled by the alternatives by which they were confronted—to abandon their Methodist fellowship, from which their consciences recoiled in horror, or to allow the Societies to move away from the Church. "We knew not what to do, that peace and union might be preserved" ran the Minutes of the Conference of 1792, recording the critical discussions of that year—"almost all the preachers were in tears".

But here we must pause awhile before we continue the story.

---

* That there was pressure from the preachers, and the form it took can be seen by the question asked at Conference in 1781—"Can we erect a school for preachers' children in Yorkshire?" and the suggestion is not unsympathetically received—"Let our brethren think of a place and a master and send me word".

We get a hint of what was in their minds from words used some thirty years later when the school in Yorkshire was established, when it was said that the situation of Kingswood had prevented many of the preachers from sending their sons to it "on account of its distance from their stations, which would have kept them from seeing their children for years together, or have taken them from their circuits to the injury of the people, and would have been attended with an expense they were not well able to bear".

"The school at Kingswood was not a success," said Lecky, and the adverse verdict on the school of Wesley's day has often been repeated. The historian's estimate of any institution depends more largely than he is always aware upon the sources from which his information is drawn. The story of early Kingswood lends itself more readily than most to distortion. Wesley carried far the search for edifying accounts of religious experiences, and as we have seen encouraged the masters at Kingswood to supply him with accounts of revivals among the children which simulated the strange phenomena of early Methodism in the societies round about; and to them he gave wide publicity. Then too, for reasons not entirely clear to us and perhaps unwisely, he saw fit at two periods, once at the end of the first three years, and again at the end of the Simpson regime thirty years later, to put into print his criticisms of the masters of the school. It has been easy for the biographer of Wesley or the historian of Methodism to draw on this material for striking quotations suggestive both of religious excess and of dismal failure, and to dismiss the school accordingly and to write it down as a failure. As the reader will have seen, this is altogether too sweeping. Numerous references express great satisfaction and approval, but these are brief, and do not afford the racy quotable material of the indictments. Once the school had survived the crisis at the end of the first three years it was always full, and often there was no room for those whom Wesley wished to send there.

Looking back in the light of McGeary's success over the last decade of Wesley's life it is not difficult to arrive at a more just assessment, or to discern some at least of the causes of the earlier setbacks. For many years, and notwithstanding his own deep interest in and knowledge of educational practice, Wesley chose masters primarily for their piety rather than for their ability as schoolmasters. It was a mistake easy to make in the eighteenth century, when parsons were often also schoolmasters. Even so it might have served tolerably well if Wesley had left his masters a sufficiently free hand; John Jones was a man of width and learning, James Rouquet certainly did not lack personality, and Joseph Benson, though very young when in charge at Kingswood, possessed qualities which were later to carry him far. In the third decade Simpson does appear to have been given more latitude, and his tenure lasted for twelve years before the final breakdown of discipline. It was not until McGeary's appointment in 1783 that the school really found its feet, and the secret seems to have lain, not, as we might have expected, in a modification of the famous rules, but in the choice of a man as headmaster who had real ability as a schoolmaster as well as the piety that commended him to Wesley. It ought not therefore to be said, as has too often been said, that the rules were unworkable. For McGeary did work them, and the school under him was without question, and by all ordinary standards, a success. It is with the school under McGeary in our minds that we should look at Wesley's courageous re-statement in 1783 of his ideals in *A Thought on the Manner of Educating Children.**

Wesley had come to realise that "what is commonly called a religious education frequently does more harm than good"; and he had taken his stand upon the theme that of course this will be so, if either the religion wherein they are instructed, or the manner of instruction therein be wrong. In most of what are termed religious schools there was a grand error in either the former or the latter instance—

Unless religion be described (he wrote on the first head) as consisting in holy tempers, in the love of God and our neighbour; in humility, gentleness, patience, long suffering, contentedness in every condition, to sum up all, in the image of God, in the mind that was in Christ; it is no wonder if these that are instructed therein are not better, but worse, than other men.

And as for the instructors, even if they know what true religion is, they may still be mistaken as to the manner of instilling it into children—

They may not have the spirit of government, to which some even good men are utter strangers. They may habitually lean to this or that extreme, of remissness or of severity. And if they either give children too much of their own will, or needlessly and churlishly restrain them; if they either use no punishment at all, or more than is necessary, the leaning either to one extreme or the other may frustrate all their endeavours.

* *Works*, Vol. XIII, pp. 434–7.

H

Having enunciated these great truths—both so often to be lost sight of in the schools of nineteenth-century England—Wesley harked back to his mother's teaching concerning the correction of aught amiss—

As far as this can be done by mildness, softness, and gentleness, certainly it should be done. But sometimes these methods will not avail, and then we must correct with kind severity. For where tenderness will not remove the fault, 'he that spareth the rod, spoileth the child'.

Let parents therefore from the time that children begin to speak or run alone begin to train them in the way they should go, to do everything in their power to cure their self-will, pride, and every other evil temper—

Then let them be delivered to instructors (if such can be found) that will tread in the same steps; that will watch over them as immortal spirits, who are shortly to appear before God, and who have nothing to do in this world but to prepare to meet Him in the clouds, seeing they will be eternally happy, if they are ready; if not, eternally miserable.

IV

OLD KINGSWOOD AFTER WESLEY

FOR SIXTY YEARS after the death of Wesley the school remained on its old site on the outskirts of Bristol.

When Wesley died in 1791 Thomas McGeary was still
headmaster. "The present headmaster", say Coke and Moore in
their *Life of Wesley* of 1792, "is well qualified for his office and
has ever given, since his first appointment to it, great satisfaction."
In their account of the school they mention that the sons of the
preachers then made about three-fourths of the children, and
that many useful preachers "who must otherwise have sunk
under the weight of their families" had thereby been enabled to
devote their whole lives to the immediate service of God. The
Conference of 1791 appointed a Committee to superintend the
school for the ensuing year—Henry Moore, Thomas McGeary,
John Valton, and Thomas Roberts and John Ewer of Bristol.
The assistants of the school, it was laid down, and the servants of
the house, shall be under the control of the master, and account-
able to him for their conduct.

But in 1794 McGeary ceased to be headmaster. It was a year
when the leaders could scarcely hold the Methodist societies
together. In Bristol the tension was especially grave, and
threatened to disrupt the whole Connexion. Joseph Benson found
himself at Wesley's New Room there with a minority "Church
party", whilst others, including the Methodists at Kingswood,
were urgent for steps which could only mean separation from
the Church of England. Benson played an important part in
healing the breach between the two parties. "Mr. Bradburn,
Mr. Moore and I met at Kingswood this forenoon at eleven
o'clock", he wrote in his diary on February 21, 1795, "and had
much conversation together. We agreed upon a letter to the
preachers containing general outlines of a plan upon which, it
appeared to us, all parties might unite, and by means of which
a division of the Methodist body might be prevented." It was
a momentous meeting, for the plan went on to become the Plan

of Pacification which carried the day. It permitted a measure of choice to each local society. Now for the first time the sacrament was permitted to be administered by duly authorized Methodist preachers, whose authority did not, however, flow from episcopal ordination. The Kingswood society was among the first to take advantage of the option, and the school had clearly to accept the practice of the society with whom it shared the use of the chapel. Life cannot have been easy in those years. McGeary left; he is said to have become a school master in Keynsham, and in any case he did not live long, for he died in September 1797, and lies buried in the chancel of Keynsham Church. Adam Clarke's father, a schoolmaster by profession, came from Coleraine to Kingswood for a year or so, but it was not a success, and he soon left.

While he was alive Wesley had, in practice, taken personal responsibility for the school; latterly he had run it through a headmaster, one or two assistants, and a housekeeper. Now that he was dead, and the faithful McGeary had sided with the Church or minority party—for that is what his retirement to Keynsham must surely mean—the Methodist Conference decided to continue the school and to control it through a resident Governor and his wife. Joseph Bradford was the first to act thus as Governor, 1795–1802. He enjoyed great prestige as one who had acted as Wesley's travelling companion and it may well be he who stands by Wesley's side in the print of 1790. He was chosen President of the Conference in 1795. A vivid little vignette of Bradford in action at the school has happily come down to us. He was to be seen, we are told, stalking into the dormitory, clad in a straight-breasted long-tailed coat of a bluish-grey colour, a red waistcoat, leather breeches with red stockings, and large buckles on his shoes. One stroke on the ground with his staff was expected to rouse the boys. He waited two minutes whilst they dressed. They were then bidden to their knees, and thence to the long "gallery" open to the outer air, where they washed. Here certainly is still the flavour of the eighteenth century, and the "severe simplicity" which Wesley had desired to impress upon the school.

Sometime in the nineties—Myles says in 1796, and it may well have been on Bradford's initiative—the school was wholly set apart for the sons of the preachers. Whether this actually happened until some years later is open to question. It is not surprising that amid the uncertainties of the times the school was not at first full, and it was laid down that if a preacher could not give a satisfactory account of why his son should not go to the school he should forfeit the grant of £12 a year made for his education.

In 1797 it was decided to publish annually a report on the affairs of Kingswood School, and the accounts appear for the first time in the Minutes of Conference of the following year, showing expenditure of nearly £900 on thirty-two boys. Lest this should seem extravagant, and it was quite a large sum, a quaint addendum appeared below—

"Family at Kingswood School

A preacher and his wife to superintend the family; two masters; two maidservants; one manservant; and thirty boys.

N.B. In this account there are many expenses included, which are not incurred in other schools; such as clothing, washing, boys' pocket money, travelling expenses for removing the boys to and from school, the master's attendance upon the Conference, the postage of letters, implements for the school &c. There being no vacations, the boys are perpetually at the school, which occasions another large extra expense; and also every boy, when he leaves the school has six new shirts, six new pairs of stockings, two pairs of shoes, two hats, pocket handkerchiefs &c."

"Whoever properly considers this", it was added in 1800, "will be convinced that the public contribution for the support of this school is managed with the greatest frugality."

Bradford's detailed accounts have survived, and it is possible and rewarding to take a closer look at the domestic economy of the little school in its still largely rural setting, not far from the Avon escarpment by Crew's Hole and Baptist Mills. It was, we must remember, a time of continuous and desperate war with revolutionary France, and at the end, with the whole of Europe. The accounts of Eton and Westminster have been used as national indices for the period, and those of the very different little school at Kingswood, conducted with the utmost economy at this time of vital national struggle, may have some scarcity value. It was a community without vacations. The food, said an old boy, was "nothing to complain of". In 1795 £270 was spent on it; in the next three years not more than £180 in any one year. Of the £270 some £98 went on meat, largely beef, but including pigs;

£83 on flour; £37 on butter cheese eggs and milk; £28 on vegetables, mostly potatoes, but including some turnips, peas and beans; £13 on sugar and tea; £2 5s. 6d. on fish, sometimes red herrings, and £6 6s. 0d. on rice. The appearance of rice is interesting for the Privy Council had turned its attention to rice when the price of wheat soared from 49 shillings an imperial quarter to 75 shillings or more. In July 1795 all families were implored to abjure puddings and pies, and the poor were to be taught to make soup and rice pudding. Rice was a new and as yet little used commodity, and the Government promised a bounty to keep the price at 35s. a cwt.; perhaps Bradford bought too soon, for he paid 59s. a cwt. that September. What seems a disproportionate amount, £65, was spent on drink other than the highly expensive tea. Even allowing for a late bill (part of the £33 malt and hops in December) the sum is large; nearly £50 of it on malt. There was also a hogshead of cider, and a kilderkin of porter, and the cooper's bill was £3 15s. 0d. Later on (1813) the school stopped brewing and paid £5 5s. 0d. to the Subscription Brewery instead. The water was perhaps always suspect.

The accounts tell us something of what the boys must have looked like. This year £122 was spent on boys' clothes. £47 went on cloth, £25 of it on wool including worsted, £9 10s. 0d. on fustian (in later years velveteen or corduroy); £2 12s. 0d. on thickset (a stout cotton), and £7 on linen. The tailor's bill was for £28. Forty pairs of stockings cost £3 6s. 0d., thirty-six handkerchiefs £1 5s. 0d., sixty-seven new pairs of shoes 4s. a pair, twenty-four hats 3s. 6d. each, an especially cheap lot. There was a quarterly bill for new shirts of about 16s. There was the mending too; almost £20 was spent on that. A boy who left was fitted out with a suit of new clothes which cost £6 11s. 0d. This year a "coat and waistcoat of superfine cloth" cost £3 8s. 0d., and a "Florentine or satin waistcoat and breeches" cost £3 3s. 0d. A little later suits included velveteen, probably for lapels and/or cuffs such as a Christ's Hospital Grecian still wears. Caps made of leather would soon appear for the first time, at 2s. 3d. each, cheaper than the hats. Caps were perhaps for every day wear and the sailor-like hats for occasions, no doubt much as can be seen in pictures showing British boys watching the troops in battle pieces of the period. Jackets or long coats were of fine wool, worsted, or as in 1799, broadcloth, or of a fine woollen

twilled cloth for summer wear; breeches below the knee of corduroy or doeskin, i.e. a smooth closewoven woollen cloth; long
stockings, and rather flimsy shoes which needed constant repair.
They carried handkerchiefs and wore linen shirts. No mention
was made of underclothes. Hair was worn long, restricted by
cutting twice a year.

The multiplicity of the demands made upon Bradford and his
wife emerge with striking clarity from every page of the old
leather-bound account book. There were resident, no doubt under
Mrs. Bradford's eye, Sarah the cook-maid, Sarah and Catharine
housemaids, and A. Sage manservant; they were paid around
£5 or £6 a year. Mrs. Bradford paid, rarely, an additional char-
woman (the term is used) and we must picture a group of other
women engaged for most of the year as sempstresses, mending and
making shirts and suits and handkerchiefs. Year after year Sally
Pool was baking and brewing, and the Leonard family mending
shoes. The school had enough land to run a small holding. The
pigs and the horse had to be cared for, and the pigs killed (that
cost 1s. 6d. a pig); potatoes had to be planted and dug (Sally
Pool did some of that); thorns had to be bought for the hedges,
and cabbages planted. In 1795 taxation was light compared with
what was to come. Window tax was £5 12s. 0d. The Governor
objected to this, and the account book shows a payment of half
a crown for waiting on the Commissioners for a repeal of the
window tax. Little relief did he get, for the second instalment was
increased to £6 1s. 6d. Coal was 7s. 6d. a load, fifty loads in
1795–96; in later years "box-heaters" appear, some form of
brazier perhaps.

The Bradfords' management seems to have given great satisfaction. "The domestic department", said one of the preachers in
appealing for support*, "is directed by a Governor" (i.e. Bradford)
"whose praise is in all the churches; the other departments by
proper masters. A superintending Committee investigate once a
quarter, or oftener if they choose, the state of the school, and make
an annual report. What I believe is peculiar to this school, where
the chief design is to form the man, and to plant the scholar thereupon, the indiscriminate use of the pagan poets is unknown. After
an initiation into the languages, by grammars composed on purpose for the school, the scholars are led into the Latin by the aid

* Thomas Roberts, *Wesleyan Methodist Magazine*, 1804, p.201.

of judicious extracts made by Mr. Wesley from the earliest Latin authors; from them they are led on to an acquaintance with the beauties of the best Latin poets. The Holy Penmen conduct them to the fountains of Greek erudition. When their minds have been cast into the mould of the Gospel by the simple phraseology of St. John, their taste is cultivated till they can relish 'the immortal tale of Troy divine'."

Quill pens were bought in quantities that seem to us amazing; 1,600 in one year at five a penny, and 2,000 in another. The boys must have spent hour after hour squeaking away with their quills! The masters in Bradford's day were young men whose piety was unquestionable. W. M. Johnson, who followed McGeary, soon left to take orders in the Church of England, and Andrew Mayor, 1796–1801 was a Methodist preacher seconded to act as schoolmaster at Kingswood. They were assisted by a succession of youthful ushers, ex-pupils of the school. More will be said of them later.

Numbers were rising; there were forty-six boys by 1802, when the cost was £953 1s. 6d. The collection on which the school now relied was prominently reported in the Minutes of each Methodist Conference. The Kingswood collection had moreover to find £12 a year for each of the growing number of preachers' sons who did not go to Kingswood, as well as £8 8s. 0d. for daughters. During this first decade of the new century the whole system was sometimes in jeopardy. "Let the preachers state to the congregations the great increase of the children", minuted the Conference of 1805. In 1806, when there were 589 preachers and 149,666 members belonging to the English Conference, it appears as as follows:

The four Conference collections this year were

	£	s.	d.
The Kingswood Collection	2,676	12	0
Preachers' Fund Collection	1,922	7	6
Yearly Subscription	3,263	16	9
Mission Collection	2,909	4	6
Total	£10,772	0	9

The parents of boys at Kingswood were called upon to find £4 4s. 0d. for each of the boys towards the provision of clothing and travelling expenses. This must have been a sore trial. To send a boy to Kingswood meant sending him off for up to six years, forgoing the £12 a year they would otherwise receive for his education, and now finding £4 4s. 0d.

"The boys are perpetually at the school"—a boy at Kingswood might not see his parents for the whole time that he was at the school. At the Conference in 1803 it was asked

"What directions are to be given to enable the boys at Kingswood School to visit their parents?"

It was decreed that the boys should have a vacation of two months every two years. But a year's experience of this arrangement convinced the authorities that the vacation had been "highly detrimental to the morals and learning of the children", and the rule was repealed. It was not until seven years later that parents were allowed to have their boys home "by permission of the Bristol Committee". In 1811 the holiday month was fixed for September, and later it was sometimes April, or May, or June. The boys of those days thus often spent their years at the school without a sight of their parents, and Kingswood became a home to them.

Such a one was Joseph Beaumont, who was at the school from 1803-9. His father was a Methodist preacher stationed in the North of England, whence Beaumont travelled down with several others—"the journey was the more pleasant", he wrote, "as we went all the way in post chaises". He seems to have taken kindly to the life of the school and he found happiness in his garden— "he was well known not only in the precincts of the school, but in the neighbourhood for the care with which he cultivated his little garden . . . and afterwards frequently reverted to this earliest distinction, and would tell how his carnations in particular used to be purchased at prices which must have formed no unimportant part of his small resources". The time came to leave—

"At length", he writes, "the long-looked for time arrived—the Bristol conference—when I was to be loosed out of what I thought was my prison, and be made completely happy. And lo! I saw my father and mother; the former I had not seen all my time at the school before, five years, but I did just know him . . . Conference being nearly concluded, I bid farewell, a long farewell, to my old school, to dear Kingswood."

No long holiday awaited him at home; five days later he was packed off to Macclesfield to embark on an apprenticeship that his father thought too good a chance to miss. In his diary he continued to apostrophise the Kingswood which held for him the brilliancy which, in life as in nature, adorns the early morning—"Kingswood School, art thou fled for ever? Where are the pleasing shades of the sycamore and the glen?" This affection for the school he retained throughout life, as he did the ardent love of knowledge that he had acquired there. About a year before he left he had been converted—"a few of the boys began to be serious . . . and being of the number I was awakened to see in what a deplorable state I was". They began "to meet in class"; and soon afterwards, after hearing Mr. S. preach, Beaumont says that he "went from the Chapel to the school that night determined to take no sleep till I felt the great load removed, and no sooner did I get into bed and the master was out of the room than I knelt upon the bed. . . ." From this time, says his biographer, his life was continually pervaded and penetrated by the love of God. He became one of the best known and most loved Methodist ministers of Victorian times.

When Joseph Bradford left, the post of Governor was filled by another of the senior preachers, John Pritchard, 1802–7. At his side was a saintly supernumerary, William Stevens, whose health was not equal to the itinerancy, and who both helped Pritchard with the accounts and acted as writing master.* The demand for quill pens rose even higher, and some 13,000 were taken into stock in 1804–5 alone! For the rest the school relied on a remarkable ex-pupil, William Horner, later a well-known mathematician. He was appointed usher in 1800 at the age of sixteen, and his modest remuneration was gradually increased until in 1806 it exceeded that given to Stevens, and Horner could be called "headmaster". It was clearly Horner who kept the school going, and of his influence we shall shortly have more to say. In 1807 Governor Pritchard retired, perhaps after illness, and another veteran preacher, James Wood, at the time prominent in Methodist affairs, took the school under his wing, though he does not seem to have been described as Governor. (He was even permitted to break the strict rule of the itinerancy, so expedient was it considered for him to stay another year in the neighbourhood in the interest of Kingswood School.) It was perhaps on his initia-

---

* For an appreciation of William Stevens and his influence see *History of Kingswood School*, 1898, p.89.

tive that one William Wragge was installed at the school; first as Governor, and from 1809 as Headmaster. In 1810 it was settled that Wragge should have what must have seemed to the preachers the unprecedented salary of £150 a year, be non-resident (save that he should "dine with the children"), and that the preacher resident for the time being at Kingswood should keep the accounts and supervise the house.*

William Wragge is a mysterious figure. Was he perhaps already a schoolmaster by profession, and had it been represented to the Committee that what the school needed was an experienced man with a broader outlook to take charge? We do not know. At first all went well. A change in the atmosphere begins to be perceptible through the accounts. There is for example an attempt to give the boys some entertainment, six shillings for a visit to a museum, and they went bathing at Baptist Mills. There is extra money for "censors", whatever that may mean—was it some first glimmer of a prefect system? These had to be supplied with slippers, perhaps a status-symbol? The committee expressed themselves satisfied that "the school has of late improved very much". But Wragge's lot was far from enviable. Apart altogether from war-time stringency and what often seemed the impenetrable gloom of national affairs, he had to contend with the vagaries of an annual succession of preachers in charge of the domestic establishment, and with the vacillations of the Conference about the months in which the boys should take their holidays; and he had but one young usher to assist with his forty-odd boys. The strain began to tell, and perhaps the new liberty and excitement got out of hand, for we have now the first entry for "cane, 3d.", and again, and rather ominously on the same line "Brandy, 5s. 6d., postage 1s. 9d., cane, 6d." Alternate doses of stick and reward is, as a later headmaster has been heard to observe, no way to treat boys.† By 1812 entries for numerous canes are varied by expenses to Sam Whyatt, the handyman-gardener, incurred in bringing back runaways. Three times did one Byron run away, and finally there is the disturbing

---

* The details are far from clear. Myles, who was in a position to know, lists Wragge as classical master 1807–09, as well as Governor; but the accounts show no payment to him of any kind until 1810, nor is he alluded to in any way.

† But it is risky to jump to conclusions. The brandy may well have been for medicinal purposes.

entry "chain for Byron's leg, 1s. 3d."* The Committee were already disillusioned about Wragge, for he had been getting himself into financial difficulties, and had had to make application for loans. By 1813 it was a case of his future being contingent on his keeping out of debt, and he was no longer to have his meat and drink in the school. The preachers decided to return to the former practice of having a trusted colleague to be resident Governor of the school. Wragge did not long survive the change; three years later he was charged with severity in correcting some of the boys, and he left. "He greatly neglected the school."

How easily the school might have perished! But it had, what the private school lacked, a Committee behind it, and the Committee was responsible to the Conference. The system they reinstituted, that of a trustworthy ministerial Governor in charge of the domestic establishment, was henceforth to endure throughout the century.

Whatever the troubles of Wragge's regime the tradition of scholarship had not been extinguished, and by about the time of Waterloo, if not before, foundations had been laid that were long to endure. This we know from the first recorded prize list, that of 1817. It was as follows

James Moulton	*Homer's Iliad*
William Bunting	*Greek Testament*
William Chettle	*Latin Testament*

To whom was it due? The evidence seems to point to the youthful member of the staff, William Horner, to whom reference has already been made. Horner was an exceptionally able teacher. Where he learnt his mathematics is a mystery, but he was a remarkable man, and the discoverer of a mode of solving numerical equations of any degree which was long known as Horner's method. Something happened in '09—perhaps a clash with Wragge?—and Horner left and set up his own school in a fashionable part of Bath. The Committee heard of his decision to leave with great regret. "So perfectly satisfied has it been with his conduct", it minuted, "and so thoroughly convinced of his extraordinary abilities. He has now taught the school for nine years and made that compensation to the institution and to the Methodist Connexion which no other scholar who has been edu-

* Byron stayed on for another year after this.

cated here ever did." It was during his time at the school that the Conference resolved "that if any boy shall discover an extraordinary genius he shall be allowed to continue at the school beyond the usual period, provided that his parents shall pay such sum as the Committee deem proper". It was an important decision.

But though Horner left to set up his own school he shortly afterwards appeared again at Kingswood in the role of examiner, and stern critic of the staff when it did not reach his exacting standards. We know a good deal about his views on education from his reports, which run from 1815 until his death in 1837. "I earnestly trust", he wrote in 1826, "the Committee is not wavering towards any inclination to deviate from the principle, recognised by former Committees, that this is essentially a classical school". In considering Wesley's plan for Kingswood, Horner thought it was necessary to separate his views of moral discipline from that of scholastic arrangement. The former were either theoretical or swayed by partiality for models unsuitable for English institutions. But in the latter Wesley's experience and judgment were free to display themselves:

(1) A short course of English Grammar, preparatory to the Latin, and restricted to the two lowest classes,
(2) No more English Grammar during the school course of education,
(3) Latin Greek or Hebrew every day in every class except the lowest,
(4) Arithmetic urged forwards in the middle classes.

"These four principles appear to me incapable of being altered for the better." Horner, though a mathematician of parts, had no doubts about the value of a classical education.

But whether Horner was almost wholly responsible, or whether the credit should be shared with others, this school of little boys, who mostly left on reaching the age of fifteen, was pushed to a standard of achievement in the classics—Virgil, Homer, Cicero Thucydides, not to speak of the Greek Testament—that would stand comparison with later periods. And this was done at a time when there was scant prospect that the classics would prove a path to the Universities and the professions. Here and there an individual did make his way to the University. One of Horner's brothers, who was also usher at Kingswood for a time, went to Cambridge and became a Fellow of Clare. Charles Ogilvie (1803–6) was taking a first class in Greats at Oxford in 1815, and so getting his feet on the rung of the ladder that would make him one of the makers of modern Balliol.

The increase in the number of preachers' children, and the fact that many of them were stationed in the North of England suggested the need for a sister school to Kingswood. As early as 1781 the question had been put "Can we erect a school for preachers' children in Yorkshire?", and Wesley's reply had been not unsympathetic—"Let our brethren think of a place and a master and send me word." There was evidently a great discussion in 1809. It was decided that when the numbers at Kingswood reached fifty another school should be opened in Yorkshire, as near Leeds as might conveniently be. Yorkshire Methodists, it is recorded, were sensible, hearty, and liberal, and prominent laymen from Leeds, Bradford and Halifax were placed on the Committee to consider the project. With their help and generous subscriptions from the preachers themselves the estate of Woodhouse Grove, near Apperley Bridge, was bought for £4,575. Schoolrooms had to be improvised, but the school was opened in 1812, and by 1816 there were eighty boys. The beauty of the vale, the hills and woods, and the clear water of the Aire figure in all the early accounts of the school.

Henceforth for some sixty years it was largely a matter of geographical accident whether a boy was sent to Kingswood or the Grove, and as preachers moved from one part of the country to another many of their boys went first to one and then to the other of the two schools, and often back again. The early regime at the Grove shows that its founders followed, as was natural, in the tracks laid down at Kingswood. The trustees headed by James Wood, Thomas Coke, Joseph Benson and Henry Moore, who were all very familiar with Kingswood, included also a great majority of others interested in the school as old boys or parents. At the Grove the boys rose at six. There was a public prayer meeting at six-thirty, reading and exercises at seven, family prayers and breakfast at eight, and school work proper began with Latin at nine. The evening routine was similar to that of the morning, but there was a half-holiday on Saturday.

As we shall see, the Grove in its early form as a school for the sons of the preachers was ultimately to be merged with and become part of Kingswood, but meanwhile it was to prove a formidable rival. It was for a time the larger of the two schools.*

Like Kingswood, Woodhouse Grove was essentially a classical school, where short holidays, long hours in school and steady application were the order of the day. "I had my breakfast with the other boys," wrote one new boy, "of butterless bread and milk, and at nine o'clock entered the school, where I was put into a class and an Eton Latin Grammar was placed in my hands with instructions to learn by heart so many lines."

An external examiner was appointed, and the work was entrusted to the Rev. Patrick Brontë, then curate at Hartshead, near Huddersfield. It was in the summer of that first year of 1812 that Maria Branwell came to stay with her uncle the headmaster of the school. There were picnics, and soon there was a wedding that would give rise to a famous family.† As at Kingswood a Governor was soon given charge of the household, and the post filled by one of the senior preachers. James Wood, whom we have seen a year or two earlier taking a hand in affairs at Kingswood, appears at the Grove. He was one who believed in the virtue of the rod. To him "fighting" was a serious matter, and he would address the assembled school on the enormity of the offence whilst the culprits ranged round his desk awaited their turn for chastisement.

It was left for one of his successors, the Rev. Miles Martindale (1816–21) to shape the traditions of the school in partnership with a schoolmaster of exceptional ability, Samuel Parker (1816–32). "Eton herself", wrote one of his pupils, "could not have lodged the contents and meaning of her grammars more assiduously and effectively in the memories and understandings of her alumni." Progress depended on the boy himself. "I knew the construction of the Latin and Greek languages", wrote another of his pupils, "about as well as I knew my A.B.C. With slight intervening preparation I entered St. Catherine's Hall, Cambridge, at sixteen,

* J. T. Slugg, *Woodhouse Grove School*, 1885; H. W. Starkey, *Short History of Woodhouse Grove School*, 1912. See also a very clear account included in *Methodist Secondary Education*, F. C. Pritchard, 1949.

† Mrs. Gaskell, *Life of Charlotte Brontë*, 1893; and for a recent biographical account of Patrick Brontë, with many interesting references to Woodhouse Grove, *A Man of Sorrow*, John Lock and W. T. Dixon, 1965.

and afterwards migrated to Sidney Sussex College, where I obtained a Foundation Scholarship." He passed an exacting viva with the help of his training in the classics under Parker.* But Parker also instituted weekly science lectures, and one of his pupils, J. W. Draper, achieved great fame as a scientist in America.

Many families connected with Woodhouse Grove were long prominent in Methodism and in wider spheres—the names Morley, Stamp, Waddy recur with many others. Old boys of the Grove were to be to the fore later in the century in the movement which pressed for changes in the system, and led to the merging of the old Grove with Kingswood in the eighties. But to follow its story further in any detail would overload our narrative, and for the present we must return to earlier years.

Both school prospered. At Kingswood, the first of its uninterrupted series of resident Governors, the Rev. Robert Johnson (1813–1820), was "of a kind and gentle disposition; cheerful, instructive and pious in conversation; diffusing something of that happiness around him which he enjoyed so largely himself". The headmaster, the Rev. John Lomas (1819–23) who had been an assistant master since 1813 was equally beloved; though no great scholar, he was "an universal favourite". As a contemporary report states, "the masters appear to take pleasure in their work and rule the boys in love; the boys seem highly satisfied with their teachers". The Conference was of course sometimes held in Bristol. The boys were admitted to the Conference of August, 1819; two of them in the name of their schoolfellows delivered orations, one in Latin and one in English. "Patres reverendissimi," began Richard Teffry, "Regiosylvenses sumus Discipuli; hoc nomine gaudemus", and after a friendly reference to The Grove spoke of the unique privilege that Kingswould could claim—"quod auctorem commemorare licet, Reverendum JOHANNEM WESLEY . . . hunc, inquimus, illum Britanniae Apostolum, quem pro pietate erga Deum, pro morum sanctitate, pro laborum magnitudine, et vitae utilitate, non nostrum est justis laudibus ornare . . . ." Upwards of seventy years

* The Rev. W. M. Shaw, Vicar of Yealand Conyers, quoted by Slugg, p. 105. The account is interesting as showing that the route to Oxford and Cambridge was then open to a boy from Kingswood or the Grove with but a year's interval between school and University.

had elapsed, the fathers were reminded, since Wesley had founded the school—"nor can we without peculiar delight remember that some in whose presence we now stand refer to the instructions received at Kingswood School those impressions of early piety, which have since formed their character and marked out their path to that dignified station they now occupy".

If the facility in Latin is now for too many Kingswood boys a thing of the past, we have yet a reminder in the old breaking-up song—

> *Omne bene, sine poenae*
> *Tempus est ludendi*
> *Venit hora, absque mora*
> *Domum rediendi.*

The song is still popular among old boys of the school. Washington Irving had heard a party of northern bound schoolboys singing it on the coach before 1819, and the song was in use at Harrow and elsewhere in the 1820's. Its vogue at Kingswood may well, therefore, be a direct link with that already remote day.*

The external examiners no doubt played their part in achieving this creditable state of affairs. Horner examined in the classics from 1815. Another of the examiners was Mr. T. Exley. "He was a fine old gentleman and a profound mathematician. He used to walk into the school, clad in a swallow tail coat, his face beaming with good humour, and his tails bulging with examination papers." The system lasted from 1815 until 1855, and no doubt helped to save the school from lapsing from the high standards of the beginning of the century.

A new schoolroom was built in 1822, in keeping with the traditional arrangements of the times—desk for the headmaster at one end and desks for the assistant masters at the other end. The old schoolroom was converted into a laundry. Another important addition was made to the main building in 1828, along the whole of the eastern side, providing additional space on the ground floor and dormitories above, but spoiling the original symmetry of the building. A comparison of the later prints with McGeary's print of 1790 shows this alteration clearly. A substantial stone staircase was substituted for the early wooden one, and

---

* See *Kingswood Magazine*, Vol.XIX, p.496, and Vol.XX, p.301, where the spelling *rediendi* (rather than *redeundi*) in the last line quoted finds confirmation.

the lavatories modernized. The Committee felt that in the old outbuildings of Wesley's day "the fence of modesty was broken down". The dormitories were low, and by the time the plans were drawn, overcrowded; "number four" was only seven feet high, and a boy standing on his bed could touch the ceiling with the palm of his hand. The beds were mainly of the semi-detached kind known as double cribs; a board ran down the middle as a partition.

V

THE 1820's AND 30's

THE HAPPY days of the early twenties were not to last. With the appointment in 1823 of Jonathan Crowther as headmaster there was a lapse. He was a nephew of Jonathan Crowther, author of the well known *Portraiture of Methodism.* Although himself Horner's favourite pupil at the school and for a brief period a master at Woodhouse Grove, and although destined later to prominence in Methodist affairs, young Crowther's unwise and cruel use of the cane led to definite riots; he was hooted, and his windows broken. His reign lasted only three years, but the bitterness caused is a measure of the new and happier standard that had begun to develop at Kingswood.

Memories of Crowther's days smouldered on through the century, and formed the basis of a book published anonymously in 1862, entitled *How it was done at Stow School,* wherein the mingling of fact and fiction led to much resentment on the part of those who believed their characters to have been unfairly delineated.* As history much of it must be discarded, and as to its authorship we shall have more to say later. But first let the reader judge for himself whether the passages which follow have not the note of authentic reminiscence.

We begin with a description of the new boy's departure from his happy home—how his father drew a letter from his pocket to announce a vacancy for his youngest son at Stow : how wearisome the waiting, and how great the excitement when the day came for Frederick to take his place in the Royal Mail for school—

"His mother's earnest grief, and his father's thoughtful, anxious looks, contrasted strangely with the merry, buoyant, bustling bearing of the boy himself, who was confident in his own joy, and wondered at his mother's tears. Circumstances rendered it necessary

---

* *How it was done at Stow School*—Hamilton Adams & Co., 1862, 2nd edition, 1888. There is, of course, no connection with Stowe School, founded in 1923.

that he should travel all night; and frequently did his guardian urge him to lie back in the corner of the coach and sleep. But excitement kept him awake, as the mail rattled along the hard roads, fenced for scores of miles, on either side, by tall bushy hedges, white with the dust of many weeks. The monotony of the horses' tramp and of the rumbling wheels was seldom broken except by the coachman's curse, or the guard's horn, as the vehicle approached some snoring gatekeeper, or was about to enter some town. At eleven o'clock the coach dashed through the streets of a midland city, and drew up at a princely hotel, where the passengers took supper. A delicious fowl, fresh from the spit, invited Frederick."

But the thoughts of his coming greatness had destroyed his appetite, and he was restless—

"until the next day brought him within sight of a large quiet-looking mansion, whose ample gardens and magnificent timbers at first inspired the most pleasant thoughts of enjoyment and of new delights."

He was, as the reader has no doubt guessed, soon to be disillusioned. We need not linger over his early troubles, but pass at once to the coming of the new Headmaster, whose reputation had preceded him. The boys had resolved that the best thing they could do was to render him powerless on his first exhibition of cruelty—

"The day was particularly fine. We were busy with our studies, expecting the new Head Master; of whose arrival we had already been apprised. A fever of excitement raged in the school; and each time the door creaked, a multitude of faces—some flushed, some pale—turned round to catch a glimpse of the great unknown. What a morning was that! The first hour appeared a month. The monotonous ticking of the school clock was intolerable. Had it gone faster, we could have been content. But to go so much slower than usual, it was mocking us.

"At last—and O the stillness of that moment!—the door opened in reality; and there walked up the main aisle of the school a human form, different from, but ten thousand times more dreadful than the being we had pictured to ourselves. Our utmost imagination had never carried us beyond six feet of stiff black hair, with huge whiskers and beard. But Mr. Nicholas Stern, whom we now saw, was neither black nor bearded. Yet one glance sufficed to fill us with terror; for there was a cold, calm, settled, resolute fierceness about his look, which told its own tale, and at once proclaimed what we might expect.

"He had declined all introduction, preferring to appear at his desk, as if he had been long familiar with it; and on this, his first entrance into the school, he walked its entire length with his hat on; having a huge Schrevelius with a bunch of keys in his left hand, and a formidable cane in his right hand. The boys on his right instinctively drew back as that cane passed them. Poor fellows! They had strong presentiments.

"Every eye was fixed on Mr. Stern when he turned in to the Head Master's desk. First, he laid down his cane, gently, as a mother would her only child. Then followed his Lexicon, put at once into the place which it ever after occupied. Next, he applied keys to various locks. And having finished that work, he unbonneted. We saw our man in a moment. He was above the average size, though not tall; square-shouldered and muscular . . ."

"'I have only to say, boys,' he began, when he was fairly settled at his post, 'that I insist upon the most perfect order in the school; and that the first boy who talks, or is otherwise disorderly, will be flogged.' Not a whisper had been breathed since he entered; and for the next hour, you might have heard a pin drop. Then a little unfortunate wretch, to whom the silence was most distasteful, and who could bear it no longer, began to talk to his neighbour.

"'March this way, sir,' was thundered from the head of the school; and poor Voules, pale and trembling, walked up to Mr. Stern's desk.

"'You heard what I said just now, sir; that the first boy who talked or was disorderly should be flogged.'

"'Yes, sir,' said Voules.

"'Very well, sir; I am always as good as my word. I never break it for any one, or to any one.'"

So Voules was flogged, in such a style that everyone's nerves seemed to tingle at the sight, and "after it was over, silence, interrupted only by Voule's bitter sobs, reigned supreme until the morning studies were ended".

Afterwards they discussed what to do, and it was agreed that the next time Stern attempted to thrash a boy his ears should be saluted with a general hissing and scraping of feet on the floor. A brave young spirit volunteered to provide the occasion. They brightened up, and no one could have supposed that those cricketers and fives players were the broken-hearted students of the morning. The first bell rings, and the second bell; and they are all at their places.

"Suddenly, when we were all fairly seated and at our work, a boy's voice is heard at the lower end of the school: 'I say, Poppins, lend us your Hutton.' Then follows a shout from Stern: 'The boy on the tenth form who was talking, march this way.' Nothing loth or frightened, Stephens leaves his seat and walks briskly up the aisle of the school.

"Now there was a sensation. We all felt that the time for action had come. What thoughts then whirled through our brains, no memory, however faithful, can call up. But little Stephens had done his part so nobly, that we were bound to follow or be cowards for ever . . . Before the blow fell on Stephens's back, the whole school had united in such a hearty hiss, with most vigorous shuffling of the feet, that it was impossible to mistake the meaning.

"Stern paused, and shouted in his most violent tone, 'Silence'. But the hissing rose higher . . . Then the tyrant found that he had not reckoned for accidents of this kind; and he unloosed his hold of Stephens. The blood forsook his cheeks and lips . . .

"It was in vain to contend with them. And the Head Master—humbled instead of humbling—returned to his desk, made no further effort to regain his authority, and called up no classes; but after spending a few minutes in the vain attempt to read some book, he at last left his throne in a state of agitation not to be described, and retreated to his home."

Happily for the cause of order in Stow School, one of the young masters present—there seem to have been four present in the schoolroom that day—was a resolute spirit who commenced with great tact to put a stop to the hissing and shuffling amongst the lowest forms, though into the upper "he wisely did not enter". When five o'clock came there was a general rush to the head-master's desk, on which, in his hurry to escape from the scene of defeat, he had left his watch and his cane. The latter was instantly broken into a hundred pieces, every boy claiming a bit. The watch too was appropriated, to be held as hostage.

"We were shortly after summoned to supper and prayers. These finished, we began to march in bands up and down the playground, defying all the masters, but specially singling out Stern, of whom we very speedily prepared an effigy. 'Down with old Stern!' we cried, as with stout cudgels we belaboured his Guy. 'Down with old Stern! Horse him! Crack his skull! Make him feel it! March this way, sir!' And we repeated our blows until Mr. Stern's double fell headlong to the earth. Then we stood before his rooms, challenging him to come out; and when there was no reply, we sent volleys of stones at his windows, demolishing every pane of glass. Whether he or any of his family was struck, we could never tell. Not a light was seen, not a movement heard. But this destruction of glass seemed to satisfy us; and when Jones proposed that we should dash the watch to pieces, there was a general refusal. It was urged that the watch should be kept as a sort of hostage, until we had extorted the promise of no more flogging.

"We were in a high state of excitement when the seven oclock bell summoned us to evening studies, and took our places with as much disorder, as was consistent with the very important stand we had this day made against tyranny and law."

There followed an uproar which would have occupied the whole evening if four or five of the older boys had not risen from their seats and quietened the school with the plea that it was not the master on duty but the Headmaster against whom the grievance lay.

"It was determined the next morning, that none of us should go into school without first bringing the Head Master to terms . . . The second bell rang. And we, who had never dared to question the authority of that summons before, now stood firm as a rock."

One of the assistant masters thought he could take no very great harm, if he stood at the door and summoned them—it would be something to his credit too, if they came when he called.

"But alas! alas! how vain is all our fancied greatness . . . As he was in the very act of shouting 'All in', holding his hand by the side of his mouth, to make his voice sound the louder, or to prevent 'the wind carrying it away', as it might already have done in the case of the bell, forty or fifty stones flew about his head, and chest, and legs, several striking his person, while others rattled against the door behind him or entered the school.

". . . What was now to be done? The masters, altogether beaten, were at their wits end. There was but one course open to them—to acquaint the Principal. It was true that he had not much influence with the boys: but they respected him; and he might, perhaps, be able to bring them to reason. He already knew something about the disturbance; but not much. For it was a regular part of the masters' policy to keep their difficulties to themselves, lest the Principal should trouble them with his advice, or should in any way interfere with their system. Now, however, they had no alternative."

The boys stood perfectly still as he approached—

" 'Sir,' said Brewer, whom we had requested to be our spokesman, 'we came here because Mr. Stern began to use the cane as soon as he came into the school. He flogged one boy yesterday morning, and was going to flog another in the afternoon; but we hissed him and broke his windows, and do not intend to go into school again unless he promises that there shall be no more flogging.' "

What passed between the Principal and the Headmaster they never learnt. The Headmaster had "only acted upon the plan usually adopted in public schools . . ." though he could not consent to abolish the cane entirely yet he would never use it to any boy in the upper school. Would that satisfy them?

" 'No, no, sir,' said all the little boys. But so indeed it was settled. For a month the headmaster abstained from punishment, but two other masters soon fell into their old plan of bullying and brow-beating. They gave a few canings also in private, but attempted nothing of the kind in public until the headmaster himself had set the example. This he did first in a case of notorious misconduct with which the boys were themselves disgusted, and which Stern very wisely laid hold of as a suitable occasion for recommencing his use of the rod. "And it cannot be denied", continues our author, "that the boys also felt relieved. To be a whole month in the school without a thrashing was an unnatural state of things. The place seemed under a cloud; and no boy was sorry when he heard again that 'once familiar sound'."

How it was done at Stow School was written by Theophilus Woolmer, who was a boy at Kingswood 1823–9, three years under Crowther, and three years under his successor, Edmund Shaw. Many years later, when himself a Wesleyan minister, he was Governor of Kingswood after it had moved to Bath, and we shall meet him again. "I was the youngest of five brothers who were all educated there," wrote Woolmer,[*] "the eldest entered in 1811, so that for eighteen years in succession my father's home was continuously represented at the school; and for a good portion of that time by two of his sons together. We heard from others—as it may be supposed—many stories about the school, and we had some to tell ourselves. Not a few of them have already appeared in a half-crown volume entitled *"How it was done"*, which professes

[*] *Kingswood Magazine,* Dec., 1889.

to relate the experiences of several boys at various public schools."
Of Crowther he continues "I dare not trust myself to speak in
these pages, except to say that for the three years of his reign he
ruled us with a rod of iron; and excited so bad a spirit in the
boys that they broke out into open rebellion, which it was no
easy matter to quell."

Nor does Woolmer's testimony stand alone. In another account we hear of the new boy arriving in the spacious and well-
wooded playground with its avenues of elms, and of his introduction to the Governor and then to the Headmaster, the Rev. Jonathan Crowther. "He, being a friend of my father, received me
kindly, and led me to my place at the bottom of the school. I was
not long in discovering that the discipline of the school was decidedly severe, indeed far exceeding in severity all my previous
experience and darkest forebodings. The cane was in daily and
vigorous use, and Solomon himself had been shocked had he
witnessed the frequent and cruel castigations inflicted on small
boys under the sanction of his name, and often for what still
appears to me very trivial offences."*

Those who remembered the twenties seem to have accepted
Stow as a faithful reflection of Crowther's regime. Its motive
was to expose the cruelty of the system, and the inadequacy of
the masters to their task; and it contains much moralizing omitted
from the extracts quoted above. But it was deeply resented by
some who felt that it combined fact and fiction in such a way as
to denigrate, not only the Headmaster, but the Governor and
others whose work was remembered with gratitude. "It abounds
in evident facts," wrote one who was at school a little later, "but
so overdrawn at times . . . I gloried in looking back, because of
having bravely withstood the ordeal and such endurance at Kingswood instructed me in self-denial and hardihood . . . it must be
remembered that the employment of stern and inflexible methods
towards youth was not only sanctioned by law but deemed a
virtue."† But then the writer had, as we have noted, been at
school a little later; and as we shall see, witnesses are not wanting
for gleams of sunshine at Kingswood in the thirties.

There are in *Stow* other glimpses that can only be Old Kings-

---

* Ibid., Apr., 1890.

† Sir John Akerman, K.C.M.G., quoted *History*, p.193.

wood. There is a fight on the grand scale when nearly all in
the school were engaged with the boys and men of the villages
around—

"In our neighbourhood there were several blast furnaces, whose
lurid glare by night, and dirty smoke by day, as it rolled in darken-
ing clouds over miles of hill and vale, robbed the country of its
beauty, and gave an unreal aspect to scenery which might have
been called lovely and romantic. Coal-pits abounded within three
or four miles of these furnaces, and the blackamoors who worked
in them seemed to be possessed with a spirit of hatred to the Stow
boys, which every now and then broke out into a desperate conflict.
We were, however, generally victorious; and, after repeated trials
of strength, obtained at last the name of 'cocky boarders'—a distinction of which we were not altogether ashamed. Our fists were the
principal weapons in these battles, though sometimes sticks were
used; and, when we carried on warfare from a distance, stones."

It is easy to recognize the Governor and his wife—

"To both parents and scholars, Mr. and Mrs. Goodenough always
maintained that the domestic arrangements at Stow were ample and
on the most liberal scale. And they took pleasure in showing the
dormitories, which were always clean and very cold. The schoolroom
was said to be warmed by hot air; but the hot air was so long in
reaching some parts of it, that we should never have known the fact,
if we had not been told. So we went shivering from the cold schoolroom to the cold dormitory, where we hastened into bed, to forget
the sorrows and disappointments of the day in sleep. And to many
of us, sleep was the only luxury and the only friend we had. All
day long, we were wishing it was bed-time; and to nothing did we
listen so unwillingly as to the 'All up' of the master, who called
us in the morning."

There was, however, a happier side to the picture, which finds
support from other sources:

"Not far from the gates of our playground there lived a little trades-
man, who found it greatly to his interest to keep a large stock of
provisions on hand, for the special use and advantage of the scholars.
And here in Mr. Profit's house might be found every Saturday
afternoon, from two till five o'clock, dozens of the older boys, rich
in their own and their slaves' pocket money, discussing a large
variety of dishes. Mrs. Profit, with benevolent forethought, always
prepared a small room—half kitchen, half sitting-room—for her

juvenile customers. She took care also to have a bright, clear fire, such as would be best for cooking purposes, and provided gridiron, frying-pan, and saucepans, with plates, and knives and forks in abundance. Crusty loaves of new bread, Yarmouth bloaters, rashers of bacon, mutton and pork chops, eggs, cheese, and other dainties were in great request. Every boy cooked his own dinner; and chops, rashers, eggs and bacon, herrings, and Welsh rabbits, were put upon the table in a condition that would not have disgraced even Soyer himself. Vast quantities of treacle and butter also, properly compounded, were converted into toffy for use during the week. And Mrs. Profit, who was skilful in making tarts, custards, two-penny puffs and fourpenny puffs . . . did a considerable business . . ."

How, too, midnight parties crept down to the pantries "out of which they brought a huge round of beef, with bread and cheese", and sitting round the table like Trojans, though the carver always took care to leave the beef with the same surface form that he found. "Smile not, Gentle Reader," says the author, "remember that we were like other boys before we went to Stow."

If memories of Crowther's reign bit deep, at least it was brief. As we follow the story of the school through the next couple of decades a much more homely light is thrown upon the scene. The break with the Church of England was virtually complete, and Methodists were increasingly regarded by others if not by themselves as nonconformists. Methodism developed more and more a life of its own, in which its hard working itinerant ministry played a vital part ; and a connection with one of the two schools, to have been there oneself, or to have a boy there, was one of the strongest links.

The boys wore olive green coats with short tails and brass buttons, and light drab or green corduroy trousers. When he left a boy had a tall hat with a set of new clothes and must have cut a proud figure when he arrived back at the manse. The Rev. Robert Smith was the Governor from 1820 to 1843. He was, we hear,* a dear old gentleman, exceedingly well suited for his post, a very patriarch in appearance—"to us boys a man of vast cir-cumference—he was unable to see his feet without sitting down and elevating them for that purpose—with a face as bright as the

* *Kingswood Magazine*, Dec., 1889

sun, and a most beaming countenance." He had a most melodious voice, and visitors who joined the school for family worship "invariably expressed their admiration of the manner in which he conducted our singing, his voice taking the lead and retaining it throughout, and guiding without a jar or a mistake, eighty or a hundred other voices; including, in addition to the boys, the Governor's family with the masters and servants". We see him solemnly administering occasional chastisement—"he first steadied his greatness with care in the aisle, and then struck backwards upon the desk-hoisted victim and breathed hard." At his side was his "Dame", about a quarter of his size and clean as a new pin. The boys ragged her sometimes. One morning she found herself standing between two dormitories where the masters had somehow overslept, and boys were snoring audibly and yet calling "Dame, Dame" the moment her back was turned. Vainly attempting to identify a transgressor she electrified them all with the oracular deliverance, "Dame is an honourable name", and retired with dignity amidst vociferous applause. Trifling as it is, the incident helps us to picture the life of the school.

The boys were isolated from their homes to a degree it is difficult to grasp. "Left absolutely alone at eight years of age amidst the constant bustle of a great school," wrote one who joined the school in 1843, "I had a few days of utter misery. I have never known such a sense of utter desolation since. My home was utterly gone from me . . . ." The journey had involved two days of travelling by coach; he was indeed the only boy who had so much as seen a railway train. There was no penny post; a letter home would cost a shilling; and even writing paper, sealing wax, and wafers were a costly luxury. To have sent a letter, whether home or elsewhere, without its being submitted to the censorship of the masters and the Governor would have been a crime certain to meet with condign punishment. No holidays long enough to give a chance of a visit home were to be expected until the midsummer vacation; and at that age nine months must have seemed an eternity. The discipline, it is interesting to note, this little boy regarded as strict, but no great hardship, for he had been two years in the Bedford Free Schools, under the Harpur Foundation, where he had seen more corporal punishment than he did in six years at Kingswood. The masters cuffed the boys now and then. Another who arrived in 1839 records his good fortune in the possession of an ample store of marbles brought from home—"little as I was, not one of my treasures was ever imperilled through the darkly pictured bullyism so often attributed to those remote times." There were many homely touches; in the domestic regime of the school there was a quaintly unconventional simplicity, and the picture is anything but forbidding. The Governor was awe-inspiring from his sheer immensity of proportions; but he had a placid benevolence of feature, and a kindness of smile that soon inspired confidence.

Crowther was followed as Headmaster by Edmund Shaw (1826–30) and he in turn by a strong minded and distinctly able man, Samuel Griffith (1830–44). He had a reputation for knocking boys about in his impatience, though the Committee admired his "mild but effectual system of discipline". Griffith married the Governor's daughter, and in 1838 his salary had risen to £300. He now attained a position where the word "Headmaster" could properly be spelt with a capital "H". He won undoubted success as a teacher; he could show these boys, young as they were, how to enjoy an ode of Horace, and some of them respected his memory when they were old men. His eyes were dark and penetrating, and when in class they flashed under the provocation of a false quantity, guilt and timidity alike quailed. One of his pupils has left on record how he came to associate Milton's conception of Satan with his raven-locked Headmaster. "How anxiously we scanned his dark visage for some gleam of sunshine," he wrote years later in a vignette which makes the old schoolroom live again, "and especially on an after-dinner Greek afternoon, as standing round the terrible desk we pursued our translation in monotonous cadence, . . . with what a fearful snatch of joy we watched the gradual closing of the great grey eyes, till Jupiter himself actually nodded, and terror vanished before the potent influence of the sleepy god."

The school was never more than just sufficiently staffed. But at a time when the normal staff for a grammar school was still often but Headmaster and usher, with the occasional help of a writing master, Griffith was supported by a Classical Assistant, a Mathematical Assistant, a Commercial Master (another name for the writing master) and two Junior Masters, or ushers. There was often at the school a scholar of stainless character, promising gifts and adequate attainments awaiting his promotion from the Sixth Form to the master's stool, and his transfer, we are told, was effected with singular simplicity and ease.* His father appeared upon the scene and signed a legal indenture for his son to serve the Governor as a junior master for a term of years at a nominal salary; and the Governor engaged for his part to teach the youth the art and mystery of the profession. The new junior master then doffed his olive green coat with its rudimentary tails and bright brass buttons, and slipped off his nether garment of green corduroy; and then, attired in a less brilliant and more dignified costume, with starched shirt front, stand-up collar and silk necktie, the metamorphosed youth marched up the schoolroom escorted by the patriarchal Governor. "Profound attention was instantly accorded, all eyes were fixed and ears open, when the supreme authority, waving his hand in the direction of his young companion, broke the oppressive silence, saying in sonorous and impressive accents, 'Boys, Mr. T.'" The emphasis laid upon the prefix "Mr." conveyed to the school all that was intended. The scholar was a boy no longer. A great gulf had suddenly opened between him and his old companions. He henceforth lived apart. He moved in a higher sphere and with statelier mien, and he speedily grew sleek on more generous and dainty fare. He was a Master! invested with authority to teach and with power to punish. The Governor having seen his apprentice ascend the platform, perch upon the vacant stool and take possession of the empty desk, withdrew. Mr. T. henceforth enjoyed all the dignities privileges and emoluments of his order, which in the estimation of the boys were neither few nor small. The two junior masters were supposed to teach everything to the younger boys, to light the school lamps, and to repair the school books with paste and tissue paper when required.

There were six divisions; "reversing the practice of other public schools, we called the highest division the First, the Sixth being the lowest". In Latin it was Eutropius, Caesar, Virgil, Livy, Sallust, Horace; in Greek, St. John's Gospel, Xenophon, Herodotus, Demosthenes, Thucydides, with Homer and Sophocles. There is even mention of translating speeches from Shakespeare into Sophoclean iambics. If one raises an

* *Kingswood Magazine,* Feb., 1890.

eyebrow, one is assured that "we had long hours and steady discipline, and years of consecutive study, and it would have been strange if we did not do well". Some at least of the younger members of the staff were fit to stand comparison with junior masters anywhere and of any age. One of them was Thomas Sibly, later to become the first Headmaster of Queen's College, Taunton, and to make a name for himself in the educational world of the sixties. Some account of his personality has been rescued from oblivion by Pritchard in his pages on the Taunton venture.* In the sixties Sibly gave evidence before the Schools Inquiry Committee, and one can still sense from what he said in praise of geometry the vigour of his teaching. He taught his boys of fourteen the Binomial Theorem, Maxima and Minima, the method of Indeterminate Co-efficients, and the Differential Calculus. A good disciplinarian, he dispensed with corporal punishment, and in later life, when he left Taunton and founded Wycliffe, he "ruled with the authority of a king and the wisdom of a sage". Another young master was J. H. Rigg, whose years as a boy and a master just covered the thirties. He was a mere boy set in authority; but the day would come when Gladstone would say that when Dr. Rigg had spoken on the subject of education there was no need for any other person to speak on the same side! Not all the young masters were of this quality, and they were very young; this was not peculiar to Kingswood, for all over England schools were being conducted on the same economical principle. Some of them undoubtedly abused their disciplinary powers, and left unhappy memories behind them.†

Was the school unduly pious? The records over a long period —that is to say from Crowther's time until well after the middle of the century and the removal to Bath—point to a mingling of piety and severity which was characteristic of the times; those who are interested will find many instances noted in the old *History*. There were periods when many of the boys found within the forms of contemporary Methodism, with its class-meetings and prayer-meetings, a welcome means of self-expression. It was rather encouraged than otherwise by the Governors of the day. Though it is clear that in some cases these influences led to dedicated lives, others reacted adversely and seemed to

---

* *Methodist Secondary Education*, F. C. Pritchard, 1949.
† See pp. 134–5 of the *History of Kingswood School, 1898*.

recall nothing but the severity in their time at school. Both the piety and the severity were widespread in this early Victorian England: neither should be over-stressed. There is equally evidence of a happy life in these hard years in the earlier half of the last century. If one of the boys had to be sent round at six o'clock in the morning to break the ice and pump the water into the washing trough, there was cheerful song as they deluged each other with the icy water—

> "Away with melancholy,
>   And let our hearts be jolly,
> And let us gladly sing,
>   For time is on the wing.
>
> The packet's on the river,
>   The coach is on the way—
> We'll sing heigho for ever!
>   Upon that jolly day."

A few minutes later the hundred boys, in masses of four deep, would be rushing with all possible force against each other until the outwitted party fell in a confused heap on the ground. "Enough has been said", writes one of our witnesses "to show that we were a merry lot of boys, hardy and spirited." Strange as it may seem, he tells us in another place, his schooldays were exceedingly bright; "vivid remembrances recur to me of times when, soliloquising on present and future, I wondered as a Kingswood boy whether when I grew to manhood, it would be possible for me to be happier than I then found myself". When early piety and Spartan severity, Classic learning and sheer happiness can reach such heights, one wonders whether such may not be the best form of schooling after all.

VI

WIDENING HORIZONS

FOR ALL that the record shows the school might have been almost cut off from the outside world. But it is time to pause and take other factors into account.

Throughout the first third of the century Methodism had been making rapid strides. It was building chapels everywhere in the great cities of the North and of the Midlands, in the country towns, and in the villages, and stimulating the older nonconformist bodies to similar activity. By the year of Waterloo the rigidly controlled membership of the societies* had risen to some two hundred and thirty thousand, more than three times as many as the seventy thousand or so at the time of Wesley's death in 1791. Methodists in America were as numerous as in Great Britain. In the period after Waterloo and throughout the years of Reform the movement went from strength to strength. In these years, when the ancient aristocratic control of Parliament was successfully challenged, the question of sharing the revenues of the established Church with those outside was one not lightly to be set aside. Some thought with Dr. Thomas Arnold, that it was only a matter of time. Among the factors that seemed to make the question urgent was the spread of Methodism. In 1828 Kingswood, and its equally vigorous sister school Woodhouse Grove were each enlarged to take a hundred boys, and were widely known. Indeed, since the dissenting academies of the eighteenth century had now largely died away, and only here and there did a grammar school take boarders in any numbers until much later in the century, these two schools are not without interest as a type of boarding school education alternative to that of the old public schools, whose fortunes ebbed and flowed until the reforms later in the century. At varying dates in the thirties

---

* Now known as Wesleyan Methodist to distinguish them from the Primitive Methodists, separately organized in 1812.

K

and forties Charterhouse, Westminster and Harrow all dropped below a hundred boys.* Nor did the grammar schools provide an acceptable alternative. Their efforts to broaden their curriculum were defeated by a ruling of Lord Eldon's in 1805 which restricted the use of their endowments to the teaching of the classics, and the ban was not lifted until 1840. In many cases they were all but deserted. Bristol Grammar School, for example, was closed altogether from 1829 until 1848.

It was in such a context that Dr. Thomas Arnold went to Rugby in 1828. We have no evidence that he owed any direct debt to Wesley in the formulation of his educational ideals, but the air he breathed was full of evangelical ardour. He was well aware of the activities of the Wesleyans, and he may have regarded Kingswood and Woodhouse Grove with a mixture of admiration and anxiety for the future of the national Church. Arrived at Rugby he began to preach sermons to the boys; from the autumn of 1831, when he took over the chaplaincy, he preached almost every Sunday of the school year to the end of his life. The preaching of sermons by the headmaster to the boys was not unknown in the old public schools, but Arnold's use of it was without precedent. He made the preaching of sermons in chapel central to the life of the school, as it had been at Kingswood since Wesley's day.

There was, too, another circumstance connected with the rise of the Victorian public schools which may have owed something to the example of Kingswood. In more than one of the new foundations now about to appear on the scene, the desire to provide educational opportunities for the sons of the less affluent parish clergy played a prominent part. Marlborough was founded in 1843, and two-thirds of the boys were to be sons of clergy, who paid less than the others. It does not seem altogether fanciful to suppose that, while the very general growth of the demand for education was chiefly responsible, some additional stimulus may have come from clerical homes where it was realized that in Kingswood and Woodhouse Grove, with their free classical education, the Wesleyan ministers had stolen a march upon their opposite numbers within the national Church. The model once established could readily be transferred to another profession; in 1853 came

* Vivian Ogilvie, *The English Public School*, 1957.

Wellington College to assist the widows of soldiers with the education of their sons. Was the development perhaps in some small measure due to those who set a standard at Kingswood in the years after Waterloo and that made schoolmasters all over the country apply for boys educated there to be their assistants.*

The reader may, however, have caught hints that not only was the Kingswood of the 1830's and '40's a very different school from that of earlier days, but that the character of the neighbourhood had greatly changed. The Bristol riots of 1831 made themselves known by fire and smoke from afar. The Bishop was unpopular on account of his opposition to reform, and his Palace was burnt by a mob which dominated the city for several days.

An outbreak of cholera caused much anxiety at the school—"the wasting pestilence extended its march to within a few yards of the House, and seemed for some time to hover about the precincts".

There was, too, sometimes friction with the local Methodist community, whose radical outlook and sympathies were often in conflict with the Tory allegiance of the Wesleyan Conference and of the school. When a new and much larger chapel was built in 1844, many concessions had to be made by the school. It was reluctantly compelled to devote the old chapel of Wesley's day to other purposes. In the new chapel† the boys occupied a large part of the gallery, and the school had to stipulate that special pews on a low platform be provided under the gallery for the Governor and his family, and for the Headmaster and his family. Differences may well have been accentuated by the temperance issue, for in 1841 Conference ruled that its chapels might *not* be used for teetotal meetings, which the reformers within Methodism were endeavouring to promote. Readers of a later generation may find it hard to believe that the school may well have incurred local hostility for holding out against the reformers on this issue. In the late forties another wave of the reformist movement swept over the local population, establishing a rival Zion, and carrying with it for a while some three-fourths of the people. Here, clearly, was a situation with many elements of friction to impair the former harmony between the school and the community. By 1850 matters had gone so far that there is mention in the minutes of the

* The minute book of 1822 spoke of frequent applications from various parts of the Kingdom.
† i.e. the present Methodist Church in Kingswood, Bristol.

"strong prejudices now unhappily existing in the neighbourhood against all the institutions of our body".

The appointment in 1843 of a vigorous new Governor, the Rev. Joseph Cusworth, was therefore a momentous event in more than one direction, and the high spirited lady who was his wife was the exact antithesis of her predecessor. With their advent the ancient regime gave way to an era of progress which to the boys then in the school seemed one of revolution. Cusworth soon became the dominating personality in the school's affairs, and old anomalies fled before his approach like cobwebs from a brush. He possessed the power of vigorous, forceful speech, which made its impression; and he was pertinacious. The minutes of the Committee reflect the new attitude. The open spaces in the walls of the lavatory to be fitted with glazed windows; measures to be devised to prevent the boys wearing each other's shoes, caps or clothes; beds in future to be made by the servants; all orders for goods whatsoever to be given by the Governor; the school to be lighted with gas; a library room and a museum to be prepared. The search for water was renewed, and a paper was laid before the Committee on which the old pits on the estate were marked and the lines of the excavations traced, which seemed to make it likely that water would be found if a well were dug in a given space in the garden. (In earlier times there is continual mention of a water-cart). It was not long before Griffith resigned; he had been at the school since 1822, and Headmaster since 1830. He was succeeded by a more accommodating man, the Rev. Samuel Jones, but Cusworth had already obtained from the Conference a declaration that it should never be a matter of debate whether the headmaster should submit to the authority of the Conference or the Committee, and that the Governor must be upheld in the exercise of his supreme and undoubted authority.

Cusworth took charge at Kingswood at a time when the Methodists were thinking of education on the grand scale. In the year that Cusworth had come to Kingswood, Conference embarked on a scheme to provide some seven hundred day schools in seven years. It was a large number, comparable with the number of voluntary hospitals existing in this country before they were nationalised in 1948; and the greater part of the scheme was carried into effect. The first of the new public schools, Cheltenham College, was but two years old—there, too, there was a Governor, as at Kingswood, apart from the teaching staff. Marlborough College also was just being founded, as we have noted above. It was an age of Colleges and of railways. The building of the main line railways was, as Mr. D. C. Somervell has pointed out, important for the new schools in more than one way. It enlarged the geographical outlook of all concerned.

By 1845, the Kingswood Committee were reporting to Conference their unanimous opinion that the premises were altogether inadequate, that the school and classrooms were far too small and inconvenient, and the bedrooms badly ventilated and overcrowded; that there were no suitable apartments for the sick, and that the difficulty of procuring water from a distance— "there being no well on the premises or in the immediate vicinity" —rendered the supply too limited for cleanliness and health. A special Committee assembled at Kingswood. Some of the laymen professed themselves confounded, and declared on their return that they felt themselves disgraced by having an institution for the sons of their ministers in such a condition; they almost scolded the ministers for allowing matters to have reached such a pass. James Wilson, a well known architect, was called in and attempted plans for reconstruction, salvaging what he could of Wesley's classical buildings. The discussion was skilfully minuted:

"Plans and estimates of alterations and enlargements were considered together—

Whether a limited and imperfect alteration should be preferred on grounds of economy;

Whether either of the plans for enlarging the present premises should be recommended;

Whether a new building on a different site would on the whole be more economical."

It was resolved that alterations were needed; that a small outlay would be inadequate; that the Committee admitted the principle of removal to a new site; and "that the site near Bath which has been mentioned appears from all the information yet obtained to be so desirable, that if on full enquiry it should be found obtainable on moderate terms . . . the Committee would be disposed to concur".

Thus is mentioned for the first time the site at Bath. Much effort, we are told, had gone into seeking to obtain a site on the Bristol side of Kingswood, but none being found, James Wilson, the architect, called the attention of the special Committee to Lansdown. They were not, we are told, predisposed towards it when they met to view it; but when they *had* viewed it "there seemed to be but one opinion concerning it, and that a favourable one". The price was £1,050: but this was a greatly reduced price, offered by the liberality of Mr. Wilson and several other friends residing in Bath. It was unanimously resolved to accept the offer. A little later, whilst the Committee were deliberating on the plans, it was learnt that the school might obtain at a moderate price a piece of land adjoining the upper part of the site first purchased, which would permit of the buildings being so disposed as that they should not have to be placed upon the slope of a hill but stand upon a broad platform, thus saving the cost of excavation.

The decision, and all that had led to it were set out at length in a widely circulated statement. "We have thus stated the case in detail", said the statement, "to satisfy our friends that so serious an undertaking as the removal of Kingswood school from its present locality, and the erection of another building, have not been lightly or inconsiderately made." Appended was a list of those who had already subscribed, including many ministers who had undertaken to subscribe £5 5s. 0d. each, and a request over Joseph Cusworth's signature for the list of subscribers in each Methodist circuit to be sent to him as soon as possible.

Many had felt that nothing but absolute necessity would justify abandoning the site chosen by the Founder, so rich in associations with early Methodism. But Wesley, it was pointed out, had gone thither when the neighbourhood was almost entirely dependent on the means of grace established in connection with the school. All this had changed; there were now churches and chapels, and a spacious and handsome chapel had been built by the Wesleyan Society in 1844. And yet the old buildings could not be left without a pang. Memories of Wesley's day clung to the Chapel with its high-backed pews, the scene of many a conversion; and to the rooms used by him. There was the garret too, in which were stored the boxes, where was rung the chapel-going bell, and where too was the print of a naked foot, scorched into the wood by the Evil One. There went with the school to its new premises the Founder's portrait that used to hang in the dining hall, a number of pieces of furniture used by him, and a couple of hundred old leather bound books comprising a substantial part of the library provided by him for use of the school.

Dr. Joseph Beaumont, whose affection for the school we have already noticed, visited the old buildings with his son. The son, who had himself spent a year at the school, and was then a barrister, speaks coldly of its situation in the mining district which disfigured the charming vicinage of Bristol—"the very fag end of creation". The school had little to commend it save its tall trees, and its being the object of his father's affection. But to Dr. Beaumont it meant much, and his feelings were widely shared by many. The final closing of the old chapel was a matter for sadness. "When the last sermon was announced", says Braine,* "the chapel was filled with snowy heads, who in earlier days had sought its benefits, and were then reaping its fruits. The scene was peculiarly impressive. The old people shed tears like children, and with tremulous voices and wet faces sang old hymns with pathos and feeling seldom witnessed."

When eventually the new premises at Bath were opened, the old school was bought by Mary Carpenter, a well-known Unitarian of philanthropic bent, and a Mr. Russell Scott, with help from Lady Byron and others, and converted into a reformatory. Wesley's room was preserved untouched, and used for a while by Mary Carpenter. The great water difficulty which had baffled the Kingswood Committee was overcome by their successors at a modest cost. The main building was used for its new purposes until 1894, when it was replaced by a more modern structure; and the whole site has continued to be used as the Kingswood Training and Classifying Schools. The old chapel survived until 1919; a tablet now shows where it once stood. Two of the elms planted by Wesley and shown in McGeary's print still stand today.

* A. Braine, *History of Kingswood Forest,* 1891.

VII

THE MOVE TO BATH

THE OLD road from the high ground to the North traverses the plateau of Lansdown and commands a broad sweep of country as it drops down past the famous crescents of the eighteenth century. Much of the upper part of the hillside had been bought by the wealthy and eccentric William Beckford after he came in 1823 from Fonthill to live more modestly in Lansdown Crescent. On the hillside he had created gardens, grottoes and plantations. On the summit he had built the tower which is still such a prominent feature of the landscape, a hundred and twenty feet high, and crowned by a model in cast iron of the Monument of Lysicrates at Athens; the rooms below had been crowded with some of his choicest books and pictures such as The Doge by Bellini, now in the National Gallery. From the Crescent the elderly but still active connoisseur would walk up through his landscape gardens and meadows, sweet with thyme, to his retreat at the Tower, where he would peruse his treasures. From the top on a clear day he could see the Welsh mountains, the estuary of the Severn, and the rolling downs of Wiltshire. A visitor once asked him what it was that reconciled him to the loss of Fonthill. His eyes lit up as, pointing to the great sweep of country which lay before them, he answered "This! this!—the finest prospect in Europe".*

Now Beckford had died in 1844, and it was in consequence of the break up of his estate that Wilson and his friends were able to offer the school a site on the upper slopes of Lansdown. Bath was no longer the centre of fashion that it had been a century earlier, but it was in the forties and fifties a prosperous city, and the Great Western Railway had arrived in 1840.

Wilson set to work to produce a design worthy of the site. He

* For an interesting discussion of the route see *William Beckford; some notes on his life in Bath*, 1822–44, by Peter Summers, privately printed 1966; see also *Views of Lansdown Tower, Bath, from drawings by Willis Maddox*, description by Edmund English, quoted in *Life of William Beckford* by J. W. Oliver, 1937.

was much in demand, and had been responsible for Cheltenham College, the first of the new public schools, founded in 1841.
For the Wesleyan Methodists he had designed the new Theological College at Richmond, opened in 1843, and the ambitious undertaking at Taunton, part school, part university, known as
Queen's College. The new training college for teachers in Westminster was also entrusted to him and was opened in 1851. To all
these the design now prepared for Kingswood would bear some
resemblance. The first plans were, as was perhaps to be expected,
too elaborate for the Committee. "We began freely to cut down
on the design," they said later, "one member of the Committee
struck his pencil through some turrets—another through some
battlements—another through pieces of tracery—another through
the pinnacles—until Mr. Wilson had to begin to design anew.
But his genius, out of all our cuttings and parings produced this
simple, chaste, and beautiful building." Kingswood could be described, as in Bryan Little's informative book on the architecture
of Bath, as bridging the Georgian and fully Victorian phases of
the Gothic revival. A little earlier Wilson had built St. Stephen's
Church lower down the hill; a little later he was to design the first
block for a new public school, Lansdown College. It was opened
in 1857, but did not prosper, and Wilson's building was bought
to become the home of what was first called the Military Female
School. It has since of course become the well-known Royal
School for Officers' Daughters. A comparison of the designs of
the two buildings affords therefore an object lesson in the progress
of a movement that governed much Victorian architecture. Kingswood was fortunate that it was built when it was, when the style
retained a certain lofty simplicity inherited from the past by
which it was inspired.

Building was begun in 1850. A foundation stone was laid by a
Methodist member of Parliament, Mr. James Heald. Flags
marked the boundary of the site, and there was an evergreen arch
surmounted by an imperial crown in a floral device, a symbol of
loyalty to the spirit of the times. The boys moved in on September 8, 1851, when much still remained to be done, and a cere-
monial opening took place on October 28, 1852. Many prominent
Methodists were present; speech-making went on after lunch
until nine o'clock, and full accounts appeared in the Wesleyan
Methodist weekly *The Watchman*. The entire cost was £16,000;

£2,000 for land, £12,000 for buildings, and £2,000 for furniture, etc. Above £8,000 was collected by Cusworth, towards which the ministers themselves subscribed out of their small resources no less than £2,500. Some of those who had promised did not pay, for the raising of the money had coincided with a period of unhappy controversy within Methodism. Its importance should, however, not be exaggerated. "It must, doubtless," commented *The Watchman*, "appear to persons unacquainted with the real state of the Wesleyan Connexion somewhat strange and inexplicable that at times of reputed disruption and danger it should have been engaging itself successfully in large and costly undertakings. . . .The great body of Methodism is still healthful and sound."

The buildings were of stone faced with that from the Combe Down quarries. They took the form of a very wide letter H, prominence being given to two well proportioned rooms, dining hall and schoolroom respectively. The school was planned for a hundred and thirty boys. The central tower was an integral part of the heating and ventilating system, and was provided with spacious flues to draw off vitiated air from all parts of the building—a system which soon proved a failure. The architect was especially proud of the enriched oriel window of two storey height, which adorns the base of the tower, immediately over a deeply recessed and moulded doorway. (We hear that all ornaments were paid for by private individuals.) Beneath the tower he provided a dignified entrance hall and central staircase; arranged, however, in such a way as to reserve enjoyment of them to the Governor and his guests, and to confine the "students", and incidentally the masters, to an altogether inferior passage through the back of the main building and under a dark tunnel beneath the Governor's staircase. This tunnel was a defect which no one has yet found a means to correct.

Much of Wilson's building still stands just as he built it, but behind the main frontage a very different scene would confront the visitor. No high buildings at all, no great block of Upper, Middle, and Lower House dormitories, no enclosed "Junior Playground", and none of the present buildings to the west of it. The main building would end at the swing doors close to the present School House junior day-room. The area we have just traversed in imagination would be occupied by a farmyard, by the well, and by arrangements for sanitation so unsatisfactory that they would be replaced before many years had passed, (The latter have always been known at Kingswood as "pets"—a survival of eighteenth-century usage for the "little houses" or "petties", i.e. petits.) Sanitation, well, farmyard; perhaps it was the obvious place to put these things, and perhaps it was not quite as bad as it sounds. The records of the Governors for the next half century are choked with ever-recurrent problems of water supply and sanitation, and with accounts of epidemics, the causes of which were obscure, but which were often attributed to defects in these matters. But to proceed. The "Patch" would be there, but scarcely recognisable, for it would be a steeper slope, and not yet macadamised. It had however to serve as play ground and playing field, for the wall marked the boundary of the estate, and beyond it were sloping fields not yet the property of the school.

Passing into the buildings the visitor would be bewildered chiefly, perhaps, by two things; the secluded air and general magnificence of that part of the buildings where the Governor dwelt apart, and the crowded and busy state of the main School-room, now long since metamorphosed into the Moulton Hall. Here, on a kind of throne behind a railed off space, sat the Headmaster. Here he taught; at other points round the great room were arranged the lesser masters. There were at this time six, besides the Headmaster. The Schoolroom, the Glasgow room (i.e. a tiered lecture room), and one other small class room; that was all that was expected in 1850. No provision was made for the Headmaster to be resident in the building. He was given a cot-tage which stood on the site of the present sanatorium. The only provision for resident masters was in small rooms adjoining the dormitories (now the School and Hall Houses). The dormitories themselves, with their cubicles and individual washbasins, were in accord with the most up-to-date ideas, and have withstood the test of time. There was, of course, no house system; its place was taken in part by greater emphasis on academic status or order in school. Boys slept in school order in the dormitories, and sat accordingly at the tables set lengthwise in the dining hall. Nor of course were there any day rooms, until quite recent times.

The building of a chapel was postponed to save a further expenditure of £875. It had been proposed to build it near the east front (i.e. the dining hall) in line with the corridor and connected with the building by a short cloister. Instead the boys went off down the long hill on Sundays, and filled the galleries of the two large Methodist chapels in Bath—the seniors to King Street, and the juniors to the slightly nearer Walcot. The arrangement was, of course, not unwelcome to the Methodists in Bath, and the presence of the boys became a feature of the services there. The walk down the hill into Bath in "divisions" afforded an outlet for the boys' energies, and rivalry soon developed between the divisions in the time taken to climb the hill again. Later, but not till much later, the organization by divisions was abandoned, and boys were trusted to make their way down and up again of their own accord. Occasional services were held in the dining hall at the school, usually in the evening.

VIII

THE FIFTIES AND SIXTIES

NEW KINGSWOOD seemed to all outward appearances a great achievement, and an intense pride was felt by Methodism in its school. No more coffin bedsteads; each boy had a neat iron bedstead and a cubicle and a washbasin to himself. No more rushlights in perforated shades on the floor as the only light in case of need, but a well-arranged system of gas lighting. A perusal of the old *History* will soon show, however, that for another quarter of a century—that is from 1851 until the reforms of 1875 during Osborn's headmastership—the school was far from finding its feet. It had its ups and downs, much hard work was done, as always at Kingswood, and life had its lighter side. But as we shall see, many thought of it as a hard, cruel place, more like a prison than a school. The old "Patch", with its limes and elms and chestnuts had been exchanged for a narrow bare walled-in space; and no use was made of the open country of Lansdown. The reasons for this state of affairs do not appear from the old *History* with any clarity; but we can see today more clearly, with the help of a wider grasp of what was happening to the public schools in the period in question, the proportions of events.

The fact is that in the middle of the last century no one really knew how to handle more than a small number of boys boarding together, though Arnold at Rugby in 1828–43 had been demonstrating some of the principles upon which the public school system, as we have understood it for the last eighty or ninety years, has been based. In the old English public schools the number of those living in college was comparatively small; there were seventy scholars each at Eton and Winchester, and forty at Westminster. Yet even so, life in the old Chambers or dormitories was often rough and callous, and the absence of any supervision at night led at times to cruelty. At Eton commoners boarded out, and the system permitted the boys to enjoy the freedom of the countryside, and to engage in many forms of sport. This, of course, brought its own troubles. At Winchester as early as 1740 an attempt had been made, almost in the spirit of Wesley, to check vice and idleness by bringing the commoners into a single enclosure. But where boys were gathered together into anything resembling barrack conditions trouble was endemic. The classic case is that of Marlborough in the 1840s; to make possible relatively low fees, for two-thirds of the boys were sons of clergy, all the five hundred boys were lodged in a single large dormitory block run by the school. Until the arrival of Cotton from Rugby, the school was in deep water. "The boys were a mere crowd", as Mack has put it in his book on the public school and British public opinion, "without communal solidarity or esprit de corps, or traditions of decency and morality. There was no prefect system, and no games . . . chaos dominated Marlborough." Cotton created a tradition and the school prospered. Its early history helps to explain much at Kingswood; why it was that the new Kingswood of the fifties and sixties was driven to dire expedients, and even took on features suggestive of a prison until it, too, learnt from Arnold some at least of the things needed to achieve success.

What the public schools gradually learnt, mostly from Arnold and his lieutenants, was this: firstly, the importance of the school chapel, and the need to use it as the means of a direct appeal to the boys' sense of loyalty; secondly, the necessity for a body of masters who would take a lively interest in the boys in school, and more important, out of school; thirdly, the difficulty, the virtual impossibility of achieving any such real contact without splitting up the school into houses of something like fifty boys, each with its carefully chosen housemaster to set, and to some extent to control the tone among the boys; fourthly, the need for prefects with real authority and of sufficient seniority to rule the boy-commonwealth with some degree of self-restraint in the use of their powers. After Arnold's day, the deliberate use of games came to be regarded as essential to the plan, and certainly often helped. In the seventies it was realized that boys of what we now call preparatory school age should be handled separately from the main school. What gradually became clear was that without these things a school will become a mob, or will have to be turned into a prison.

None of this was self-evident in 1851, and the successive Governors of Kingswood deserve our sympathy. The Headmaster, we must remember, was still a more or less subordinate figure, and was only now beginning to claim a position at all comparable with that of the Governor. The latter had a hundred and thirty boys under his care, most of whom left on attaining the age of fifteen, though the need for scholarships to enable some of them to enjoy extra years was beginning to be recognized. He inherited from Wesley himself a direction that the boys were to be under the constant supervision of a master, and the office of Governor seemed to carry with it a paternal duty, and to inhibit its delegation to the masters, among whom there were certainly some with the qualities needed for the tasks we now entrust to housemasters. In the smaller buildings at Old Kingswood, the system had intermittently achieved a considerable degree of success; there had been something of a family atmosphere, and the life of the school had in a real sense centred upon the old Chapel. At New Kingswood conditions were far less favourable for this intimate conduct of the school. There was no school chapel. The architect provided the Governor with a fine set of rooms and a grand entrance lobby carefully segregated from "the students". The struggle to combine the old spirit of family control with the new arrangements continued year after year; at times there was serious stress, and something near mutiny. If only one of Arnold's men could have come to show the way at Kingswood, as Cotton did at Marlborough! But it was impossible that one should come, for the Conference was committed to the idea of a Methodist minister as resident Governor, and many years were to pass before they would entrust the sole care to a Headmaster. Nor, one suspects, were the successive Governors well posted as to what was happening elsewhere; at the most they may have read Stanley's *Life of Dr. Arnold,* and have heard from time to time of the exposure of abuses at the old public schools. Kingswood would have to wait many a long year before a stir would be made and a demand arise for a school where boys could stay until they were old enough to go on to the University, and which would conform at least in part to the new pattern set by Arnold. Had the stir come twenty or thirty years earlier the history of New Kingswood might have been very different.

With such considerations in mind let us look at the Kingswood of the fifties and sixties. Half-a-century later Dr. J. S. Simon would recall the terrible Crimean winter when the boys were strictly forbidden to go into the playground, and when some bold spirits forced their way out and made a slide in the deep snow, fancying themselves sliding in the trenches of Sebastopol. It was a primary concern of the authorities to maintain control over the boys. No advantage was taken of the new situation of the school, and the boys were kept herded within the walls. "Never outside the playground except on Sundays," writes a boy of the sixties, "in food scanty, in thrashings oft, in holidays few and far between, the boys of those days deserved to be called heroes." Much more testimony to the same effect has survived, coupled with evidently sincere tributes to successive Governors and Headmasters.

Upon their personalities we can touch but briefly here. Cusworth was Governor himself for the first seven years in the new school; he belonged to the older world; he could promise the boys a glass of wine all round to celebrate his son's success in an examination, but his geniality alternated with grimmer moods. Punishment was, we are told, usually administered on the spot, and no ill-feeling remained; out of doors he carried a stout walking stick which did good service. But Cusworth was getting older, and perhaps losing his earlier grasp. The records do seem to show that in these years the school was a rough cruel place. Faction fights formed a savage occupation in play hours; boys got out at night, and some inscribed their names on the Monument at the far end of Lansdown. Two were caught at Bristol endeavouring to board a ship. One morning when the Crimean War was over, Cusworth called for three cheers for peace. A little boy at the far end of the long dining hall mistook the words for "three pieces each"—meaning three pieces of bread for breakfast—and cheered as loudly as anybody. In 1857 Cusworth died in harness at the age of 67; "beloved by everyone in the place; under his gruff exterior he had the very kindest heart."

On Cusworth's death the Rev. Theophilus Woolmer was appointed to Kingswood. He had for many years owned a private school, and had entered the Methodist ministry relatively late in life. A man of fine presence, nearly six feet tall, with a chest measurement of fifty-two inches and a wider outlook than many of his predecessors, he set himself to promote "high tone and gentlemanly feeling among the boys"; he was fair and just to all. He, or his biographer, must have caught some touch of Arnold. Woolmer, the reader may recall, was the author of *How It was Done at Stow School* and had suffered under Crowther in the

WILLIAM BECKFORD'S TOWER ON LANSDOWN
from an engraving by Thomas H. Shepherd, 1829

JOSEPH CUSWORTH
from the portrait painted by W. Gush
engraved by J. Cochran

twenties. "As I had the most vivid remembrance", he wrote, "of my six years residence at the old school, with the cruelties there practised, and the tricks that were played, and the irreparable mischief done to scores of boys exposed to the brutalities of their bullying seniors and to the snubbing and flogging of injudicious masters, I thought it not impossible that I might be of some use in rectifying such a state of things if it still existed." Attempts were made to improve the clothing arrangements and the food, despite the stringent economies enforced upon the school. The funds upon which the school depended were hard put to meet the claims made by the growing numbers of ministers' children, and it was no easy matter to keep Kingswood solvent. Woolmer devoted the whole of his modest salary (he seems to have had some independent means) to providing a meat dinner on Saturdays in lieu of the traditional bread and cheese. Nor did he spare himself when many boys and all his own seven children were ill with scarlet fever in 1860.

Scarlet fever was indeed a serious matter in the middle of the last century. A second outbreak occurred in January 1863. The Rev. Francis West had followed Woolmer, and had that winter just been granted leave to travel to the continent on account of his own health. He reached Milan when he was summoned back by telegram. There were twenty-four cases of scarlet fever, and four boys died. Their deaths are recorded with detail that helps us to picture the consternation of the authorities. ". . . He was delirious all day till evening when his father arrived . . . on Tuesday he died . . . the case was so virulent that immediate interment was necessary." Another was so weak that he required a good supply of wine and strong nourishment, but there was a relapse and he died while the Governor was committing his soul to God. "I thought it my duty", wrote West in his report, "to be almost continually with him these two days." The Committee were satisfied that more tender, prudent and assiduous management could not have been exhibited than was furnished by Mrs. West during the long, anxious and painful dispensation.

"Whenever fever breaks out", commented the Governor, "there is a disposition to charge faultiness on the drainage, or something of this kind." He did not believe there was room for more than minor improvement in these matters; though it was desirable that a connection should be formed with the town main sewer as soon

L

as possible. Better sick rooms were needed. Mrs. West had had the greatest difficulty in resisting a parent who wished to bring her son into the private rooms of the Governor; and convalescents had had to be sent into lodgings in the country at great cost and inconvenience. Two years later there was a third outbreak; two nurses were engaged, a sheet hung upon the door of the sickroom ; all that could be done was done, but a boy died. There was another "long conversation" on the sanitary condition of the premises. We know now, what the authorities of those days could not know, that the spread of scarlet fever is not to be attributed to sanitary arrangements.*

From these calamities successive Governors emerge with credit. Of West's devotion to the interests of the school there can be no question. He was in many ways an enlightened man, and it was he who introduced music into the curriculum. But there was unhappy tension in his relationships with the boys, and he encountered hostility. Incidents are recorded which indicate the state of affairs.

In February 1861 a boy loaded a pistol with powder and shot and put it in his pocket. He was later seen "letting off" powder over a gas fire, and was reported to the Governor and duly flogged. The Governor little knew that the pistol, loaded, capped, and cocked, was in the pocket of the boy he was flogging, but so it was. It spent the night under his pillow, and the day following, the inevitable happened. Boys sitting round the big gas stove at the top of the schoolroom heard a report, and a boy came running in to say "X has shot his hand off". He had blown the palm away. In the coolest manner possible he picked up the pistol with his other hand, and went his way whistling to the nurse's apartments. The next day the whole school were made to sit in silence whilst the Governor questioned them one by one in his study about this and kindred matters that now came to light.

The following year a dozen boys due to leave held an illicit midnight feast in the tower just before the midsummer vacation. A light was seen by one of the maids, and the Governor was

---

* After 1837 scarlatina was of a severe and very grave type in Great Britain. A very high peak of mortality was reached in 1863. Whole families were sometimes wiped out by it. About this time a future Archbishop of Canterbury lost five of his six children from it within a month. Since 1885 the virulence, if not the prevalence, of scarlet fever has steadily declined—Singer and Underwood, *History of Medicine*, 1963.

summoned. He unwisely attempted to drench the boys with the
fire hose. One of them resisted. Next day this boy, though an excellent scholar, was expelled; and two others dismissed, though
not technically expelled. Old boys of the nineteenth century were
never tired of telling how the chief delinquent, J. L. G. Mowat,
became a Proctor at Oxford; and one of the others, W. T. Davi-
son, a leading Methodist theologian and President of the Methodist Conference. It was always known as the Great Tower Row.

The school was sometimes near rebellion. One day Mrs. West
noticed a rope hanging from one of the gargoyles over the schoolroom. The Governor assembled the school and demanded an explanation. None being forthcoming, an expected holiday was
declared forfeit. Thereupon the culprits confessed; they had been
holding a smoking party in the roof, and the rope had played its
part in providing access to a manhole, but had escaped in a gust
of wind. The culprits stood their punishment, but the holiday was
still denied. This the school took to be an injustice. They refused
to leave the playground, and windows were freely stoned. Every
pane of glass was broken in the chemical laboratory and much
damage was done to its contents, for it was the Governor's hobby
to spend some of his leisure there.

The suppressive system was maintained in full vigour, says our
informant,* and what spirit was at any time manifested by any
unlucky wight was immediately crushed by the strong hand of
authority. Silence was far too much insisted on. Silence was the
rule in the dormitories from the moment they were entered at
8 p.m. till the moment they were vacated in the morning. Silence
was strictly enforced in the dining hall during meals, and in the
schoolroom during school hours, at all times of assembly, and even
in walking to and from chapel on Sundays and weekdays.
Corporal punishment was far too frequently resorted to, and
sufficient distinction was not made between venial offences and
grave moral delinquency. The boys were goaded into rebellion.
When Mr. West left in 1867 the stringency of many rules was
relaxed.

The first Headmaster at New Kingswood had been Henry
Shera. His reign was brief, for he soon left to become headmaster

* The Rev. W. Goodhugh Dawson, *Wesleyan Methodist Magazine,* February
1899.

of the already prominent school, Wesley College at Sheffield, where he long enjoyed considerable success. In exchange Henry Jefferson came from Wesley College in 1855 to be headmaster at Kingswood. The school had still to make its name. Jefferson was twenty-nine, and possessed just the scholarship and vigour that were needed to make an impression. "Up to that time", writes one of our witnesses, "we had been unaccustomed to the sight of academicals, and we were duly impressed when Mr. Jefferson sailed up the central aisle of the schoolroom." He had a London M.A., with a double first in classics and mathematics. "I am bound to say", continues our witness, "that the disciplinary powers of the new headmaster were soon sorely tested. There was an unusual amount of flogging, but it was richly deserved." From the turmoil the short, virile figure of the young headmaster emerged triumphant. As the boys reached the First Division they came to know Jefferson better, and respect for his scholarship grew upon them. He was fortunate in having among his pupils some of more than ordinary ability. "I well remember Fletcher Moulton profiting by his instruction. Moulton was wonderfully quick, but Mr. Jefferson more accurate if more slow. Master and pupil respected each other's abilities, and differences of opinion were always friendly . . . I very soon found I had no ordinary teacher to instruct me . . . He first taught me how to learn . . . We had come into a new dispensation, in which the art of learning was greatly simplified."

Jefferson protested with vigour against the rule that ended the school career of most of his boys at fifteen, and it was largely on this account that he resigned in 1865. The narrow means of the boys' fathers, he thought, prevented their doing the school justice in after life. There were exceptions. A few were finding their way to the universities, and attaining distinction. Fletcher Moulton we have just mentioned; he came of a brilliant family, was Senior Wrangler by a legendary margin of marks in 1868, and President of the Union. He was on the threshold of a career that led on from one honour to another.* Three years later a boy from the sister school at Woodhouse Grove, T. H. Grose, was President of the Union at Oxford. He was one of the most influential figures in the Oxford of Jowett's day, and his portrait hangs in a place of honour in the hall at Queen's.

* See also p.203.

Old boys used to say of the fifties and sixties that if it was dry bread and skimmed milk twice a day, yet the education was splendid. In Jefferson's time the Oxford Local Examinations were first organized. He saw in these examinations a field in which the school, handicapped as it was in other directions by the early leaving age, might perhaps make its mark. The examinations, too, gave a new direction to the arrangement of subjects in the school teaching, and helped to free it from rigid adherence to the old classical routine at a time when the provincial grammar schools had not yet awakened from their long slumbers. More room was found for mathematics, which was soon to become the chief distinction of Kingswood. Boys who came out top of the Honours Lists of the Oxfords began to get letters from Balliol offering them awards. The examinations acquired a glamour that later filled too much of the horizon; and compensation for lack of success in other directions was found by dwelling overmuch on the results obtained against competition that was none too exacting. The old public schools, we must remember, stood loftily aside from what they regarded as middle-class examinations. Kingswood was among the first of the schools to make a success of taking external public examinations, and that it is these examinations which pioneered the way for the present nation-wide system of "O" and "A" level examinations.

Boys also sat for the "Matric" of London University. Between the years 1864 and 1897, when a count was made, Kingswood and Woodhouse Grove passed 533 boys, and eleven times in the thirty-three years took the first place in honours. Every third year, commented the *Magazine,* was something of which they might well be proud. Records of subsequent careers are far from complete, but analysis shows that of some 288 boys about whose careers we have sufficient data, about one-fifth obtained university degrees of one kind or another, many of them the external degrees of the University of London then being made available. About a fifth also became Wesleyan ministers, or took orders in the Church of England. About mid-century, too, many sought careers overseas, again amounting to about a fifth of the total. These proportions would remain fairly constant for the rest of the century.

IX

THE MERGING OF THE "OLD GROVE" WITH KINGSWOOD

IN 1866 the school entered on a new era with the appointment of Thomas George Osborn. A nephew of the well-known Methodist Dr. George Osborn, and that year tenth Wrangler and a Fellow of Trinity Hall, Cambridge, Osborn was of a different calibre from his predecessors, and capable of imparting his lively personality to the school. The circumstances of his appointment were unusual. On Jefferson's resignation the Committee had appointed William Elton; but his health quickly gave way, and it was suggested that Osborn, then studying for the Bar, should come for the time being. As he himself said later, he had no intention of becoming a schoolmaster, and had counted on taking up his Fellowship at Trinity Hall. It was when he was walking with Fletcher Moulton in Jesus Lane, he recalled years later, that the latter had first put into his mind the possibility that he might become Headmaster of Kingswood. So Osborn went to Kingswood, and remained, despite the untoward circumstances—"from the illness of the master, and from other causes the school had gone down somewhat". He was but twenty-three when he thus came to Kingswood.

But before we go further with Osborn we must glance at the Governors with whom he would have to work. The Rev. William H. Sargent (1867–73) was a shrewd and dignified Governor, combining a natural heartiness of disposition with an old-world courtesy of manner that was sometimes peculiar, but always kindly and pleasant. He introduced a system of permits, whereby boys who had not blotted their copy-book too seriously were allowed to escape from the premises on half-holidays—Wednesday had been added to Saturday in 1853. Permits were henceforth much used for explorations of Wick Rocks, Hampton Rocks and Sham Castle. The Cleveland Baths were much patronized. Sargent was followed by the Rev. J. H. Lord (1873–85) during whose long reign the mellowing influences became much more pronounced. He was held in great affection by the school. Working through a batch of boys he had to cane he would come upon one smaller than the others, look up and ask appealingly "How can I cane a little boy like this?", and bring the punishment abruptly to an end. Fighting was, however, regarded by the Governor as a grave offence; "directly after breakfast", records a boy's diary of 1876, "H. and E. were flogged publicly for fighting". H. had cut E. above the eye, and given him two black eyes on the preceding Sunday afternoon. It must not be supposed that the Governor, for all his gracious courtesy, lacked strength of character. His voice took on an indignant ring when he spoke of anything small minded or ungentlemanly. We catch the Arnoldian echoes.

With such Governors as Sargent and Lord, and with Osborn steadily increasing in stature as Headmaster, the school was able to make real progress in more than one direction. A new interest is apparent in providing facilities for games. A pioneer cricket eleven had taken the field in 1862, in red flannel caps with a white star on the top—"the first properly organized cricket eleven at Kingswood." In 1863 the field next to the school (where the Ferens buildings now stand) was bought, and in 1870 the slope that constituted the playground was made comparatively level. This change of level meant that the openings from the piazza were sacrificed. The first bathroom appeared in 1868; a small room at the foot of the stone staircase was used, and two large lidded baths were installed, in each of which two boys washed at the same time. Improvements followed fast one upon another and science began to figure more effectively in the curriculum. "The years of my stay at Kingswood were halcyon", wrote one who was a boy in 1866–72, recalling "that prince of schoolmasters, T. G. Osborn, with not only the honours of scholarship, but that which thrilled the boys, athletic prowess". Osborn was to see the school emerge from the mediocrity which threatened to settle upon it in the middle of the century into a spell of achievement which will always be associated with his name.

In the twenties and thirties Kingswood and Woodhouse Grove had had relatively few rivals. But by the sixties educational reformers were to be found on every hand and rivalry between this school and that had begun to create a competitive atmosphere which has been maintained until the present day. The Clarendon

Commission reported in 1864 on the seven old public schools—
Winchester, Eton, Westminster, Charterhouse, Shrewsbury, Harrow and Rugby, with the two large London day schools, St.
Paul's and Merchant Taylors. Another body, the famous Schools
Inquiry Commission ("the Taunton Commission") undertook an
exhaustive investigation into all other secondary schools and reported in 1867. It at once put its finger on the weak spot at Kingswood and The Grove, the fact that with few exceptions boys were
required to leave at the age of fifteen. Always on the low side for
a classical school, the age limit had not perhaps been gravely out
of step with the common practice of many schools of the first
half of the century; but the Commission thought that boys in
second-grade schools should leave at sixteen, and at first grade
schools at 18 or 19, so that they could pass on to the universities.
Thus quickly had opinion altered since the thirties, and Kingswood and the Grove, though both had been expanded, had been
left grievously behind. A fresh impetus was given to the consideration of these matters by the prospect that Gladstone would remove
the remaining restrictions imposed upon nonconformists at Oxford
and Cambridge, and with the passing decades Methodists had
increasingly come to be regarded as nonconformists. It was
natural therefore, that the position of Kingswood and Woodhouse
Grove should be reviewed.

Mr. H. H. Fowler of Wolverhampton,* who had himself been
at The Grove, urged the Wesleyan Methodist Conference of 1871
to appoint their own Commission of Enquiry. He wanted them to
look into the question of the leaving age and consider amalgamation of the two schools, perhaps making one preparatory to the
other, thus avoiding duplication of staffing, and enabling boys to
be adequately prepared for the university. Fowler saw too, that the
schools suffered from the economy of their administration, and
that if they were to be put into a position to compete with the
rapidly multiplying public schools many changes would need to
be made. The schools, he said, ought to be the very best of their
kind in the kingdom, turning out boys who were at once scholars,
gentlemen, and Christians. The sons of the Wesleyan ministers
ought to be enabled to fight their way to the University, to the
Civil Courts, and to the higher walks of life generally. A certain

* Later Sir Henry Fowler, M.P., and Lord Wolverhampton.

proportion would enter the Ministry, and to it they would bring the advantage of their better education.

In the discussion that ensued it was urged that boys could and did go forward from the two schools as they were—why "unsettle the system?" The National Commission had been appointed to enquire into the public schools because of the existence of evils which in the lapse of time had arisen there, but these had never been alleged against Kingswood and Woodhouse Grove.

The Conference was not convinced by the objectors, and appointed a Commission of Enquiry. It comprised three prominent Wesleyan ministers, the Rev. Benjamin Gregory, the Rev. W. J. Tweddle, and the Rev W. Fiddian Moulton; and three laymen, Fowler himself, George Lidgett (father of Dr. John Scott Lidgett) and P. W. Bunting. The Commission modelled its procedure on that of the national bodies which had been attracting so much attention. It set to work to collect evidence and to interview witnesses. It showed its quality by calling into consultation leaders of the educational world of the day. Dr. C. J. Vaughan had been of the inner circle of Thomas Arnold's favourite pupils at Rugby, and had very nearly been appointed his successor there. He had gone instead to Harrow. Dr. Alfred Barry had been one of the early Headmasters of Cheltenham College. Mr. J. G. Fitch, as one of the Commissioners of Endowed Schools, had played a major part in moulding the future shape of many of the public schools. The views of these three men were expressed in forthright terms, and none were better qualified to advise on the principles which might lead to success.

The Report of the Commission was an epoch-making document and 3,000 copies printed by order of the Conference were widely distributed. Its recommendations deserve to be recorded in any history of the school, and are not without interest today.

First the Commission noted the early age at which the boys left; and, what was obviously bound up with it, the lack of a proper system of monitors or prefects, and an obsolete conception of the function of the Under-Masters. The fact that the schools did not—with few exceptions—offer education beyond the age of about $15\frac{1}{2}$ was a serious handicap for those destined for the universities, the professions or the Civil Service, who were generally obliged to dislocate their course and seek elsewhere a final preparation for College. But it was also a loss to the schools "for it is mainly to boys who have reached sixteen or seventeen and are passing into manhood . . . that the school looks up. Without them speaking generally, the school has no social organization".

Hence, thought the Commission, the system of government was too close and repressive—"the whole school life is passed under the close inspection of the master, and indeed almost entirely within the ring fence. Many old pupils speak strongly of this imprisonment; and it needs only a very slight knowledge of the playground life of a healthy public school to condemn the close system entirely. Dr. Vaughan and Dr. Barry, schoolmasters of the highest reputation and character, unite in reprobating it."

There lingered in Kingswood and The Grove, said the Commission, as in many other schools, traditions of the pedagogue entirely out of keeping with the times. The Under-Master, they continued, needed the whole of his time out of school hours to freshen his mind by reading and by converse with his colleagues, by preparation for his immediate work, and for the higher posts for which he ought to aspire. He should be the professional equal, though the subordinate of, the Headmaster. At Kingswood and The Grove salaries were too low and half the assistant masters were under twenty-three years of age. Reform was overdue.

"The getting of good Under-Masters", commented Dr. Barry, "is rather a question of the character and reputation of the school than of salary. Very good men can be obtained at a comparatively low rate (I do not think that less than £100 a year with board etc. should be offered) if it is worth their while to have been at the school. They will not stay long; but if the chief Masters stay for a considerable time, change in the juniors is no great evil."

The Commission passed on to consider the system of dual government. The objection to dual government was not merely theoretical. At Winchester the dual system of government had led to serious difficulty. It had been tried with even less success at Cheltenham, where it was at first deemed best to place the moral and religious supervision of the boys in the hands of a Chaplain, and leave the Headmaster responsible for the secular teaching only. It had had to abandoned, and the school placed under a single clerical Headmaster. But whatever the arrangements might be it would be well to assemble the boys once on a Sunday for preaching by the Governor or Head Master. "The bringing together of boys in a public school is always accompanied by religious dangers which require discretion and tact, breadth and force of teaching, and a wise use of the pulpit . . . the great schoolmasters of England have based their government on their pulpit authority, and would have parted with any instrument of power rather than that."

These were large issues, but there were others of great importance. The schools were, it was agreed, each too small; and the witnesses concurred in thinking that whilst some of the public schools were too large for the best management, 250 to 300 was a very good number to aim at.

The Commission concluded that the best practical step was to make one of the schools a Lower School, and the other an Upper School; and this would permit of the Upper School being divided into Classical and Modern sides. On this topic they had very full advice from Mr. J. G. Fitch, who supplied them with copies of a scheme which the Endowed Schools Commissioners had prepared for Sherborne as a First Grade classical school. His scheme for Kingswood was on similar lines. It provided for an Upper school as follows:

Course of Instruction
In both Departments, Mathematics; English Language and Literature; One branch of Physical Science; French.

Modern and Scientific Department
Other branches of Physical Science; German; Pure and Applied Mathematics; Economic Science.

Classical Department
Latin; Greek; Ancient and Modern History.

Fees for Scholars being sons of Laymen—For tuition, not exceeding £15; for boarding, exclusive of tuition £45.

It will be noticed, perhaps with some surprise, that Mr. Fitch's scheme provided for the admission of the sons of laymen at a fee of £60, for both tuition and boarding. He had "the strongest opinion" about it. A change to the admission of, say, 50 per cent of laymen's sons would bring in new and valuable elements, and need not cause the sacrifice of any of the distinctive features of the school. Dr. Barry also urged this course; it would be good— very good—to have them. The Commission agreed. The change, they urged, would not be contrary to, but in accord with the intentions of the original foundation of Kingswood.

The force of the argument was strong, but the practical difficulties seemed insuperable. There was the awkward factor of size. If the two existing schools became one they would be about the right size, but admission of the sons of laymen seemed to be bound up with a different plan, the retention of two schools, each with some hundred or more laymen's sons. It was an open question whether such numbers would be forthcoming. Provision was already being made for such boys from Wesleyan homes in the North at Wesley College, Sheffield, and in the West at Queens' College, Taunton. At this time, too, the Wesleyan leaders were committed in another direction. They were anxious to establish a public school in close connection with either Oxford or Cambridge. In 1874 donations were solicited for "the proposed Wesleyan first grade school at Cambridge". In 1875 the Leys Estate was bought and Dr. W. F. Moulton, brother of Fletcher Moulton, was appointed its first Headmaster. The difficulties about the admission of laymen's sons at Kingswood and the Grove were thus real enough, and some of those who had advocated their admission changed their minds. Moreover, and most unhappily, the presentation of the Report of the Commission in 1873 coincided with increased financial stringency.

There was room for much diversity of opinion. Should the schools be concentrated on a single site, or should the Grove become preparatory to Kingswood? It was first resolved that the Grove be sold, and Kingswood extended as might be necessary to take three hundred boys, but the proposal to give up the Grove came as a shock, for it was deeply rooted in the Methodism of the Northern counties. A great agitation arose, protests flowed in, and postponement was decreed. A year later it was resolved to retain the Grove as preparatory to Kingswood. In 1875 this plan took effect, and Osborn became Headmaster of the combined school. The old Committee disappeared, and a new minute book commences entitled, for a while, Kingswood and Woodhouse Grove School. The boys who came from the Grove brought with them no mean tradition of their own, and meant for Kingswood an influx of new life and vigour.

X

ADVANCE UNDER T. G. OSBORN

THE COMMISSION had given a clear lead in many matters and momentous changes took place. Looking back today we should say that by far the most significant was the ending of the old attempt to ensure continuous supervision by a master, and the appointment of prefects. Thus came to an end a feature of life at Kingswood that the school owed to Wesley, and which, continued into conditions quite unlike the early days, had been the cause of untold misery and the loss of many a master. Eight prefects were appointed. "The name of prefect was assigned to those boys whose responsibility it was to turn the stream of popular opinion into worthy channels, and to put down all offences against public good manners." At the top of the list was W. T. A. Barber, later to follow Moulton as Headmaster of The Leys.

There were other changes. Butter appeared on the breakfast table; though the Commission had said that butter was not necessary where milk was available, and that it would be a retrograde step to spend money which was wanted for education on things unnecessary. The supper bun was first distributed, for it had been said that the regimen was too severe, and "it would be well to temper it with a little supper". The rule of monastic silence in the dining hall was allowed to give way to "cheerful talk". A change in school hours set free the time after lunch each day.

Games were further encouraged; already in 1868 or 1869 a code of football rules had been drawn up for the use of the school, but they had proved quite impracticable, and the boys had fallen into a kind of spurious Rugby. When in 1877 the school was invited to play a neighbouring school at Rugby football, fifty boys, all expecting to play, accepted the challenge. Their somewhat shocked opponents explained, that before removing their jackets (they had no football clothes) they must select a short list! Comments in the *Magazine* enable us to recapture something of the phraseology then in vogue. "Owing to the state of our ground", we hear in 1880, "we have been able to practice comparatively little; shortness of breath is a defect common to almost all, and, owing to this, forwards have not the persistent pluck for which they have been famous of old." Against The Hermitage one Watson played well, "collaring our big opponents in capital style". Cricket was about on a par with football; good hitting power, we are told, was almost altogether wanting, and the team indulged in that fatal practice of reckless and indiscriminate slogging so characteristic of young and inexperienced players. It was not until 1891 that the school acquired ten acres on the top of Lansdown by the gift of John Cannington of Liverpool.

But if cricket was taken more seriously, the traditional trial of Guy Fawkes before the twelve jurymen had to give way. The beloved pageant in the hall used to be followed by a bonfire lit by the head boy in the name of "Our gracious Queen and the Protestant Religion, and to the confusion of all foreign tyrants and spiritual usurpers". The celebrations were done away with and a missionary meeting took their place. Straw hats were tried in the eighties, but the dye used for the ribbon proved not to be fast, and a school cap was substituted—"it will be a black polo with a shield in front". The black polo was found to be much more satisfactory than the straw. Bicycling came into favour. "The numerous disasters attendant upon the pursuit seem to inflame rather than to diminish the zeal of its votaries, whose only talk is of 'croppers', 'boneshakers', 'pedals', 'brakes', and such like mysteries."

Despite, however, all that had been said about dual government no change was made in the system, and the Rev. J. H. Lord continued to be Governor at Kingswood, with his counterpart the Rev. George Fletcher at the Grove. It was no simple matter for Osborn as Headmaster to supervise from Bath a Lower School in Yorkshire, but he was fortunate in having able and loyal colleagues. James Deaville's thorough and masterly work at the Grove made his top class the foundation for the greatest successes at Kingswood. A. S. Way, later known for his verse translations of the classics, was appointed second master at Kingswood.* The curriculum was bifurcated to make a modern as well as a classical side. Osborn could now keep more of his boys until they

---

* Deaville later became the first Headmaster of Kent College, Canterbury, and Way of Wesley College, Melbourne.

were old enough to go on to the universities. Coming from homes
of the kind depicted in E. E. Kellett's lively descriptions of mid-
Victorian Wesleyan Methodism, they found at Kingswood every
encouragement to work at their classics and mathematics, and to
cultivate among themselves a wide range of literary interests. The
roll of Presidents of the Senior Literary Association goes back
to 1868, and ante-dates the first regular captains of cricket and
football by some ten years. Public opinion in the Senior Literary
Association insisted on manuscript contributions to its journal
from all its members. Many boys have ever since traced to this
journal, as contrasted with work to be shown up to a master, their
first serious efforts at literary style or philosophical speculation.

With a great thrill the boys began to realize that Oxford and
Cambridge were indeed open to them. Away over the hills at
Marlborough boys from the parsonages had already, under
Bradley's headmastership there (1858–70), made the reputation
of their school for scholarship. The parsonages with their narrow
means, bred boys, as F. B. Malim has reminded us, who were
not only simple in their pleasures, but intelligent, industrious and
ambitious. Their future depended on their own efforts, and to
them the gateways to the learned professions were the universities.
It had been a great day when an eager throng walked out miles
on the Ogbourne road to welcome the first two Marlburians who
had been elected at Balliol. In the Methodist manses all over the
country these influences were as strong as in the parsonages, and
often the literary flavour of home life was even more marked.
At Kingswood also excitement ran high when academic successes
were achieved. "We were all arranged along the carriage drive
to give him a welcome, and when at last the carriage drove up
with the hero of the day we gave him a ringing cheer." There used
to be a small desk in the Schoolroom occupied by the two top boys.
In 1880 one of the places would be occupied by W. P. Workman,
who would go on to be Second Wrangler, Fellow of Trinity, and
come back as Headmaster; and the other by F. W. Kellett,
classical scholar, Fellow of Sidney Sussex, and "the ablest of them
all". Becoming a Methodist Minister he went out to the Madras
Christian College and fell a victim of malaria. In 1883 the
two who occupied the top desk went on to become First and
Second Wranglers—A. C. Dixon, Fellow of Trinity and F. R. S.,
and W. C. Fletcher, Fellow of St. John's, and later a well remem-

bered Chief Inspector of Secondary Education. For a long period there was scarcely a year when the school could not claim either a Wrangler or a first class in mathematics at Oxford; by 1898, when the *History* was written, fifty-one awards had been won at Oxford, and six Fellowships; and at Cambridge sixty Scholarships and seventeen Fellowships.

It was of this period of the school's history that Kellett was able to write in a passage that has been more than once quoted,* that among the twenty or thirty boys with whom he was brought into more or less close association "one who could foretell the future would discern two Fellows of the Royal Society, three Fellows of Trinity, Cambridge, four or five Fellows of other colleges, five or six professors of various subjects, some eminent headmasters, and several distinguished doctors, lawyers, and educationists". The school all but succeeded in becoming a household word for scholarship and an acknowledged rival of the leading public schools. If it failed to do so it was because it did not take its chance to develop an upper school comparable in scale with others whose senior forms were being rapidly expanded. Kellett was at Oxford in the eighties. "It was the mode to pretend a hatred of all enthusiasm," he wrote, "the university has always been, in a special sense, the home of lost causes; at any rate it was the custom to talk as if all causes were lost, and as if no cause were worth the trouble of working for." The boy from Kingswood was forced to examine his preconceived ideas and to effect a new synthesis, itself a highly educational process. Many moved forward thence into positions of responsibility. Over fifty boys from Kingswood and the Grove became headmasters of public or secondary schools in the latter half of the nineteenth century. But candour compels one to admit that the school itself long failed to reap the full benefit of this enhanced contact with the universities. Could she have found means to offer some of them posts with the scope they found elsewhere she might have reaped a precious harvest.

The happy arrangement whereby Woodhouse Grove acted as a Lower School to Kingswood was not, however, destined to be permanent. Steps taken to establish the finances on a sounder

* E. E. Kellett, *As I Remember*, 1936, p.263.

NEW KINGSWOOD *c.* 1850
from a painting by J. Syer, engraved by J. Shury

T. G. OSBORN
Headmaster 1866–85
from the oil painting
at Kingswood

THE TOWER
from a photograph by E. A. Eachus, Bath

basis were frustrated by increasing demands on the funds.* Matters came to a head at the Methodist Conference of 1880. Those who sought a solution by reverting to two schools and admitting laymen's sons to both were still vocal. But those who, like Dr. W. F. Moulton and Mr. P. W. Bunting, had seven years before been attracted by such a plan were now convinced that the difficulties were insuperable; they could not so expand both schools without much expensive building and success would be problematical. The only solution seemed to lie in concentration of the whole body of ministers' sons at Kingswood.

The Conference of 1881 met therefore in an atmosphere of crisis. The old boys of the school had prepared and published a petition urging the giving up of Woodhouse Grove and the enlargement of Kingswood to take three hundred boys as the only solution that would not be destructive of all that for which the school stood. Dr. Moulton spoke in measured terms; how the school had never been so good as it was then, how they could not go back, how impracticable were the alternatives, how calamitous it would be if Osborn were to leave. Amid great excitement the vote was taken—243 for, 80 against. The new arrangements were to take effect in 1883. The tension subsided, and Conference addressed itself to finding ways and means. It was decided gradually to reduce the number of boys on the foundation to 250, and to cut the number of years allowed to a boy from six to five.

Here, therefore, we bid farewell to Woodhouse Grove as part of the story of Kingswood. A new school in Yorkshire, the present Woodhouse Grove School, was opened in 1883 with sixty-four boys mostly drawn from Lancashire and Yorkshire. It is now a public school in its own right, represented on the Headmasters' Conference.†

---

* Among them was the assumption of responsibility for three small schools for ministers' daughters. One of them was called Queenswood, and items sometimes appeared in the magazine from "Our sisters at Queenswood". Some years later (1893) the ministers' daughters were concentrated at Trinity Hall, Southport, and Queenswood was reopened as a proprietary school with a number of places for ministers' daughters at reduced fees. It is now of course a well-known public school for girls.

† There has sometimes been an understandable difference of opinion whether the story of the old Grove 1811–83 belongs to Kingswood, or to the school which inherited its site and buildings. Strictly speaking it belongs to Kingswood, for the old school was wholly merged into Kingswood, and its boys (except the very few who left and entered the new Woodhouse Grove School) were transferred to Bath. Of this there never was any question in

M

It was not in the circumstances surprising that the new dormitory block at Bath was of the simplest possible character. Various schemes were canvassed. At one stage it was suggested that Wilson's two wings should be carried back and a quadrangle created. The objections are interesting. They were that it would destroy the farmyard; that the only view from such buildings would be of the dingy quadrangle itself; and, no doubt conclusive, that it would be more expensive. Another plan envisaged extension of the dining hall "at the side" (we can but speculate what this would have looked like), the provision of a gallery in the Schoolroom to take fifty boys, and the building of classrooms out into the playground with dormitories above, roughly where the library now stands. Eventually the plans were settled, and work began on the ungainly, if severely practical, block containing the Upper, Middle, and Lower Dormitories one above another. The *Magazine* carried a description. "A long line of new building runs out of the back of the old at right angles, starting from close by the bathroom, and reaching to within a short distance of the farmyard, the Eastern side of it going along the site of the beautiful Beech Avenue that used to run from the drying ground northwards. The Beech Avenue and the garden on the left of it and the turf of the drying ground are all cleared away." The new buildings had stairs of oak up to the dormitories above, where was room altogether for one hundred and sixty-eight boys "each of whom will have one of the wooden constructions with other arrangements similar to those of the old dormitories". The elongation of the dining hall is noted. The scheme included the building of a sanatorium, and the cottages at the back of the grounds were assuming the form of a Swiss chalet for use for this purpose. It was said at the time that if the wind had risen the roof would have risen with it.

When, therefore, the school re-assembled in August 1883, for its second "half" there were close on three hundred boys in the building. The accommodation was overtaxed, and the hot water pipes had to be used as seats. The sole provision in the new buildings for resident masters consisted of a small room apiece,

---

the minds of the boys of the old Grove. But the new Woodhouse Grove has indeed strong links with the old whose name it took and Kingswood need not grudge it a share in the story of the earlier school.

situated near the central stair on each of the three floors. Boys slept in the dormitories according to school, not house, order. Indeed there was as yet no house system. The Governor remained responsible for the life and discipline of the boys, with the help only of the resident masters, most of whom were young men who had little choice in the matter. The Headmaster was to continue to live in Burton House, and to be responsible only for work in school as hitherto. Osborn had indeed pressed upon the authorities that instead of building large "barracks" they should build three or four good houses along the road at the top of the field, and let the masters take laymen's sons and ministers' sons—"in fact that the school should be conducted somewhat after the style of Clifton or Bath College". It would of course have been a new idea, and the authorities were not prepared for it. "They move very slowly", he permitted himself to say, "and have very conservative ideas. They will do something like this in the long run, but it will be many years yet." Had they done so there would have been no misappropriation of funds, for the school had no endowments, and the point would have been met by making the laymen's sons pay such fees as would cover the entire cost. In fact the profit would have relieved the ministers. There was, thought Osborn, no very strong reason why they should not have done what he suggested; but there were other Wesleyan institutions which were doing very well, to which the school would have been a formidable rival.

Let us return to the *Magazine*. Known hitherto as the *Kingswood and Grove Quarterly*, it was in 1883 re-christened *The Kingswood Magazine*. It contains, like all school magazines, literary effusions relevant and irrelevant, mingled with school news and "Gleanings" invaluable to the historian. Here the school world of the day at once comes to life. The changes, it commented, were not as great as outsiders might think. As the stone weathered the new work had already begun to look less uncouth. The boys from the Grove seemed to have a faculty for appreciating the traditions of the place. Here are letters from the universities, here is reflected the deep interest taken in the missionary efforts of the times. There are accounts of visits by men like Owen Watkins (father of a future chairman of the Governors) with his twenty oxen drawing the twenty-foot-long wagon to Pietermaritzburg, and appeals from the youthful W. T. A.

Barber to other boys to join him in China. There is a letter in similar vein from A. W. Lockyer in Panama, where he found the climate soft and delicious; he had died of yellow fever before his letter had been printed in the *Magazine*.

Here, too, in the reports of cricket and football are the first appearances of schools which have long been friendly rivals. In the summer of 1883 is the first mention of Wycliffe College, with the very modest scores indeed on both sides. But this seems to have been an isolated event. Next year comes a victory over Monkton Combe by fourteen runs on the first innings, and in the autumn the first encounter with Monkton at Rugby football. It took place on their ground, and was a lamentable affair. Monkton scored seven tries nearly all at the corners, and Kingswood were unable to score at all. There are numerous references to the levelling of the field (i.e. the "Lower Field" on which the Ferens buildings now stand) and to the leasing of various fields on the top of Lansdown, and it is not surprising that games made slow progress. In 1885 Bristol Grammar School appears in the list of cricket fixtures. It was a severe defeat, on their ground—"we think it only right to say that the ground was execrable, indeed it was scarcely possible for it to have been worse. It may give old boys some idea of its character to say it was no better than our pitch in the Lower Field used to be two or three years ago. . . ."

But suddenly, in April 1885, there is the announcement "We regret to state that Mr. Osborn is going to leave us at Midsummer".

It was indeed a shock. Osborn had naturally come to believe that the successes of the school under his headmastership, and the repute in which he was now held in Methodist circles,* would persuade the authorities to entrust to him the single-handed control of the school when, in 1885, the Rev. J. H. Lord reached the end of his second term of office as Governor. But they had referred the matter to a Committee. The Committee, pondering the difficulties of dual control, yet still unable to abandon the old conception of a ministerial head of the establishment, put forward as a solution the management of the school by a

---

* He had been a member of every Conference since laymen were first admitted, and elected at the head of the poll.

single head or principal "who should be a minister". It was a singularly inept conclusion. They may have been influenced by the success so evidently attending Dr. Moulton's appointment as headmaster of The Leys, and in fairness we must remember that lay headmasters were still rare in the public schools. But as applied to Kingswood it was a disastrous proposal. For Osborn was not a minister, nor a man likely to accept a subordinate appointment, and the recommendation was tantamount to an invitation to him to resign. He did so with the deepest regret, on March 14, 1885. The Governing Body seems to have felt powerless to intervene. They acquiesced, and set about appointing a successor.

Osborn thus left, and founded Rydal, now a public school with many links with Kingswood. "I leave the school with very great regret, I cannot say how much", he said in the course of an interview,* "I am going to Colwyn Bay, it is a promising place in the North, and I hope to get a number of pupils there . . . Of course in all these years I have made a good many friends among the Wesleyans, and even now I have promises of pupils from all parts of the country. . . ."

What had been the secret of his success? Hard work had been a factor—"I cannot lay claim", he said, "to any secret beyond that of downright hard work. I have worked, as few men I think could have worked, for years. Except for public duty or some such call I never go out, I have abjured society and everything. I begin before seven in the morning, and I rarely give up work till twelve or halfpast twelve at night, and I have been doing that for nearly twenty years. Any man, if he will only cultivate the habit of hard work, may do a great deal." Yes, that was true enough, but other schoolmasters worked hard, and still fell far short of Osborn's results.

Was it better to lead than to drive the boys? "My idea has always been," said Osborn, "not so much to teach the boys as to teach them to teach themselves . . . if you stimulate a boy's ambition his interest is excited, and then one hopes to see good results after he has left school . . . It has been a very interesting process to watch a boy—perhaps a careless idle boy—get into the vortex, as it were, and become surrounded by these influences.

* At Burton House, on the eve of his departure, *Bath and Wilts. Chronicle.*

Such a boy often gets quite transformed . . . The tone and spirit of the school has got gradually to be in favour of hard work."

He had been hampered by the early age—sixteen—at which most of the boys left, but now that their parents could secure them a longer stay by payment they could sit for scholarships—five open scholarships that year, including the top mathematical scholarship at Trinity, Cambridge, and the top classical scholarship at Christ Church, Oxford. The strain must have been very great? "Yes, I have to examine every class, which I do as a rule once a week, and at the same time to teach my own class." Discipline? "I do not profess to have got so far as to be able to abolish corporal punishment altogether, but I have sometimes done without it for years. I never will consent to say that it is done with. If I said that, I should have trouble the next day. The fact that it is there and may be used is a very great help. There are certain natures among boys that cannot do without it." He had felt deeply the limitations placed upon his work by the system of dual control. "My greatest difficulty has been that I am only a visiting master", he said. "I live here in Burton House and have nothing whatever to do with the boys out of school, so that I cannot get that hold upon them that I should like . . . If you can imagine Dr. Arnold managing a school he did not live at, I think you will see what I mean. Dr. Arnold used to say that the chapel at Rugby was his special means of working the school. I never occupy the pulpit here."

That Osborn did in fact preach to the school on at least one occasion shortly before he left we know from vivid recollections cherished by E. W. Thompson.*

"All that I knew", wrote Thompson recalling the occasion, "was that the school had had a very great Head who had raised it to eminence, and that we were not likely to see his equal again.

"It was a lovely evening in the late summer of 1885 when Osborn rose up in the dining hall to give us his last sermon.

"We were gathered in the dining hall, because that alone would contain our three hundred. The sun was blazing sideways through the great South window, causing every coloured pane of glass in its ornamented borders to glow like a jewel. There were five long tables, ranging from the window towards the doors. We were six rows

* The Rev. E. W. Thompson became a Methodist minister in 1894, served in India, and was Secretary of the Methodist Missionary Society 1919–34. He penned the words quoted in 1962 after an interval of some seventy-seven years.

of boys, three rows on the one side looked across the hall to three rows on the other. In the centre, near the entrance was the short masters' table. Looking up the hall the first long table was that on the right along the wall, the top end by the great window. From it the majestic Sixth had their seats downward, and I as a junior in the Fifth only just managed to be allowed a seat at its bottom end by the doors. But my lowly position had this advantage, that when Osborn rose up at the end of the masters' table to give us his last charge I was almost on a level with him and could see and hear him perfectly.

"Osborn was not tall: he was rather short and stocky. He wore two moustaches, which curled in Victorian fashion round the corners of his mouth. He had a beautiful speaking voice, a voice of dignity, and full of authority. I never heard it raised in anger, for he always spoke with the assurance of being instantly obeyed; but I did imagine that if he were moved to wrath by disobedience it might have been terrible in its devastating power. My form was too low down in the school order to have much direct teaching by Osborn, but we had one hour a week when he took us in Greek Testament as we stood before the blackboard and the old school motto *In Gloriam Dei,* in the top right hand corner of the Senior Schoolroom as we called the Moulton Hall."

Osborn spoke in his sermon of false values and false standards. He spoke, too, of the corporate life of a great school, and of its influence on the individual. The advantages of massing large numbers of boys together for the purposes of education were many; for instance, the feelings inspired in boys by the past history and successes of their school. He was unquestionably Kingswood's Arnold—"in a few remarks on the prefect system, which he had done a great deal to introduce into the school, he begged us not to bring about its discontinuance by any unpleasant or small feelings that might creep in amongst us unless we kept on our guard against them."

Kingswood as Osborn left it was not a large school, but had the authentic note of a great school about it. Its scholarship was beyond dispute. The name of one of its boys, A. E. Hillard, was to be familiar to generations of schoolboys as joint author of the once famous text-books of Latin and Greek prose composition; and the name of another, A. E. Taylor, as the author of a standard work on Plato; and these are but random examples. This was no accident, as Hillard would assert years later when himself High

Master of St. Paul's. The thoroughness with which they did things in those days was explained by the hours put in voluntarily in the big Schoolroom from 5 a.m. all the summer months. Osborn, thought Hillard, understood a boy's pride, and what induced a boy to do his best for himself; and he understood, too, a boy's temper.

During Osborn's headmastership there had come to the school the self-government among the boys which had long been recognised as a principal mark of a public, as distinct from a private, school; and it had come at a time when the school was conducted on a sufficient scale to give it real meaning. Hillard had been the first Senior Prefect after amalgamation with the Grove. It was then that he had learned what he called the whole trick of schoolmastering—how to call for silence, and how to have silence when he called for it. There did exist in some measure what we should regard today as unduly demonstrative piety, more perhaps than we should think is good for boys; but such was not confined to Kingswood. All through the middle of the century since Arnold lit the flame at Rugby piety had been spread abroad through most of the old and nearly all of the new public schools by Evangelical (and sometimes Tractarian) headmasters. At Kingswood the difference was that it took a Wesleyan rather than an Anglican form. Waves of revival making their way through the English-speaking world were reflected in similar waves at Kingswood. Boys were converted, and many went out later to play their part in carrying the message overseas. The atmosphere at the school at this time was probably more open and healthy than at many schools. The failure to throw the school open to any other than the sons of Weslyan ministers certainly did not result in any lack of tone; but had others been admitted in this era of change, as some had wisely counselled, the school need not have waited until the present century before it could develop an upper school big enough to take full advantage of its privileges. It is a topic to which we shall have occasion to revert.

XI

W. P. WORKMAN, 1889–1918

IT IS strange indeed that having lost Osborn over the issue of dual government the authorities went back on their decision and appointed both a Governor and a Headmaster. For a further fifteen years control was vested in ministerial Governors—the Rev. Dr. George Bowden, the Rev. Wesley Brunyate, and the Rev. T. Ferrier Hulme, and the Headmaster continued to live in Burton House.

The Rev. Dr. George Bowden was a man of strong personality. In his late fifties, tall, of good address and a florid complexion, he wore side whiskers, and his hair, we are told, looked as if just dried from the bath. He was indeed a great believer in the cold bath and physical fitness, and naturally of a somewhat choleric disposition. Breakfasting in hall with his wife and two girl wards he made no attempt to disguise his disgust at the late arrival at his table of any unfortunate master who had overslept. The Doctor, as he was known, owned a farm in the West country, and used the school field for his carriage horse and his experiments in the growing of new crosses of grass. When out visiting, mounted with his wife and the young ladies behind him in the wagonette, sitting erect with whip and reins in hand, he "looked and probably felt no end of a toff". He was of a kindly nature quite innocent of any desire to take undue advantage, but it was perhaps inevitable that he was sometimes tempted to overstep the proper limits of his authority, and interfere in school, as distinct from domestic matters. The last years of the eighties and the first of the nineties were full of anxiety for him; his wife's health gave way, and the Doctor was compelled to retire before the end of his full term of office.

The routine of life at the school had now acquired many of the features that were to last through several generations, and the moment is opportune to glance at it. There was morning school before breakfast. Then came the mug of tea, not too warm and very sweet, a pat of butter the size and thickness of a couple of pennies, and a slice of bread. Too often no second slice was offered; the maids went round with shallow baskets of cut slices "and if all were taken before she reached one's seat she retired and no more came". The same fare served for tea. On rare whole holidays boys walked to Bristol, or made their way to Castle Combe or Bradford-on-Avon, to arrive back with varied excuses for non-arrival before the time limit had expired. Provision for out-of-school activities was sadly deficient, and Dr. Bowden established a workshop. It was through the generosity of his friend Mr. John Farnworth, a former Lord Mayor of Liverpool, that the school acquired a gymnasium and reading rooms above it. The buildings were in Swiss chalet type similar to the sanatorium, in sharp contrast with the stolid dormitory block next to which they stood.

In 1892 the fatherly and white-bearded Rev. Wesley Brunyate took over the Governorship. He was already an elder statesman in Methodism when pressed to accept the Governorship at Kingswood. He had had sons of his own at the school who had gone on to distinguished careers (two of them knighted, for services in India and Egypt) and Mrs. Brunyate knew how to ask boys to breakfast once a fortnight with cold steak and kidney pies and lashings of jellied gravy—never to be forgotten pies, and coffee and marmalade too. Brunyate grappled manfully with a whole series of problems; fever again, improvements to the sanitary and catering arrangements, the removal of the farm buildings from the immediate vicinity of the dormitories to the far end of the field. To him as Governor it fell to administer discipline on the "house" as distinct from the "school" side, and his quaint old-fashioned ways of discharging this duty gave rise to many "Brunyatisms". But he was a man of resolute intellectual energy and possessed a lofty conception of the Christian life that made a real contribution to the life of the school.

Meanwhile there had been the gap left by Osborn's departure to be filled. What were the authorities to do? Incredible as it may seem they re-appointed Jefferson, now nearly sixty.* Their action promptly incurred criticism. Successful as he had been in his earlier days it was a very different matter to re-appoint him now. It seems just possible that they were already looking again to Cambridge, where one of Osborn's most brilliant pupils, Walter

* See p.155–7 above.

Percy Workman, had just been elected a Fellow of Trinity, and they may have thought of Jefferson's appointment as an interim measure. But there is no evidence that this was in fact so. Jefferson was re-appointed, and his second headmastership lasted from 1885 to 1889.

In the summer of 1889 W. P. Workman, now twenty-six, was appointed Headmaster. He had had a brief glimpse of school-mastering (at The Leys with Dr. Moulton), and was a gifted and conscientious teacher, remembered as a whirlwind of gown and chalk at the blackboard. He was later to become the author of a widely used *Tutorial Arithmetic* and of other mathematical textbooks.

Workman showed great courage in coming to Kingswood when he did and devoting his very considerable abilities to the service of the school. The end of dual control was not yet in sight, and the financial crisis which had dominated the eighties still remained. Numbers dropped back, and it was not until 1896 that the full six-year term for a boy at the school was restored. There were renewed outbreaks of illness, including scarlet fever, and critics were complaining that food was sparse, sanitation already obsolete, and discipline often severe.

The young Headmaster was undaunted by the adverse circumstances. He belonged to a generation that had caught from Osborn a sense of pride and purposefulness and a great belief in the future of the school. He found, too, support in the warmth with which the old boys of Osborn's day, then establishing themselves in their varied careers rallied to the support of the school. They had sometimes been called upon to express opinions on matters of policy affecting the school, but no efficient organisation existed. In 1894 it was taken in hand by a young barrister, W. Addington Willis,* with the active co-operation of the Headmaster. The new body was known as a Union rather than as an Association, to mark the fact that it was a union of two streams, including with the ministers' sons educated at Kingswood those educated at the Woodhouse Grove of the old dispensation, prior to its final merger with Kingswood in 1883. Their motive was described as the wish "to benefit the school from which they had derived so many advantages and to which they owed their success in life".

---

*Later Sir Addington Willis, Q.C., a leading authority on the law of Workmen's Compensation.

Though the membership did not for some years rise greatly above two hundred, the Union soon began regular dinners in London and elsewhere. The first provincial dinner was at Manchester in 1898, and Yorkshire was not long in following suit. Interest in the school games has always been a strongly marked feature of the Union, and gifts from the old boys through it have meant much to the school. A pavilion on the Upper Field was an obvious need. "If any old boys will take a stroll up the hill as far as the cemetery, and cross the stile into our Upper Field, which we can truly call our own", the *Magazine* had commented a little earlier, "they would be considerably surprised at the numerous changes which have taken place. Of course there is the same old wind which never seems to drop, the same old trees lining the road and casting their shadows over the field. As they cross the stile they will still see the quarry, but this we hope will soon be filled up. What will strike them as strange will be the sight of a football pitch . . . on the other side of the field another football pitch, parallel to the one we have just mentioned. This is the First Club pitch, and will be found to be equal to our old one, which was undoubtedly the best around Bath. Between these, and in the neighbourhood of the two wells, they will see men at work upon the new cricket pitch, the generous gift of the Old Boys Union." A cricket pavilion was provided by the old boys in 1898, and was used by all school teams on the Upper until a larger pavilion was built on the opposite side of the old field in 1962—also the gift of the old boys.

There was as yet no proper history of the school, and Addington Willis played a notable part in this matter also. Together with the Rev. A. H. L. Hastling and the Headmaster he was responsible for the publication of the *History of Kingswood School* in 1898. It was described as being the work of "Three Old Boys". Its value was greatly increased by steps taken by Hastling to encourage those who had been at school in the earlier years of the century to contribute to the *Magazine* their reminiscences of a period before the magazine existed to reflect the day to day life of the school. On this material the authors of the *History* were able to draw freely. They adapted the plan of splitting the story into three well defined periods; Wesley's day, Old Kingswood after Wesley, and New Kingswood after the move to Bath, and each period was handled under half a dozen subject headings. This unusual plan obscures the narrative of the school's history as a whole, decade by decade. But it is admirably adapted to the thorough treatment of each topic in turn. To the *History* of 1898 the present writer owes an incalculable debt; and to it must be referred the reader who wishes to probe further into the different facets of the internal life of the school. The curriculum, the dietary, the personalities of the Governors and Headmasters are here recorded in fascinating detail. The picture which emerges of life in nineteenth-century Kingswood seems harsh; but it may be noted that to one who had been a boy and master from 1855–75 and was well placed to comment it seemed scarcely harsh enough.* But through it all the *History* conveys a deep pride in the school and its achievements; "We are sure", wrote the authors in their preface "of the name and fame of Kingswood. We are sure that she is worthy of our absolute allegiance. We are sure that she stands, and shall stand, strong in the reality of her life, in the loyalty of her sons, and in the moral greatness of her aim." Here is the accent of the school of the late nineties. The publication of the *History* went far to restore perspective, and to reduce to their proper proportions the exaggerated criticisms which had been current earlier in the decade.

When Brunyate died in office in 1901 many felt that dual control should end. The Rev. T. Ferrier Hulme was indeed appointed Governor, but he let it be known that he came intending to prepare the way for Workman to take over the sole responsibility. His three-year tenure of office was marked by many changes. The old system of tables set in collegiate fashion lengthwise down the hall was exchanged for the present system. Incandescent burners appeared in the schoolroom, and it was found that it was more brilliantly lit with ten burners than it had previously been with thirty-seven—"the effect in revealing the proportions of the remarkably handsome room was very fine". Straw hats were introduced for Sunday wear in place of the ancient pork-pie. "I had a lot of unpleasant work to do", Ferrier Hulme wrote later, "in breaking down old prejudices . . . I know this made me unpopular." In 1904 the

---

* The Rev. W. Goodhugh Dawson, in an extended review in the *Wesleyan Methodist Magazine*, April 1899. This review is an important source for history of the period.

office of Governor was allowed to lapse, and was replaced by that of Visitor.

The Headmaster now moved from Burton House into what had always been the Governor's apartments to the right of the front entrance of the main buildings. The change marked a new era, and the years that followed were happy ones. Modest as were the numbers—the total dropped to its lowest, 155 in that year— there was soon an upward trend. By 1909 they had reached 250, and the masters' dais had to be moved from the centre of the dining hall to make room for more boys. The Hall House dormitories, closed in 1902, were reopened to take the youngest. In everything the Headmaster's wife shared to the full, for there was then no matron in the modern sense of the term. In 1897 he had married his cousin Amelia Mary. Her winning disposition quickly had a marked impact on the school, which should not pass unrecorded in its story. "I want to be your friend" was the long remembered theme of a courageous little speech which she made to the assembled school. She possessed an exceptional ability to interest herself in the individual, whether master, boy or servant, and to Kingswood she brought her unobtrusive but unmistakable piety. Her help was thus of the first importance to the Headmaster when he took charge of the residential side. Workman never had more than a minimal staff to assist him with all sorts of problems, and from now on we can catch glimpses of him closeted with Hinton the engineer and caretaker, attempting to grapple with matters far removed from the proper sphere of a headmaster.*

The boys, Workman could tell his Governors, had grasped the intimate connection between the Christian life and the faithful discharge of daily duty. That this was no idle boast was borne out by the high proportion of the able boys of those days who devoted themselves to various branches of the service of the Church. Many, for example, found their way at this time into the educational work of the Methodist Church in India, and to some of them it fell to exercise widespread influence.† The emphasis on hard work, always present at the school, received fresh emphasis. A boy who came to

* E. P. Aust joined the staff at Kingswood in 1905. His reminiscences *The Bursar Remembers* (1946) afford many sidelights over some forty years, and have been invaluable in affording material.

† The Rev. J. S. M. Hooper, for example, would play a large part in founding the Church of South India.

Kingswood late in his school career with the experience of three other large schools, one of them an important public school, commented that at Kingswood a boy was looked down upon if he did not work, at other schools he was looked down upon if he did; "I am sorry," he said, "I did not come here five years ago."

It was a period that rivalled, if it did not equal, the successes of Osborn's days. By 1909 Workman was able to report thirty-two awards at Oxford and Cambridge during the earlier phase of his headmastership. It was not of course comparable with the successes won by the larger public schools, but it was a real achievement for a school of the size of, and subject to the limitations imposed on Kingswood. Workman's own teaching of mathematics and his interest in physics were rewarded by a long list of successes culminating in a record of elections to the Royal Society of which the school could well be proud; when in 1941 a count was made of the number of Fellows and the schools from which they came, Kingswood was among the leading schools.

Nor were out-of-school activities neglected. Schoolmasters used to wonder whether the time given to such activities as the collection of fossils and the pursuit of photography were really worth while, but the story of Kingswood in this period affords several striking examples to prove their value. A geological collection was arranged during the years that H. H. Swinnerton was a boy at the school; throughout a long life he was to be one of our leading geologists and author of widely read books. A Photographic Society appeared, and C. E. K. Mees went on to become the inventor of Kodachrome, Chief Scientific Adviser to Kodak, and F.R.S.

At Workman's side throughout his headmastership was the heroic figure of Frank Richards. He had come to the school in 1884, when Osborn was Headmaster. "Rix", as he was always known, had like Workman been at Trinity, Cambridge, and was steeped in the classics. His spare figure, his remarkable countenance, his utter loyalty to his Headmaster, and his transparent devotion to the school made him memorable to many generations of boys. As he progressed slowly up the hill, with his hands behind his coat tails, and his body inclined forward, arms flapping occasionally, he would be meditating some classical theme and ranging in thought up and down the ages; if ever a man breathed the *largior aether* it was he. His abstracted manner did not mean that he could be trifled with; when, as Second Master he became responsible for discipline during the absences of the Head it improved. But relaxation was possible, and there might be heard coming from his classroom the occasional burst of uproarious laughter. When the ill-prepared translation faltered and stumbled so that all the form grew tense and the school donkey could be heard braying in the fields, Rix's staccato "One at a time, please!" could bring the house down, and the story be told for generations afterwards.

Richards became non-resident in 1903, after twenty years service. He continued to preside over the classical work of the Sixth as though no other occupation had ever occurred to him. A visit to Greece prompted an article in the school magazine which can still be read with pleasure. Here is Lycabettus flashing its welcome light across the hushed city to the sea, and a reference to

the rocky brow
That looks o'er sea-born Salamis

will recall to many the very accents in which he used to chant his favourite verses.

He wrote, too, in 1907 a succinct and refreshingly vivid account of Kingswood as he saw it, which deserves to be rescued from oblivion*. He tells us how Wesley's plan had recalled in many respects the comprehensive and marvellously sanguine scheme sketched by Milton in his famous letter to Samuel Hartlib; how in the nineteenth century mathematics had become the chief distinction of the school, and Kingswood had won its first public fame with the successes of its old boys at the universities; how now at last the school had been given a single head, who with his monarchical powers and personal popularity could control and reform at pleasure. It is a fascinating sidelight on the school of the period, not perhaps quite what the reader would have expected.

In the middle years of his headmastership Workman was able to embark on a series of modest improvements to the fabric. Although the administration of the school was conducted by the Managing Committee with a strict regard to economy, Workman found in the Visitor, the Rev. W. Marshall Hartley, one who could lend a sympathetic ear to the claims of the school on

---

* *Wesleyan Methodist Magazine*, 1907, p. 404.

THE WEST FRONT FROM THE FERENS BUILDINGS
photograph by Cyril Howe, Bath, taken in the 1930s
before the Library was built

H. A. WOOTTON, Headmaster 1919–28
on the occasion of the visit of H.R.H. the Prince of Wales in 1926
Also in the photograph are the Rev. Owen Spencer Watkins, Hon. Secretary
to the Governors, and E. W. Eltham, F. S. Cook and R. Dodds

*Photograph by
Cyril Howe, Bath*

SCHOOL CHAPEL
1922

Photograph by Cyril Howe,

The wide horizon is a constant feature of life at Kingswood

Methodist funds, and the two worked closely together to ease the position whenever opportunity offered. A lucky windfall provided "a splendid wing of class-rooms". They included better provision for the physical laboratory, for ever since he took over the headmastership Workman had been concerned to build up a modern side with adequate facilities. Two light and airy wards were added to the sanatorium—till then it had been little more than a chalet. Numerous much needed changes were made in the hinterland of the main buildings; ceilings of passages were raised in 1910–12, and the external appearance of this area was improved by battlements in keeping with the buildings of 1851. (The whole of this main traffic artery had received but scant attention in the original design.) A new organ was given by the old boys, and placed in the dining hall, and in 1908 a carved oak screen was erected. The oak panelling of the hall was carried out in instalments, chiefly by Flexen, the school carpenter, and the hall assumed its present appearance. The window at the South end of the hall was replaced by the present stained glass. It was felt to be a great improvement. More windows by H. J. Sainsbury followed in memory of T. G. Osborn and others who had served the school. Frank Richards spoke of its gradually growing beauty, and of the aesthetic merits of the new windows. In it, we must remember, were held the regular fortnightly Sunday evening services which now played a formative part in life at Kingswood. The music and singing of the school had made great advances under Alfred Beer, who had published through Novello a small collection of Kingswood tunes.

It remained only, thought Frank Richards in 1907, to build a chapel worthy of the school—"the most startling omission at Kingswood among the requisites of a great school". The idea of a chapel continued to be canvassed until the Rev. W. T. Derry moved a resolution in Conference and sanction was given. But the year was 1914, and the chapel remained to be built as a War Memorial.

The improvements made in the dining hall, and indeed, all that was done in the decade before the war, were part of a sustained effort to civilise life at Kingswood, and Workman was justifiably proud of what had been done. Looking back now we may wonder that concern was not felt about the total lack of day-rooms. The need was not felt. When the boys returned to

N

school in 1907 they noted that the dormitories were more like lions' dens than ever before—"formerly we had wire-netting in the windows, while now we had strong iron bars as well. Midnight strolls are to be no more . . ." Nor can we note without surprise that when in 1912 a large house known as Westwood, situated just above the school, was burnt down by suffragettes an offer by the owner to sell the eight acres to the school at £150 an acre did not apparently receive more than cursory consideration before it was rejected.

But in 1911 the Headmaster's wife died. Her gentle nature, combined with a remarkable force of character, had given her a special position in the school, helping the Headmaster on the side on which he most needed it. A man of restless intellectual energy, his interests always lay rather in his teaching and the things of the mind than in the everyday life of the boys, and he now became increasingly withdrawn. His niece, Miss Ruth Deniss, came to live at the school and to take care of his little daughter Paxy.* The gap left by Mrs. Workman's death could not be filled, and many have attributed to it weaknesses in the life of the school which were soon to appear and of which we shall have more to tell on later pages.

Had the responsibility been effectively shared with housemasters the impact of Mrs. Workman's death might have been less serious. But there was as yet in the school no adequate conception of what housemastering should mean. "Housemasters" did indeed exist in name but under the system whereby all effective control was concentrated in the hands of the Governor their opportunities had been limited. Nor when the office of Governor lapsed in 1904 was the opportunity taken to give them proper authority, and the old centralized control was vested in the Headmaster. It was a serious omission and one for which the school had to pay dearly. The position of the assistant masters still left much to be desired, and the failings of the system are only too apparent. A review of staff salaries was undertaken in 1910, whereby graduates in First or Second Class Honours of Oxford and Cambridge, (or Masters of Arts of London University) were placed on a

---

* She had in 1909 been admitted a pupil of the school. It was long thought that her case was unique, but there had been girls in the school in its earliest days.

scale of £120 per annum rising by £8 annually to £200; and there were three lower categories, in which were found stalwart members of the staff, whose pleas to be up-graded were disregarded. Residence was an obligation imposed on the latest recruits; there were to be not less than five resident masters, i.e. one to be "housemaster" in each windy dormitory. "Non-residence", reads the printed statement of conditions, "cannot in future be granted unless a master has served a minimum of six years in residence." The supply of men willing to spend long years in bachelor quarters devoting themselves to their teaching and the maintaining of discipline was clearly beginning to fail. When J. A. Knowles was granted permission to marry it was on condition that he remained a resident master and spent only the weekends with his wife. Those who took an interest in the welfare of their boys were all the more notable. Such a one was G. R. H. Nicholson, to whose inspiration both as housemaster and historian a future headmaster owed what he described as an incalculable debt. Early in 1914 Nicholson crossed the Atlantic and later founded another Kingswood in West Hartford, Connecticut, now a flourishing private high school.

Enough has been said to show that, despite much advance and continued academic success, the school was, by comparison with the now greatly enlarged and multiplied public schools of the pre-1914 era, seriously handicapped in many directions; and but imperfectly aware of the character of these handicaps. From 250 the numbers had slipped back again, and by 1914 there were but 178 boys in the school. A proportion of these, too, were below the age usually admitted to public schools, and would elsewhere have been in a preparatory school.

The reader may be forgiven for wondering why, when numbers were well below capacity, Workman did not re-open the question of the admission of the sons of laymen. That the boys from the manses imparted a quality of their own to the school few would wish to dispute. But numbers are not irrelevant, and to rule out, as Workman seems to have done, the admission of others at a time when such action could have helped the school so materially must surely be held to be evidence of a limitation of outlook. He belonged to a generation that was quick to think of the admission of boys other than ministers' sons as dilution, and as calculated to destroy the esprit de corps of the school. "It may be", it was said at an Old Boys dinner in 1906, "that under some panic legislation the essential distinction of Kingswood might be done away with. If the school is once opened to the sons of laymen, it may retain its name, but it will never be the same school." The admission of laymen's sons was postponed for a generation. The school did survive and the expansion did eventually take place. But it was in more ways than one a close-run thing.

Games flourished. They had been relatively slow to develop at the school, but the beginning of competition between "houses" in 1895 and the provision of a cricket pavilion in 1898 are signs of a new attitude, and the school *Magazine* begins to carry extended accounts of matches in a vein which has changed little in more than half a century. Monkton Combe and Bristol Grammar School make their regular appearances in usually well-contested games; other schools and clubs come and go in the record. The movement gathered momentum, and by 1904 the Headmaster, on the advice of the Games Committee, was making football compulsory for the whole school. It had been suggested in 1886, but the forces arrayed against it were then too strong. A little later on an "Alphabetical League" was formed, consisting of seven teams of approximately equal strength. On some half holidays as many as three games were played one after another in the Lower field.

The innovation met with approval. "Let no one think", said the *Magazine*, "that the leaven of the professional element is creeping in; the new system is in the right direction, seeking to do away with the loafer and the bully, and to develop the manliness and generosity which is the true ideal of sport." The award of caps for cricket and football is even accorded priority of place at the Prize-giving for several years in succession from the turn of the century; first the caps, then the Dux prizes. In 1909 the old black and silver jerseys of the first fifteen were altered to striped black and red. When at last spring came round there could be heard in the sunlit playgrounds the crack of racquets; this was bat-racquets, an excellent game which had long been a feature of life at the school. (Its ultimate demise was due to greatly increased costs.) In 1908, when a windfall permitted it, an indoor swimming pool was built. Swimming was nothing new.

Boys had long been accustomed to swimming contests at the Cleveland baths; but, with the opening of the school's own bath, swimming was pursued with a new zest. Cricket flourished, and the horse-drawn buses took the teams further afield. In 1911 there is the first fixture with Downside. It was an "away game" —"the most perfect pitch it has ever been our good fortune to set eyes on"—and opened propitiously for Kingswood, for Downside's opening batsman was well caught behind the wicket off the first ball of the match.

There is no mistaking the way the wind was blowing, and it would be misleading to suggest that in the later years of Workman's headmastership the new spirit did not trespass on the old zest for work that had meant so much to Kingswood in the past. Certainly during the second decade of the century there developed, as many still recall, a state of affairs very different from that of the earlier years. The record of academic achievement slipped back somewhat. Already by 1907 we hear Frank Richards giving it as his opinion that the disappearance of the lists of successes in examinations in which the school had formerly seemed to take "all the leading places" was to be attributed to the development of many-sided activities, victories won on the cricket and football field—"therein lies the secret". The explanation is recorded as comforting.

But, as we know today, games properly handled need not conflict with achievement in school work, and it seems probable that in those Edwardian days Kingswood was the scene of a deeper conflict of ideals than it was aware of. It was, we must recall, the hey-day of that over-valuation of games in the public schools that was still gathering a momentum it had never lost since it had first appeared in the fifties of the previous century and caused such chagrin to the more sober type of schoolmaster. It was penetrating more deeply into Kingswood every year. Workman was forced into what was no doubt from his point of view an uneasy compromise. He neither rode the tide, as did so many other headmasters to their great prosperity and renown; nor could he, nor did he wish to, suppress it altogether. To this extent, therefore, the school was, during the latter years of Workman's headmastership, at cross purposes. He, for his part, was denied the enthusiastic support another man might so easily have won; whilst the school, for its part, fell back upon respect for his scholarship and integrity in substitution for that warmth of feeling that marks a school at one with itself.

In these pre-war years the boys thus enjoyed more by accident than by design a combination of the old discipline and a new freedom that was, if not ideal, at least highly stimulating. The virtual abstention of the Headmaster and of the housemasters from any sustained attempt to participate in the boys' life out-of-school converted official discipline into a kind of game, with a gamut of excitement all its own. The boy world had its own values; the red-tasselled cap of the First Fifteen; the dignity of the Sixth Form, with its right to carry and use a walking stick; the House Tea, in honour of victories won; the occasional fight in the wood; the extravagances of the end of term permitted by tradition; the compulsory runs in wintry weather to the Monument at the far end of Lansdown; these and many other facets of school life became invested with an aura of excitement which the present school with its wider interests can perhaps hardly rival. The sudden grant of a whole holiday meant, not, as too often today, a slight change of routine, but an intoxicating gulp of morning sunlight on the hedgerows. The very look of it had been all but forgotten amid the concentrated dangers and escapes that made up life at school.

"How well I remember the massy sunlight moving up those shadowy valleys deep into Lansdown hillside", wrote one whose literary promise was cut short, recalling what he thought the sweetest place names in the world. The odour of rich midsummer days blew in upon the wholesome air of Swainswick, Woolley, Langridge, Charlcombe, Tadwick and St. Catharine's; and with it the aspect of the old places, fashioned of mist, rose living out of the past. The valley sides of Lansdown were broad meadowy declines, dipping here and there into hollows rich with blackberries, and at intervals dark with copses where windflowers strayed and primrose clumps abounded among the fern and moss. George Lowther's evocative prose is a timely reminder of the unsought bonus that had descended on the school on Lansdown, now that the boys had the freedom and leisure to appreciate the landscape that Beckford had extravagantly rated the finest in Europe. Lowther's tragic death in Floutern Tarn in July, 1913, elicited a notable tribute from his hero Edward Thompson in *Ennerdale Bridge and other poems*. The writing of verse received a fresh impetus in these years, and became something of a tradition in the school. Thompson, who had left Kingswood in 1902, would later become the intimate friend of Robert Bridges, and his biographer; and his insight into Indian history would make him the trusted friend and confidant of many Indian nationalist leaders.

When, after the summer term of 1914, the country found itself committed to war in Europe, and the army crossed to France, school work at first went on very much as usual. The Headmaster was prompt to offer the sanatorium to the authorities for use as an auxiliary hospital, and it was not long before the reality of the war was brought home by the arrival of Belgian wounded. The *Magazine* carried in heavy type a notice inviting old boys willing to enlist to write at once to the Public Schools and University Men's Brigade. The school, it must be remembered, had no military tradition; when in the latter half of the nineteenth century the idea of starting an O.T.C. in emulation of the public schools had been mooted, it had been firmly rejected by Methodist opinion; and hence, for such an eventuality as the war of 1914–18, Kingswood in common with a great part of England, was totally unprepared. The response to the call was nevertheless prompt, and the inevitable casualties began to be reported. But for many months the impact of the war was surprisingly slight, and it was not until the sanatorium was filled to overflowing with the casualties from the Somme in 1916 that its full force was felt. Thereafter the scene darkened. At Kingswood as elsewhere the losses were most grievous amongst those who were little more than boys themselves. Where so many served with distinction no record can be complete, and to single out individuals is impossible. One exception may however be permitted.

Hardy Falconer Parsons joined the school in 1912, and left in April, 1915. A quiet and unassuming boy, he was gazetted to the 14th Battalion of the Gloucestershire Regiment. On August 21, 1917, he was in charge of a bombing attack on the right flank of his battalion when the enemy attacked the position with the help of flame-throwers. "Our men", read the report, "fell back before the flames, but Hardy Parsons held the post single handed, though severely burnt with the liquid fire, and held up the enemy with bombs till the Company Commander was able to organise a new bombing party which drove back the Germans before they could enter our trenches." Hardy Parsons did not survive, and was awarded the Victoria Cross. It was the second in the history of the school.*

Through 1917 and 1918 the stress of the war was much more apparent at the school. The Easter holidays were abandoned, and term ran from January to July. Rationing was taken very seriously; even bread was limited, though it was still on sale in the shops. The younger masters had gone to the war and Workman relied increasingly on his power to hold the assembled school tense and expectant whilst he appealed to the boys' better nature to refrain from this or that of which he could not approve. But the effect was apt to be evanescent, and in retrospect it is not difficult to see that a gap was opening between the Headmaster and the school, and that much in the old regime would have to go before it could be closed again.

Workman died suddenly in harness in the early autumn of 1918, and was buried in the shadow of Beckford's Tower on Lansdown. Frank Richards, white-haired and stoical, and himself not far from retirement, was inevitably invited to serve as acting Headmaster. When the war was over and there was a new hand at the helm there would be, as the reader will shortly see, something of an inquest into the state into which it would be held that the school had fallen. There will be room for differences of opinion—how far the decline was due to the war (for other schools suffered similar troubles at this time) or how far it was due to causes which Workman might reasonably have been expected to have foreseen and corrected. The account here given will perhaps have shown the formidable difficulties with which he had to battle, and the passionate and self-sacrificing devotion to the welfare of the school which he never failed to display.

---

* The first had been won by Staff Surgeon Job Maillard, R.N., for gallantry at Candia in 1898.

XII

H. A. WOOTTON, 1919–28

HUBERT ARTHUR WOOTTON was appointed Headmaster in
March 1919. Still a comparatively young man—he was
thirty-five at the time of his appointment—he had been
educated at Nottingham High School under Dr. Gow, and
at Clare College, Cambridge, where he had been placed in
the first class in both parts of the Natural Sciences Tripos. Since
1906 he had been Senior Science master at Westminster School.
He had been in charge of the O.T.C. there, and the war saw
him appointed Commandant, Young Officers' Training School.
His abilities as a scientist were, however, of a high order, and he
was seconded to work on shell-filling with the distinguished team
under Lord Moulton's leadership that included also Professor
T. M. Lowry, F.R.S., an old boy and Governor of Kingswood.
Wootton came of a well-known Methodist family in Nottingham,
and Lowry had known him well in his Cambridge days. He had
no hesitation in urging his appointment to Kingswood. Wootton's
appointment brought changes and controversies the echoes of
which have not yet died away, and no account of the school
can with honesty evade a reference to these controversies and
some comment upon the issues. Some became and remained
ardent partizans of the ancient regime, others in their zeal for
the reforms and for Wootton's part in them have been tempted
to paint in blacker colours than it warranted the state of the
school as it existed during the latter part of Workman's
headmastership.

Wootton saw at once that the school was suffering from a
certain shabbiness, in part attributable to the stresses and strains
of the war years. But what is more important, he quickly became
conscious that much of the school routine had remained unaltered
since mid-Victorian days, and that many of those associated
with the management of the school were unaware of the character
of this legacy from the past, and of the need to review it item
by item. A brief sketch of some features of life in the school as

he found it in 1919 is therefore essential to an understanding of the changes for which he was responsible. Everything centred upon the old Senior Schoolroom, and on assembly therein at the ringing of the school bell. Here, much no doubt as in the schoolroom of the Charterhouse when Wesley was a boy, the life of the school went on. Here boys kept their property; here and in the corridors they spent much of their leisure, made their friendships, and suffered their humiliations. Here prayers were held first thing in the morning and last thing at night. The climax of the school day was reached when the whole school, save only the two youngest forms, assembled hot and stuffy for preparation in the Senior Schoolroom, and prefects and masters were tested as to their ability to maintain order. Discipline was officially based on a system of marks, distributed somewhat arbitrarily by masters and prefects and involving offenders in detention. So many marks within a week meant the loss of a boy's permit to leave the school premises, while a larger total placed his name "on the list" to attend upon the Headmaster in the library. The system, and the mechanical spirit in which it was operated, belonged rather to the nineteenth than to the twentieth century. Alongside it there had grown up authority in the hands of the prefects backed by the power to inflict corporal punishment. They carried a considerable responsibility for maintaining the discipline of the school, more than would be today regarded as reasonable. The school took an intense interest in Rugger and especially in the house matches, which were fought out with a spirit fully equal to the descriptions found in the school stories of the time; but games were loosely organized, and not so as, for most boys, to occupy more than one or two afternoons a week. The ancient and skilful but barbarous form of football known as Flab was in full swing in the playgrounds; it allowed handling provided the ball was bounced once after every three steps, and strangling an opponent in the crook of the elbow was a recognized form of tackling; and it culminated once or twice a term in a licensed battle between the Sixth and the rest of the school, a valued opportunity to pay off grudges. There was a certain amount of bullying in the school; in the absence of any organized system of fagging, the younger boys suffered a good deal from the horseplay of those immediately above them who had time on their hands.

Of commanding presence, six feet four, and the very image of what a headmaster is popularly supposed to look like, Wootton judged it his duty to intervene personally in practically every aspect of the school's life. He would appear in the classrooms, where the lack of discipline was sometimes all too obvious. He would lunch in Hall, taking note of the lack of that military smartness of demeanour to which during the war years he had become accustomed elsewhere. He would pass through the Patch at break, plainly regarding with distaste the effect of Flab on collars and ties, and meditating bringing it to an end. Most frequently of all, and with the best of reasons, he would appear in mortarboard and gown at the door of the Senior Schoolroom when preparation was in progress, or perhaps largely in abeyance, according to the capacity of the master on duty. In such circumstances Wootton's ire rose.

Happy as he often was in dealing with individual boys, in his wrath with the school as a whole he often allowed himself to use words which in calmer moments he would not have used. Here, many believed, in much provocation and in Wootton's imperious temperament, was the chief source of that indignation and resistance to his authority which marked the earlier phase of his headmastership.

But much did indeed need to be done. The old guard among the masters were mostly on the point of retirement, salaries would have to be raised to meet the post-war situation, and pensions adjusted. Wootton was quick to see the advantages which would accrue if the school could be accepted for participation in the Schoolteachers' Superannuation Act of 1919, and he was kept busy with negotiations. Participation involved, or in the confusion of the times was thought to involve, readiness on the part of the school to receive ten per cent of nominated pupils from local authorities willing to send boys and pay the appropriate fees, now fixed at £105 per annum. The taking of fee-paying pupils was, of course, a new departure, but the Governors felt that they had no option. (Despite, however, repeated notification of the willingness of the school to receive them no such pupils materialized.) It was also a condition that the school should be recognized as "efficient": a body of H.M. Inspectors arrived in October 1920, and recognition was given in March 1921.

Acceptance for purposes of the Superannuation Act followed in June, and the school was thus enabled to offer its staff participation in a pension scheme on terms materially better than those available under the schemes of most other independent schools.

The report of H.M. Inspectors was, of course, the first of its kind, and their assessment of the state of affairs was of great value to the Headmaster. He had been able to expound to them the steps he was already taking to bring the curriculum up to date, and the many defects in the premises which needed to be corrected. Their report was highly creditable to himself and his initiative, and in its references to elements of strength in the school.

Wootton also exchanged the old Oxford Local Examinations for the new Oxford and Cambridge Certificate Examination. The detailed report of the examiners was also of the utmost value, and much thought now went into the re-shaping of the curriculum. The staff, Wootton wrote at the time, were not aware of the improvements in educational methods that had been made in recent years. "My aim", he wrote, "is to evolve a curriculum with distinctive features of its own, for I believe that every school has opportunities which differ from those of other schools. In times past Kingswood was a unique school in advance of others, and there is no reason why that should not be repeated, if only I can get a staff with some enthusiasm for their work."

It was not surprising that the Headmaster soon found himself involved in serious friction with members of the staff. Always quick to think in terms of "insubordination" he proceeded (November 1920) to dismiss three of the younger masters with whom he was dissatisfied.* Such action could not but cause a commotion. The masters thus dismissed found sympathy, not only among elements in the school with grievances of their own, but among the officials and Executive of the Assistant Masters' Association, which issued a notice warning its members against acceptance of an engagement at Kingswood. This not unnaturally caused a considerable stir in the profession. But the A.M.A. had acted somewhat precipitately, and when later the masters appealed to the Governors and it fell to the A.M.A. to present their case, strong exception was taken by the Governors to the action of the Association in notifying its members before the

---

* A fourth and more senior master (W. O. Williams) left in the spring of 1921 and joined G. R. H. Nicholson in Connecticut.

appeal had been heard. The notices of dismissal were withdrawn, and the three masters were permitted to resign. The A.M.A. notified its members that the matter had terminated quite satisfactorily, and that the "former communication" should be withdrawn and forgotten.

Through the crisis Wootton enjoyed the full support of the Governors. It was fortunate indeed for him that his appointment in 1919 had coincided with that of the Rev. Owen Spencer Watkins as Honorary Secretary of the Governors. Watkins's career as a regular Methodist Army Chaplain had in the course of various campaigns from Omdurman onwards and through the Great War brought him much distinction, and he would shortly become Deputy Chaplain-General at the War Office. Himself an old boy of the school and a Governor since 1910, Watkins had for some time been dissatisfied with the control of the school's affairs. This was divided between a large body known as the General Committee, which met but rarely at the school, and a Managing Committee which included members drawn from the locality, and which sometimes seemed to press unduly its duty to secure every possible economy regardless of other considerations. Important changes were made in 1920 which saw a body of Governors appointed who should meet regularly each term at the school. It was a great improvement on the former arrangements. Wootton now co-operated more and more closely with Watkins, and the file of their correspondence throws much light on the inner history of the school. Both were forthright men, and they respected each other. "My dear Padre," Wootton would write, "I propose to take such-and-such action." "My dear Headmaster," came back the reply, "you have my full support. . . . Let So-and-so do his worst!" Co-operation between the two men became a real partnership, and contributed greatly to the rapidity and success of many of the adjustments made in these critical years. The Rev. Marshall Hartley was the third member of the trio. Appointed Visitor as far back as 1904, he had acted in effect as Chairman of the Governors for many years during Workman's headmastership, and he now corresponded with Wootton with equal if not greater frequency.

A chief topic of the Headmaster's letters was, of course, what he called the restoration of discipline. He allowed himself to speak freely of the "slackness" that he had encountered on arrival.

"As you know," he wrote to Watkins, "I do not believe in sparing the rod." The times were, he thought, particularly difficult. Incident followed incident. ". . . I had heard of this before. I had spoken plainly to certain boys whom I knew to be ringleaders. I therefore detained three forms on Saturday afternoon, administered a sound tanning to one form in addition, and dealt with the two ringleaders in the following way. . . ." Nor did he hesitate to require boys to be removed. "I do not want to be hard on anyone, but I think that Dr. Arnold was right when he laid down that the first and second and third rules for a schoolmaster were all the same, namely get rid of undesirable boys." Parents who objected to the peremptory tone of his letters, or took exception to the discipline meted out to their sons got short shrift. Yet beneath his formidable exterior Wootton possessed a warm humanity. It would be unfair indeed to suggest that he was incapable of perceptive handling of boys. Quite the contrary was the case, and he could write letters that might serve as models to any schoolmaster.

"Boys of your son's age", he could write to a parent, "often have very great struggles. During the process of growing up, they unfortunately have great moral difficulties; and their ideas of right and wrong are usually very distorted. Lying, cheating and the like are lightly regarded and often stealing is treated as nothing very serious. They require a deal of gentle handling and much kindly guidance and not always rough and ready punishment. . . . They are not really criminals. They might be made so by rough treatment. As a rule a schoolmaster is, I am sorry to say, quite ignorant of a boy's troubles and ignores all the signs of a boy's struggles. He punishes the boy regardless of reason, and stamps him as a knave at the slightest provocation. Your son's form master is markedly in contrast to the man I have depicted. He is rather too kindly, and may overlook things that should be firmly repressed. These boys need a firm hand as much as a kind one."

Wootton possessed in an exceptional measure the power of dramatizing life, of lifting the events of everyday on to the heroic scale. A boy caught smoking in the woods would be guilty of disloyalty. A boy caught gossiping with one of the school maids would find his retention in the school called in question, and the Headmaster's leniency alone would keep him there! The amusing aspect of life in those days did not escape the eye of those boys who possessed a touch of poetic genius, and Wootton was gravely troubled by the circulation of parodies of the regime.

> "This is my school, I am Headmaster here,
> The sign of awe, the embodiment of fear,"

began one widely acclaimed schoolboy effort of the period.* The newly instituted fire drill, the compulsory gargling routine that was part of the battle against recurrent infections, all afforded material for only too acute observation of the Headmaster's personal part in the "restoration of discipline".

> "The morrow morn, when that the bellman tolls
> Fresh agony to worn and weary souls,
> I rise and bent on blissful deeds alway
> Make out my list of bombshells for the day."

Rarely did a day pass without a tirade—

> "They seem to think they'll play the fool
> Like a bear garden or a council school;
> But if they chance to whet my anger keen
> They'll get a ticket for the nine fifteen!"

The schoolboy verses recapture as little else could the note so often struck in the early twenties.

No sooner had the staffing crisis been surmounted, and the four masters who had left been replaced by others,† than the school's affairs were once more overtaken by costs rising out of proportion to its resources. By June 1921 the cost had risen to what then seemed the fantastic figure of over £20,000 per annum. The school was still, it must be remembered, wholly financed out of Methodist funds, and the right of a minister to send his boy to it without charge of any kind was a much valued privilege. The strain on the funds out of which the school was financed led to renewed pressure for economies, and this at a time when the Headmaster was convinced of the need for considerable expenditure to bring the school into a proper condition. If a new block of classrooms was out of the question, at least improvements must be made in the existing premises. The authorities

---

* Known as *The Woottiad*, by A. C. Healing.

† C. L. Wiseman (later Headmaster of Queen's College, Taunton), J. H. Barnes, and R. W. Trump. E. W. Eltham had joined the staff a few months earlier.

would have to make up their mind, he urged, how many ministers' sons they could afford to maintain, and the question of the admission of the sons of laymen could no longer be evaded.

Matters came to a head in the summer of 1922. With great reluctance Watkins moved in the Methodist Conference a report which imposed a charge of £15 a year on ministers in respect of their boys. The times were difficult, ministers' modest stipends already inadequate, and it was by no means certain that the proposal would be accepted. Certain wise concessions had, however, been embodied in the scheme and the report went through. The objections so long urged against the admission of the sons of laymen seemed in the post-war circumstances to have lost their force, and in the school year 1922–23 steps were taken to make it known that they could be admitted. Numbers were at first few, but they gradually increased.

In 1922 the Chapel was opened. On coming to the school Wootton had found the Governors bent on the provision of a war memorial chapel as a first priority. The building of a chapel close to the road and in line with the Hall, had indeed been part of the plans of 1851, but had been postponed for lack of funds. For generations the boys had gone on Sundays to fill the galleries of the large King Street and Walcot Chapels in Bath; and the tramp down and up the hill had become a feature of life at the school. When, therefore, the new Chapel began to rise amid the trees near the main gates, its clean white stone marked another change in the life of the school. Visitors at the opening in June remarked upon the eager faces of the boys to whom the past meant little and the future everything. It was perhaps a way of saying that there was a new feeling about the school, a new surge of confidence, for the world of 1922 could not be satisfied with the ways of 1914.

With the summer of 1922 the first phase of Wootton's headmastership may be said to have ended. It was a notable achievement. In the three years since his appointment his impact on the school had been unprecedented; the school had been transformed and a new course set. In February of that year he had been elected a member of the Headmasters' Conference, and Kingswood had thus become for the first time technically a public school.

As we have seen, it had not been done without arousing fierce

THE DINING HALL
little changed down the years

THE LIBRARY INTERIOR
the gift of W. A. Posnett

A. B. SACKETT
Headmaster 1928–59

RUGBY FOOTBALL TEAM OF 1950
Standing (*left to right*) A. C. P. Pugh, H. Bazley, R. G. Blackmore, N. Y. Gedye, H. R. Moore, K. M. Darlington, J. A. Hackett; *centre* J. G. Smith, W. P. Cooke, S. P. Calvert, Mr W. N. Sedgley, the Headmaster, M. D. Baker (*captain*), K. Duchars, B. J. Lane; *front* M. A. Lee, C. R. Morris

controversy. He had not taken much notice, he told another headmaster, of the criticisms which had been hurled at him from all parts of the country. They had come from those who knew little of the real circumstances, and much of what was said was either wholly untrue or completely distorted. It would never have done for him to have said what he thought was the matter with the school. What had been necessary had been to stiffen things all round, and naturally enough very few people had liked the stiffening process. The difficulty for him had been that he could make no defence without causing an alarm which would have done great harm to the school. Among the troubles had been the health of the boys, and Wootton believed with justice that one of the most important things he had done had been to produce so great an improvement. "When I first came here", he wrote, "there were lots of things wrong. Feeding, ventilation, drainage, water, sick room accommodation. Fortunately we got all these things at least reasonably right."

The need to handle personally so many aspects of the school's affairs, ranging from staff and discipline to buildings and finance and domestic administration weighed heavily upon him. He had been especially troubled by the need to evolve a proper system of delegation, the lack of which had placed so great a strain on his predecessor, and by the lack of a bursar in whom he could place confidence. His first two appointments created more difficulties than they solved, and it was not until E. P. Aust returned as bursar in 1923 that he found much-needed help. Aust did not for one moment regret the passing of much in the pre-war Kingswood that he had known. His quiet competence and discretion became and long remained a source of strength to the school. The organization settled down.

Wootton could now take stock and plan ahead. But whence was to come the wherewithal for the essential physical developments, the new laboratories and classrooms? It would be a long time before the decisions taken that summer could possibly produce the margins needed to finance capital expenditure. A sum of £10,000 seemed to Wootton the absolute minimum.*

---

* This figure and those in subsequent paragraphs must, of course, be multiplied some four or five times to represent the values of the 1960's.

All through that year Wootton pondered ways and means. It so happened that the Rev. Ferrier Hulme was President-elect of the Methodist Conference. Hulme had been, as we have seen, the last of the old-style resident Governors at Kingswood twenty years earlier, and knew it well. On holiday at Freshwater in the Isle of Wight, Wootton took out his carbon-copy letter-book and wrote in his bold hand to Ferrier Hulme. Had Kingswood perhaps made a mistake in not letting its needs be known? Its real need was a substantial block to include science laboratories and class rooms, and considerable alterations in the existing buildings. It was the oldest Methodist school, and (and he thought he was in a good position to judge) the best. He had had a long experience of teaching in one of the oldest of the English public schools (Westminster, of course) and knowing others well was decidedly impressed with the possibilities of Kingswood. The school could go ahead if it did *not* get new buildings, but it was not possible without them to do as well as it might. "You are so devoted to Kingswood", he concluded, "that I am sure you will do anything you can to help." Ferrier Hulme passed the letter on to his old friend and prominent Methodist, the Rt. Hon. T. R. Ferens, for long the driving force of Reckitts of Hull. A reply came asking what the additions would cost, and Wootton had his opportunity to set out, as he well knew how, the needs of the school.* His guess was that the cost would amount to £15,000. Ferens then wrote that he was aware of the good work done by the school; two of his directors at Reckitts, W. H. Slack and Arnold Cleminson, were old boys; would Wootton get plans and tenders, and if the cost did not exceed £15,000, it would be a pleasure to him (Ferens) to meet it. A special meeting of the Governors was at once called. "I am living in a state of wild excitement", wrote Watkins to Wootton. "Hartley and I can hardly believe it is true." Wootton did indeed deserve much of the credit. "I cannot tell you", wrote Ferrier Hulme to him, "how thankful I am to you for writing to me on your holiday as you did. It was such a clear statement I was able to send it straight on as it was. . . . I highly congratulate you."

Wootton promptly paid a number of visits to other schools to see their laboratories, and to enquire about architects. The advice he received pointed to W. A. Forsyth. "Forsyth was very

---

* "This I drew up with some care and had neatly typed."

strongly recommended to me at Harrow and elsewhere as being the only man who knew anything about the building of laboratories." By the end of the year Forsyth was submitting a report of great value to the school. It praised the site—few public schools had a site equal to it—the garden setting was attractive and beautiful, the paved play yards were exceptionally large, so that the school was splendidly equipped with open spaces. The original buildings of 1850 were excellently planned, they stood as examples of well-thought-out buildings capable of simple adaptation to modern needs. Subsequent changes, however, had meant that unhealthy congestion had displaced the free and open arrangement. It was remarkable that a school with such magnificent general rooms should have a set of overcrowded classrooms, all of which were inadequately lighted and ventilated. New classrooms would be of immense value to the school. It would be possible to provide six in the new building, it would be much better to provide twelve; a complete scheme would provide single desk seats for 324 boys. The total cost of such a scheme would be £28,200. A large new building would be necessary.

The architect's report was put to Ferens. He was impressed by it. "It is a pity not to complete the whole scheme", he told Watkins, "the thing needs to be done properly." He wrote offering to defray the cost up to £30,000. The Governors recorded their appreciation, and Forsyth was free to plan a model block of laboratories and classrooms. Space was fortunately available on the small football field immediately to the west of the main buildings, commanding the full sweep of the view.*

Meanwhile Wootton had been engaged in the promotion of a scheme for a memorial to Fletcher Moulton—Lord Moulton as he became—to be linked with the school in which he had laid the foundation of his career. Moulton, as we have seen, had been the most brilliant pupil of mid-Victorian Kingswood. Coming to it when eleven years old, he had been head boy at thirteen and a half, later Senior Wrangler at Cambridge, a barrister of legendary learning, a Fellow of the Royal Society, and in 1912 had been made a Lord of Appeal. When war came in 1914 he had been called upon by Lord Haldane to fill a key role in the co-ordina-

* The Upper Field was at this time greatly extended by the purchase of additional land—in all, from ten to just on forty acres.

tion of the supply of explosives. His foresight in crises had amounted to genius and made him a national figure, one of whom it might be said that it was doubtful if the war could have been won but for his part in it.* Wootton was able to obtain agreement that the memorial fund should be devoted to the reconstruction of the old Schoolroom at Kingswood as an Assembly Hall worthy of the school. He applied himself with vigour to this scheme, waiting personally upon many men eminent in public life who had been Moulton's friends, and was able to ensure that the Moulton Hall could be opened together with the new laboratory and classroom block then building.

The Ferens buildings and the Moulton Hall were opened by the Prince of Wales on November 10, 1926. The Prince took lunch in the dining hall with the school, and a great many old boys and other guests were accommodated in a large marquee. Both Watkins and Wootton possessed great sense of occasion, and the Prince's visit was conducted with a military efficiency. It was felt to be a landmark in the history of the school.

As if he had not already enough on his hands, the Headmaster had been stressing also the need to make greatly extended provision for leaving scholarships for boys going to the universities to supplement the few that already existed. The parents of Kingswood boys were rarely in a position to find the balances needed to make up scholarships and other awards, and grants from public funds were then few and far between.† Wootton succeeded in enlisting the interest of two old boys of the school, W. A. Posnett and his brother R. H. Posnett of Runcorn, who together provided an endowment of £6,000 for scholarships. The two brothers had already made themselves responsible for the stained glass window in the Moulton Hall; R. H. Posnett had presented the excellent portrait of Mr. Ferens which hangs in the school dining hall.

* The Lord Chancellor, on Moulton's death. He said he had chosen his words carefully.

† The need for such help continued pressing throughout the following decades (until the system was changed by governmental action in the fifties) and very many old boys responded generously to a series of appeals for the purpose.

The transfer of practically all the teaching to the new block was, however, but a first step. The old classrooms could now be converted into day rooms for the various houses, a most important change for the better, but much else needed to be done. It seemed to Wootton to be merely the beginning of a series of changes in the development of the school.

"I firmly believe", he wrote to Watkins, "that this is an opportunity in the history of the school the like of which has probably never been seen before and will probably not be seen again. My opinion is very confident that if we use the present opportunity wisely we can easily put the school in a very firm position. It has advantages of site which few schools enjoy; it has now the best playing fields in the country, and will have a block of classrooms of which we can be justly proud. It has a most beautiful chapel, and if we can only get the money we can make the old block thoroughly good. It seems to me there is a chance here for good work. . . ."

The Governors at once set themselves to raise a further fund of £10,000. Ferens promised half upon conditions, and Wootton opened a campaign to raise the remainder. Success was not immediate, but later (in 1929) the two Posnetts continued their series of gifts to the school, and Wootton was thus responsible for handing on to his successor an invaluable fund of £10,000, wherewith large-scale improvements were made to the amenities of the school. Changing-rooms were doubled, and the old dormitory block extended to allow the installation of bathrooms in every house.

Two years after the opening of the Fernes building Wootton exchanged the headmastership of Kingswood for that of the Perse School at Cambridge. To many at Kingswood it seemed a surprising step, and his action gave rise to much speculation. The future of the school had never, since Osborn's brief years of glory, looked more promising. Wootton had, however, on more than one occasion disclosed to Watkins his anxiety that if he did not move on whilst still in his mid-forties he would have left it too late. He thought it a bad thing for a school and for the Headmaster concerned that a man should be appointed in his mid-thirties, as he had been, with the grave risk that he would stay on in the same place until he was sixty. His action in leaving was

perhaps precipitate, and may have been prompted in part
by personal considerations that history does not record. The
flatness of Cambridge, he told a correspondent, would give his
wife opportunities of moving about which had been denied her
in Bath by the steepness of the hills. He afterwards continued
to follow the progress of the school with deep interest, and
attended an old boys' dinner in London not many weeks before
he died early in 1949.

How did Wootton's headmastership affect Kingswood? Was
it really, as Watkins averred in a eulogy of Wootton written
after his death, a case of laying bare a state of affairs by which
the Governors were "appalled"? It was perhaps hardly that.
Both Wootton and Watkins were endowed with a strong sense
of the dramatic; Wootton loved to point the contrast between
before and after, and Watkins to improve upon it. But if here
and there a word has to be changed or a phrase toned down
to give the older school its due, the record of positive achievement
we have traced in these pages speaks for itself. The school of
1928 was indeed a different school from that of 1919 and its
future was bright with promise. Kingswood had needed a
Headmaster with the vision to see what was needed and the
determination to break with much that was rooted in the past.
Wootton possessed these qualities, and he will find an assured
place in the longer perspectives of the history of the school.

XIII

A. B. SACKETT AND EXILE AT UPPINGHAM
1928–47

T
HE NEW HEADMASTER was Alfred Barrett Sackett. The son
of a Methodist chaplain and himself a former captain of
Rugby football at Kingswood, his career at Oxford had
been interrupted by the war. Young as he was, he had found
himself in charge of what was left of half a battalion of
Lancashire Fusiliers on Gallipoli in 1915, and in France was
wounded at Ypres and, narrowly escaping capture, severely
wounded in March 1918. He had returned to Merton and had
accepted the offer of an appointment on the staff of Christ's
Hospital. Attuned by his experiences to the freer and more
democratic mood of the post-war world, Sackett was well fitted
to take charge at Kingswood as Wootton left it.

The end of Mr. Wootton's headmastership, and the opening
of Mr. Sackett's marks, however, the point at which any attempt
at a full narrative and at any sort of historical assessment ought
to cease. We are already into the period concerning living
persons, and it is a wise convention which limits discussion which,
whether by inclusion or inadvertent omission, might trespass
against the feelings of masters or others still with us. Nevertheless
much has happened in the last forty years, and the school is
widely recognized to have moved so far forward into its inheri-
tance that some account of the period is essential here. Moreover
the war carried Kingswood into a seven years exile in Rutland
as the guests of Uppingham School, and the experience of intimate contact with a school whose outlook and traditions were
quite different from those of Kingswood afforded an exceptional
opportunity for stocktaking and assessment. A backward glance
should therefore embrace both the physical extensions and other
alterations effected during the period, and an endeavour to catch
something of the significance of the exile at Uppingham.

It had been Sackett's good fortune whilst at Merton to

have fallen in with a man of quite unusual qualities, William Hamilton Fyfe,* and after the latter's appointment to the head-mastership of Christ's Hospital to have joined him there. To Fyfe the formal element in education was of little value. What mattered was the creation of an atmosphere wherein a boy's spirit might take wings and induce him to do something for himself, and it was the business of the headmaster and his staff to create such an atmosphere. If the fustian aloofness of tradition stood in the way, then it must be shattered. Fyfe knew, too, what the younger generation of officers had learnt in the war, that to lead one must first understand the led. In Sackett, Fyfe found a more than willing pupil; and for Sackett no moment was more fortunate than that when Fyfe appointed him to Christ's Hospital.

At Christ's Hospital on Fyfe's arrival it had seemed that quite suddenly the windows had been thrown wide open. Later on, a year or two after his appointment to Kingswood, it would be to Fyfe that Sackett would owe his inclusion among a body of distinguished headmasters visiting universities in Canada on behalf of the Headmasters' Conference, an experience of the utmost value to a young headmaster. Nothing could better have prepared him for the state of affairs that he would encounter at Kingswood. Great as had been the changes wrought by Wootton, the need to pull back the curtains and let in the sunshine was apparent.

"Kingswood", wrote Sackett soon after he had taken over, "has been made so good a school by my predecessor that it has now a chance to become a very good school indeed." In the light of the foregoing it is not difficult to see what he meant. The relaxation of restrictions and the creation of an altogether more friendly atmosphere was overdue. Some changes could be made forthwith. Preparation was decentralized, rules of silence were cancelled, and a prolific source of petty punishment was removed at a single stroke—the largest single source of the feeling that masters were policemen. Discipline became easier, the cane all but disappeared. Other changes could not be made so easily. There were still only five resident masters in the Kings-wood of the day, and their quarters left much to be desired. It became a primary objective of the new Headmaster to secure

---

* Later Sir William Hamilton Fyfe.

more accommodation for resident masters. Part of Wootton's invaluable fund of £10,000 was diverted to provide masters' rooms by releasing space right in the centre of the old building, and the number of men connected with the houses was doubled. It was essential too, Sackett told the Governors, that masters who were non-resident should take a full share in the life of the houses and of the community as a whole. At Christ's Hospital Sackett had worked closely with A. C. W. Edwards, a schoolmaster outstandingly successful in establishing exactly the right relationship between masters and boys, a balance between the encouraging atmosphere of a liberal regime, and firmness of discipline and control when need arose for it. *A Scheme for the enlargement of Housemastership at Kingswood* was submitted to the Governors. "There shall be two housemasters in each House", it read. The burden upon the single housemaster was to be lightened, but much more was to be expected from the new system. "This ought to be a development", continued the draft, "of the very greatest importance, more important than any single development that has yet taken place." The forecast was to be amply borne out. Life at the school became more civilized. Boys were made welcome in the Headmaster's house, and in those of married masters. Leather chairs, pictures and curtains appeared in dayrooms. In no detail was the new spirit more plainly to be seen than in the arrangements for the reception of new boys. As late as the mid-twenties no special care was taken of them. A new boy, tough or timid, was received very much as in *Tom Brown's Schooldays,* and more or less literally kicked round the passages to the accompaniment of mirth at any idiosyncrasy he might display. All this was changed, and new boys found instead friendly housemasters and matrons welcoming them and preparing them to play their part in the life of the school.

Westwood was acquired in 1933. Until then the small boys of from ten to twelve were still in the hurly-burly of the main school, a thing which would later seem intolerable. But in 1932–33 R. H. and W. A. Posnett carried further their already great and fruitful generosity by the gift of the major part of the cost of Westwood. The addition of this property was a great advance. The whole hill-slope now belonged to the school, with the greater part of the woods: there was more than a commensurate feeling of width, freedom, secure ownership and privacy. Fonthill Road, though still a right of way, became a private road along its whole length. The small boys gained what must have seemed to them a paradise; and under Hugh Clutton-Brock (enticed from Christ's Hospital) Westwood, with a floor added, became a preparatory school of distinction. All his genius for improvisation was needed: in 1935 a wing was added, which provided an assembly room, another classroom, and two large dormitories. The new regime was an immediate and lasting success. Lizards and snakes appeared in the vivarium, built by Clutton-Brock and his boys; huts in the woods, ornithology, and an owl tamed to come into the house at night—such skilled care and ingenious interest was taken in small boys as was never dreamed of in the wildest moments of 1930.

School work prospered and gradually the new leaven began to work. The boy material, the Headmaster told the Governors, deserved as distinguished a staff as could possibly be obtained: and many of the men appointed by Sackett in these years have given the school service of a high order. But what mattered above all was, as Fyfe had insisted, that boys should be encouraged to develop in their own way, which was the only way in which they could develop healthily.* In the creation of this atmosphere the multiplication of school societies and kindred activities played a prominent part. Discussion of all things in heaven and earth was actively promoted, stimulated and guided by the Headmaster, and materially forwarded in the mid-thirties by the appointment of a school chaplain well fitted to face urgent problems of current thought in discussion with representative sixthformers† With the help of preachers from the Methodist and other communions the chapel services came more and more effectively to focus the life and thought of the school.

---

* The phrase is borrowed from an address by Sir William Hamilton Fyfe. "I well know", added Fyfe, "that if I succeed in that endeavour they will probably build a bonfire and on it place all my favourite ideas and pet ideals, and when they have got it burning merrily they will probably dump me and my colleagues on top. If ever they do that, I shall sizzle with satisfaction on that funeral pyre; I shall feel a sort of pungent pleasure in the smoke, because I realize with my parting breath that I have played my part successfully and made some contribution to the great work of education." The words aptly sum up much of Mr. Sackett's own philosophy of education.

† The Rev. Rupert E. Davies, later Honorary Secretary to the Governors (1949–67) and Principal of Wesley College, Bristol.

The need for a proper library to replace the old reading room and reference library over the gymnasium had been apparent to Sackett from the moment of his appointment. A library, he had told the Governors, was as important a centre of a school as a chapel, and he left no one in any doubt that it would be a great day for Kingswood when this defect were remedied. This need, too, W. A. Posnett undertook to meet, and a beautiful building designed by W. A. Forsyth was in due course erected immediately to the west of the main buildings where glimpses of the distant landscape could filter through the windows. Books were overhauled in numbers and quality, and the library became a centre where boys were encouraged to go and work on their own without supervision. It was never locked. It was a place, too, where little boys could go and browse on their own and see what was on the shelves. The library also incorporated, on the ground floor, a meeting place specially designed to meet the needs of the literary and scientific societies, and outside a paved level area which has added great distinction to this corner of the school. Deck chairs were provided for the library lawn. At about this time, too, many individual desks made their appearance in the common rooms. The change in the life of the school resulting from the provision of the library, so much more central than the former arrangements, and the greater degree of privacy afforded to senior boys in the common rooms, was indeed profound and deserves to be recorded in any history of the school. Not only were books made more accessible, but pictures took on a new importance. The coming of the water-colourist Thomas Hennell to teach for a while, brief though it was, had left its mark upon the school.

In music, too, a great change came over the scene. The standard was lifted to a level unknown in the older school by the bringing in from outside of first-class musicians of whom the first and greatest was Myra Hess. A school orchestra took shape, and later developed to the point at which it could tackle a full symphony. This was a thing to be found at the time in relatively few schools, and the concerts given by the school orchestra became a feature of Speech Days in the thirties. Speech Days themselves became a means of throwing bridges between life within the school gates and the wider world outside. Once it was the Earl of Athlone who came, a little later it was T. S. Eliot. All this was something new in life at the school. A heroic attempt was made, too, to throw a bridge across the widening gulf between Britain and a Germany with whom all hope of understanding was fast fading. Exchanges were arranged with opposite numbers at Ilfeld, and Ribbentrop's son and Goering's nephews were among those who visited Kingswood after Ilfield had been taken over by Hitler and turned into a national political school. If the episode would soon look pathetic, it was nevertheless all part of a concerted and continuous effort to keep the school in touch with reality outside its precincts.

The more liberal regime was accompanied by a steady growth in the size of the school. Whilst the number of boys drawn from the homes of the Methodist ministers* remained roughly constant around the 200 mark, the number of fee-paying boarders increased steadily, and by 1939 the total number of boys in the school, including the younger boys in Westwood, reached 340. The proportion of time spent in the Sixth Form increased too, and the Sixth Form grew until it counted what then seemed the considerable total of some seventy boys. The changes were rewarded by an all-round advance in standards, both academic and athletic. The thirties saw a series of new high-water marks in the numbers of awards won at Oxford and Cambridge. Eight or nine in a year became frequent, and once shortly before the war the total reached twelve in one year. This, it may perhaps be said without undue self-satisfaction, was for a relatively small school, as Kingswood then was, a notable achievement. The school's games prospered; whilst Rugby football remained the school game *par excellence,* hockey was introduced and played with enthusiasm in the Spring term, and athletics provided a new and satisfying outlet for those whose eyesight hampered them in other directions. A high standard was reached, and this brought in its train Blues at the universities. "It is difficult just now", said the Headmaster in a report to the Governors, "to keep up with the enthusiasm of the boys, or to provide anything like sufficient manpower to guide and direct their interest and spirit." If, characteristially, Sackett gave the

---

* No longer Wesleyan Methodist ministers only, for with the changes brought about by the reunion with the other Methodist Churches in 1932, eligibility for places on the foundation ceased to be restricted to Wesleyans.

credit to others, the Governors were under no illusion as to the part which he had himself played. The transformation which had been wrought in the life of the school since his appointment in 1928 was apparent for all to see. "Few men", said the report of H.M. Inspectors in 1939, "could have done more for the school in twelve years than Mr. Sackett has done in every department of its life and work." The report apologized for using so many superlatives.

It was a school such as this, more self-confident than Kingswood had been for many a year, that was called upon to face the upheaval of the war in 1939. The Headmaster had warning that the Admiralty intended to move a large part of its establishment to Bath, and that besides the large hotels the buildings of Kingswood and of the Royal School for Officers' Daughters would be required. The warning reached the Headmaster in his Christmas post, but the obligation to observe the strictest secrecy greatly hampered the limited preparations that could be made. Chatsworth and other great houses, and hotels at Llandrindod Wells, were considered and rejected in favour of the acceptance of an offer from Uppingham School, made through the Headmasters' Conference, to find room for a school of about the size that the senior school at Kingswood then was. Sackett lost no time in getting into touch with the then Headmaster of Uppingham, Mr J. F. Wolfenden,* and making such arrangements as the veil of secrecy permitted. For those who participated the details of the move to Uppingham assumed epic proportions, and many an incident that cannot be recorded here will long be remembered. For others, to whom the exile was but an event reported second-hand, the interest was of a different kind—how would Kingswood fare when thus uprooted from its own countryside and thrown into intimate contact with a public school of very different traditions and outlook?

Uppingham lies in the Midlands, in the tiny agricultural county of Rutland, with its red fields, its woods and its foxhunting. The little town consists principally of a single street stretching along the edge of a long low hill. It is built of Jurassic

---

* Later Chairman of the Headmasters' Conference, and now Sir John Wolfenden.

limestone; out of term time strangely quiet, not perhaps altogether unlike the Chipping Sodbury with which Kingswood boys are familiar. In the centre of the High Street is the market place, with the Falcon, the chief of many inns; close by is the tall spire of the Parish Church, and the gatehouse of Uppingham School. In the front courtyard is the great Assembly Hall, big enough to hold the boys of both Uppingham and Kingswood and many visitors; the museum, the library and many classrooms. Here too is the Headmaster's house, and the bursary. The Uppingham boys are, of course, scattered among the school houses, some fifty boys to a house; some of the houses are to be found in the High Street, or hidden in the unseen roads that run parallel with it, and others are down the steep hill to the south. Games fields encircle the town and the cricket field with its distant views has a quiet and delicate beauty. In the school Chapel, much like a second Parish Church, is the statue of Edward Thring, the great Headmaster who developed Uppingham out of an Elizabethan grammar school into a famous English public school of the nineteenth century. Uppingham had all the merits of the best public schools of the period; its close discipline; the deeply cherished ideal of the housemaster and his family of boys; music and games of a high order; and above and beyond all this, a tradition of adaptability and generous and friendly acceptance of the stranger. This it derived from its own, now long past, but dramatic and well remembered, exile to Borth in Wales, whither Thring carried it to avoid destruction by grievous epidemic. As Borth had harboured Uppingham, so Uppingham would harbour Kingswood.

When, in the September of 1939, the train collected the boys at Seaton Junction in the Welland valley and chugged noisily up the steep one-track line to Uppingham, much improvisation was needed. Kingswood had had to bring with it from Bath all its equipment, tables and chairs, beds and mattresses, and all the paraphernalia of a sizeable school. It had needed a goods train of twenty-seven wagons, unloaded but a day or two before the arrival of the boys. A cherished principle at Uppingham, that every boy should have a study to himself, was readily sacrificed in the emergency; boys were doubled up, two to a study, and room thus made for many of the boys from Kingswood in the Uppingham houses until as time went on they could be packed into all kinds of makeshift accommodation. Others—there were two hundred and seventy altogether—went elsewhere; the Falcon, the White Hart, the Central, and many lodgings were pressed into service. One whole school house was taken over, and the semi-derelict Old Constables. The Uppingham gymnasium became the Kingswood dining hall, and facilities of all kinds—Chapel, Assembly Hall, playing fields, fives court, library—were shared between the two schools.

At Uppingham the arrival of Kingswood had been a surprise. It had been confidently predicted that the unknown school about to descend on the town would prove to be Westminster. But the surprise over, the two schools at once settled down happily together, and the unbounded generosity and goodwill shown by Uppingham left no room for the slightest misgivings as to the success of the experiment. And so it continued. A year later Sackett was able to report that relations were unclouded, and indeed the life of both schools was enriched by the sharing of many activities. For Kingswood what mattered most was that all had been kept together, that the community life continued intact. All the Kingswood staff, masters, matrons, men and maids, had elected to move with the school. School work regained its traditional momentum, and on the rugger field the school enjoyed fixtures with famous Midland schools. Its generous acceptance by Uppingham meant for Kingswood salvation from disruption in some ill-adapted mansion or group of inaccessible hotels. For this Kingswood can never be too grateful. Relations between the two Headmasters in what might have been, and indeed was, a tricky situation left nothing to be desired, and when in 1944 Mr. Wolfenden moved on to Shrewsbury he wrote a letter which deserves to find a place in any record of the exile. "Five years ago", he wrote to a Kingswood parent, "you and we entered upon an adventure; and I believe we can say with honesty and truth that of all the experiments in joint living which the war has brought upon schools this one has been the most successful and the most fruitful. . . . We have learnt much during the past five years; and I believe that all our lives are the richer from the experience of having Kingswood here. . . . Uppingham is well content if it has been able to help in some measure towards the unbroken existence of a great School."

Acceptance of the Uppingham offer had meant, of course,

that other arrangements would have to be made for the seventy or so younger boys at Westwood. It was at first hoped to move them into a large house at Oakham, and to work in with Oakham School, much on the lines of Kingswood with Uppingham. This, however, fell through, and the boys from Westwood went instead to Prior's Court in Berkshire, then belonging to Mr. Gerald Palmer, M.P. for Winchester, and placed by him at the disposal of the Government. Built of mellow red brick and dating in part from the eighteenth century, Prior's Court stands in its own spacious grounds of some thirty acres, and lies in the heart of the country—five miles from Newbury, seventeen from Reading, and twenty-four from Oxford. It was thus far from all military objectives and well suited to receive the younger boys. It adapted well for school purposes; the large billiard room, panelled in natural oak, was converted into a dining room and assembly hall, the stables and outbuildings served a variety of purposes. Within thirty-six hours of the requisitioning of the school the first van loads began to make their way to Prior's Court. There the boys from Westwood soon settled down under Clutton-Brock's care and later, when he moved on to take charge of Colet Court for St. Paul's School, of W. B. Maltby.

Meanwhile, at Bath the Admiralty staff moved into the all but empty school buildings. It had at first been supposed that the Admiralty occupation of the buildings would be but temporary, until hutted accommodation became available elsewhere; and indeed there came a moment late in 1940 when return to Bath was seriously discussed, only to fade again as the Admiralty refused permission. "Arrangements could probably be made", read a minute of the period, "to sleep in the concrete shelters which have been built on the Ferens lawn to seat 400 people." When in 1942 Bath was heavily bombed the school at Uppingham heard with relief that the then empty buildings at Kingswood had escaped with broken windows. A very heavy bomb which fell just below the brow of Van Diemen's Lane failed to explode. Before long the Admiralty re-occupied the premises, a hundred W.R.N.S.'s were installed in Westwood, and much of the detailed planning of the invasion of the Normandy beaches and of the construction of the Mulberry harbours was done in the Kingswood buildings. The invasion succeeded, tension relaxed, the end of the war came at last; and the

SUMMERHILL
The Georgian frontage was rescued from demolition at Chippenham
by Mr Ernest Cook and re-erected at Bath

PRIORS COURT, NEWBURY
Preparatory School for Kingswood

Familiar scenes: to and from the Ferens Buildings

*Photograph by
J. T. Baxter*

Uppingham authorities began, most naturally, to press for the release of their premises. Not, however, until May 1946, after nearly seven long years of exile, was it possible for Kingswood to return to its own buildings.

Departure from Uppingham was something of an occasion. Kingswood took leave of Uppingham at a joint Assembly addressed by both Headmasters.* Sackett made what an Uppingham housemaster called "the speech of his life", for much as he disliked publicity, he generally excelled on important occasions. He knew he had brought the school successfully through long and anxious years, and was taking home to Bath exactly the same number of boys as he had led to Uppingham, 278. And in his speech he matched his gratitude to one school with his pride in the other in memorable words: "Our strength is the measure of your generosity." A stone from Uppingham was taken to Kingswood and set in the Library wall, to be a permanent reminder of all that Kingswood owed to Uppingham.

The war over, the provision of a worthy memorial to those who had fallen became a matter of concern both to the school and to the Old Boys. The School Chapel stood as the memorial of those who had fallen in 1914-18; but the main entrance immediately above it had remained unaltered since it was built in 1851. The provision of a more spacious entrance in keeping with the Chapel seemed appropriate and funds were provided by the Old Boys. The design eventually chosen was widely recognized as most successful. The Memorial Gates were dedicated in September 1953 by the Rev. Owen Spencer Watkins, and a memorial tablet was unveiled by Air Vice-Marshal Sir Kenneth Cross.

A most gracious and substantial gift by Mr. and Mrs. L. W. Turner in memory of their son enabled the school to tackle the levelling of the slopes needed to provide a new Lower Field, with all the many advantages that have accrued therefrom.

---

* Mr. Martin Lloyd had succeeded Mr. Wolfenden in 1944.

P

XIV

THE RECENT PAST:
A. B. SACKETT AND A. L. CREED

BEGINNING again in Bath was difficult, arduous and expensive. Barbed wire six or eight feet high had to be dismantled, and bindweed ramped unchecked over the orchard trees. But trying as was the dilapidation, the frustration and the delay, at least the school had returned intact, its continuity of life, activities, discipline and scholarship maintained.

It had been part of the bargain with the Admiralty that the school should neither gain nor lose financially by its exile to Uppingham. During the war Kingswood had been spared increased expense. It had not however been possible to create reserves, and the sudden rise in cost after the war came as a heavy blow. It was apparent that the traditional provision for some two hundred sons of Methodist ministers could only be continued if the total number of boys were materially increased, and fees for the sons of laymen fixed at a figure that enabled the school to balance its budget. At no stage was there any lack of applicants for places. The purchase of Prior's Court in 1946 for use as a separate preparatory school permitted an increase in the number of laymen's sons who could be admitted, and their numbers grew until eventually they exceeded the number of boys on the foundation. The change implied a new era, and a greater independence in the management of the school's affairs. The Rev. Leonard J. W. Babb, another distinguished Army chaplain, had already succeeded Watkins as Chairman of the Governors; and Sir Arthur L. Dixon for many years Principal Assistant Under-Secretary of State at the Home Office was appointed to the office of Treasurer. The school was indeed fortunate that at this critical phase in its affairs it was able to enlist such great abilities in its service.

The school thus entered upon what may be regarded as the third phase of Sackett's headmastership.

An appeal in connection with the bicentenary of its school's foundation was launched in 1948, and with the generous help of the Joseph Rank Benevolent Trust important extensions were made to the Ferens buildings that played a vital part in the post-war expansion of Kingswood.* The Old Boys established, too, their own Bicentenary Fund, and through it they were able to afford substantial help to the school, especially in connection with the school games. Later on they would in this way provide a much-needed new pavilion on the Upper Field.†

The life of the school has in the post-war years fanned out in so many directions that to attempt to chronicle them all would result in a mere catalogue: of new high-water marks in scholarship matching those of the thirties and forties; of an extended games fixture list, made possible in part by the growth in numbers of the school; of acquisitions of property; of advance in many spheres of activity. Many, very many, who deserve to be remembered for their services and gifts find no mention here.

Space must, however, be found for one event of outstanding importance, the acquisition of a magnificent house and some 140 acres of park and farm land quite exceptionally well placed to safeguard the amenities of the school from potential development. How this came about, almost by accident, and at but a modest cost to the school, must now be recounted.

The late Mr. Ernest Cook, grandson of the founder of the travel agents Thomas Cook and Son, came to reside in Bath about 1930. It so happened that the park-like area that he bought lay immediately below and to the south-west of the Kingswood property, and he lived in the most westerly house in the Regency terrace known as Sion Hill Place. But wealthy as he was, Mr. Cook valued his privacy very highly, and until shortly before his death all that Kingswood knew was that Summerhill Park, as the property was known, was strictly private. Screened from the school by a belt of mature beeches, it was obviously an important and valuable property, and it did not appear in the least likely that the school would ever be able to aspire to its ownership. Even when Mr. Cook bought a magnificent Georgian façade about to be demolished in Chippenham and at great expense

---

* The Ferens buildings were further extended in 1957 with the help of the Industrial Fund for the Advancement of Science in Schools. Space for the teaching of science was thus doubled, and later a geological laboratory was included, a gift by Mr. A. L. Trump and Sir Arthur Dixon.

† The total contributed through this fund amounted by 1967 to some £50,000. The patient work of its successive officers, F. W. Greenwood, E. P. Aust, A. J. Hill and F. S. Cook, deserves to be recorded in a history of the school.

added it to his terraced house, turning the latter into a distinguished mansion and filling it with old masters, Kingswood knew nothing of what was afoot. The greater, therefore, was the Headmaster's surprise to learn that Mr. Cook was taking a close interest in the Memorial Gates being erected at Kingswood. These he so much admired that he had them specially photographed, and sent a hundred mounted copies to the Headmaster for distribution among relatives of the fallen. Other contacts followed; Mr. and Mrs. Sackett and Mr. P. G. Summers, the Bursar, were invited to see the treasures of Mr. Cook's sanctum. Then in 1954 Mr. Cook died. His pictures were left to the nation and distributed through many art galleries. No mention of Kingswood was made in his will, but it was known to his executors that he would be content that the Summerhill estate should pass into the possession of the school.

The opportunity was clearly not to be missed. Not only did Mr. Cook's estate stand in a strategically important position in relation to the school, but it included, besides the house, some half-dozen houses and cottages of great potential value to Kingswood for accommodating masters and other members of the staff. The Old Boys were consulted, and at once undertook through their Bicentenary Fund to provide £10,000, a third of the sum required; and the rest of the money needed was found partly by the sale of other property and partly by loan from the schools scholarship fund.* On an autumn morning in 1955 Mr. Sackett was able to announce the purchase to the school. Two school periods were cancelled, and the property was thrown open for all to see. A full account appeared in the *Magazine* for February 1956.

Kingswood thus became possessed not only of a landscape of surpassing beauty but of buildings which in one way and another have greatly eased the problem of providing residential accommodation. The mansion itself, known in Mr. Cook's day as No. 1. Sion Hill, has been rechristened Summerhill, as the park has long been known.† The "Chippenham" galleries are in frequent use for meetings of school societies and other functions,

---

* The property bought included a strip already scheduled by the City planning authority for development along Summerhill Road. This has since been sold on advantageous terms, and a group of pleasant houses erected to designs approved by the school.

† The original Summerhill was a large house, now demolished, some traces of which remain as a levelled area to the west of the present mansion.

and the rest of the house provides two flats for married masters and bedrooms for some twenty boys. At this same period opportunities occurred to acquire also two other houses, Beaconfield and Lewsdon, which complete the link between the school and the Summerhill estate. There were now in all upwards of five hundred boys in the school, of whom nearly two-fifths were sons of Methodist ministers.

The acquisition of Summerhill and the wider horizon that it brought with it afforded a most happy climax to Mr. Sackett's long headmastership of Kingswood. When he retired in 1959 he with Mrs. Sackett had become so deeply identified with the life of the school that many found it hard to envisage a future without his hand on the helm. Kingswood, there was no doubt, had found one who, like Osborn in the eighties of the last century, possessed the capacity to impart his own lively personality to the school. His farewell speech and moving tributes from the Governors, the Common Room, and the old boys were printed in a special number of the *Magazine* for July 1959.

By the time Mr. Sackett retired Prior's Court had become such an accepted part of Kingswood that the wisdom of its acquisition after the war had become apparent to all. Always full to capacity, and including its due proportion of minister's sons, Prior's Court under the care of Maltby and his colleagues had become a stable and happy community. The small boys were encouraged individually and incited to learn skills of many kinds; every boy was taught music; and new amenities—an open air swimming pool, for example—were added to its already great attractions. The school was enlarged and a new assembly hall and gymnasium built. Well taught and uninhibited, the boys from Prior's Court passed into the main school without further examination, and were often natural leaders when their turn came later on. When Maltby retired in 1965 his trusted colleague W. B. Mountford returned to take charge. Maltby's sudden illness and death in 1967, followed by that of his devoted wife and partner, was a severe shock to many friends of Prior's Court.

Mr. Sackett was succeeded by Mr. A. Lowry Creed, the present Headmaster, whose experience also included housemastering at Christ's Hospital and fifteen years as Headmaster of Truro School. Amid rising costs and uncertainties of all kinds the school has continued to hold its own; but the convention which limits treatment of the recent past applies with especial force to the time of a reigning Headmaster, and an adequate account of Mr. Creed's headmastership must await a future history. Sir Arthur Dixon, whose modernising regime as Treasurer, and later as first lay Chairman of the Governors, had been of formative and lasting value to the school, retired in 1966 and was followed by the Rev. A. Kingsley Lloyd as Chairman and by Mr. R. H. Bryant as Treasurer.

It was very largely due to Mr. Creed's energy and initiative that a major appeal was launched by the school in 1967 with the twin objects of providing a new Sixth Form block, and underpinning the finances by providing additional resources for support of the sons of Methodist ministers at the school. By 1969 the response to the appeal exceeded £220,000, and this made it possible to proceed. As in other schools the great increase in the proportion of boys in the Sixth Form has called more and more insistently for quiet study space on a scale unforeseen a generation ago, when the beautiful library seemed to provide all that any school could desire. In recent years the lack of sufficient space there and in the day rooms has been the greatest difficulty encountered by boys in the senior school. No difficulty arises in siting a new building close to the library and in line with the main frontage of the school in such a way that it commands the magnificent view to the south and west, and yet nestles gently into the hillside without obstructing the view from the older buildings behind and above. The work was entrusted to a Bath architect, Mr. H. Goldsmith, and was begun in the summer of 1969.

The response to the appeal included most welcome support for the school in its historic role of provision for the sons of Methodist ministers. Lord Rank made known to the Chairman, the Rev. Kingsley Lloyd, his deep interest in its welfare and his willingness to help. A gift of £75,000 from himself and his family followed. Inevitably somewhat fewer than formerly, the sons of Methodist ministers still constitute about a third of the school, and the strain placed by rising costs upon the funds out of which they are supported has more than once threatened to dictate a reduction in the numbers. Lord Rank's gift will play a decisive part in enabling the school to take a larger share in providing the necessary finances, and the school is indeed fortunate to be able to find such a generous friend.

The reader may perhaps have detected in what has been written a belief that despite its sometimes chequered story the school has a unique contribution to offer. In what does this consist, he may ask, and how far can it be said to derive from the circumstance of its foundation by John Wesley? In founding Kingswood, Wesley certainly did not at first envisage a school confined to the sons of his preachers, though later he sometimes spoke of Kingswood as existing "on purpose for them". But however this may be, the fact of its being for so long wholly devoted to the education of the sons of the manse led to the pre-servation of values that might easily have been smothered at Kingswood as so often elsewhere. Its traditions have been moulded thereby, and there has always been a marked emphasis on plain living, hard work and public service. When, therefore, in the late nineteenth century, the school was expanded and in part remodelled on Arnoldian lines, it was able to graft the new ideas on to its own already strong traditions, and to escape the exclusiveness that sometimes went with them. It was not, how-ever, until the headmasterships first of Mr. Wootton, when entry was widened and other changes made, and secondly of Mr. Sackett, when the windows were thrown wide open, that the school can be said to have come fully into its own.

Kingswood stands over against the older public schools; rooted in, and drawing her strength from, a different and no less signifi-cant aspect of a history common to them all; yet sharing with them a part of their heritage, claiming seniority as a national boarding school second only to the ancient foundations, and present achievement comparable with theirs. To the boy who comes of Methodist stock and inherits a scale of values quite other than the secular materialism of today she offers, at a level much deeper than can be spoilt by any accidental defect, a sense of underlying support. And as he grows older he will find that she accepts the need to reinterpret them and to blend them with other values drawn from other sources, so that he may easily take his place *in usum ecclesiae et rei publicae*. None who have inherited this tradition and who believe that it and its interpretation matter to the future of our country and of the world can be indifferent to the welfare of the school where it has been nurtured for over two hundred years.

APPENDICES

Relating to the Early History of the School

APPENDIX I

The Colliers' School of 1739

"WERE I TO CONTINUE here," the Rev. George Whitefield wrote in his diary on March 29, 1739, "I would endeavour to settle schools all over the Wood, and also in other places, as Mr. Griffith Jones has done in Wales. I have but just time to set in on foot. I hope God will bless the ministry of my honoured friend Mr. John Wesley, and enable him to bring it to good effect." The colliers gave him £20 in money, and promised £40 in subscriptions for the erection of a school. On April 2, just as he was leaving Bristol, the miners prepared him an unexpected hospitable entertainment, and were very forward for him to lay the first stone of their school. Early that afternoon he laid a stone, knelt upon it, and prayed that the gates of hell might not prevail against it.* Whitefield was, as he thought, on the point of leaving to return to his successful mission in Georgia, and he had already written to his friend and mentor Wesley in London asking him to come to Bristol and continue the work he had begun. Wesley had consented, and responsibility for the work in Bristol and district passed to him. Whitefield continued, however to collect funds for the colliers' school, Wesley himself sending a subscription within a few days of the laying of the stone. As late as August we hear of Whitefield continuing his discourse on Blackheath till it was nearly dark, and collecting nearly £15 for the school.†

Various references to this school are henceforward to be found in the Journals and correspondence of both Whitefield and Wesley. On April 23, 1739, Wesley went to see the stone which Whitefield had placed. "I think it cannot be better placed," he noted in his diary, "'tis just in the middle of the Wood, two miles every way from either church or school." On May 14, however,

* It was later that same afternoon, before he had heard of Whitefield's action, that Wesley made history by preaching for the first time in the open air.

† L. Tyerman, *Life of George Whitefield*, 1876, Vol.I, pp.195,271–2. Whitefield's sailing for America had been delayed.

Wesley went with others to look out "a proper place" for the school, "and at last pitched upon one between the London and Bath roads". There was evidently serious difficulty about the site, and Wesley was confronted with the necessity of pledging his own credit in the matter.

"In June 1739," he wrote later,* "being able to procure none any other way, I bought a little piece of ground and began building thereon, though I had not then a quarter of the money requisite to finish. However, taking all the debt upon myself, the creditors were will to stay. . . ."

To raise funds Wesley made application to Lady Huntingdon and her friends, "and her Ladyship, and the Ladies Hastings, with a few other persons of distinction, became liberal contributors to the schools. Mr. Ingham and Mr. Bryan Broughton were active in procuring subscriptions and many of the society in London were generous in their support of the measure".†

Thereafter Wesley was often at the site. On June 21 he was at the schoolroom, and had a large and attentive audience, "though it was uncovered and it rained hard". On the 26th he preached during violent rain under the sycamore tree near the school in Kingswood; the tree would long remain a familiar feature. In July Whitefield paid a brief visit to Bristol and after preaching to about eight thousand people dined with Wesley and many other friends at Two Mile Hill. "The schoolhouse", he tells us, "has been carried on so successfully that the roof is ready to be put up. The design, I think, is good. Old as well as young are to be instructed. A great and visible alteration is made in the behaviour of the colliers. Instead of cursing and swearing they are heard to sing hymns about the woods, and the rising generation will, I hope, be a generation of Christians."‡

In November Wesley wrote a vivid account of what had been done in Kingswood.§

Few persons have lived long in the West of England who have not heard of the colliers of Kingswood: a people famous from the beginning hitherto for neither fearing God nor regarding man; so ignor-

* *Letters*, Vol.I, p.356.
† *Life of Countess of Huntingdon*, Vol.II, p.366.
‡ Tyerman, op. cit. Vol.I, p.260.
§ *Journal*, Vol.II, p.322.

ant of the things of God that they seemed but one remove from the beasts that perish; and therefore utterly without desire of instruction, as well as without the means of it.

Many last winter used tauntingly to say to Mr. Whitefield, "If he will convert heathens, why does he not go to the colliers of Kingswood?" In spring he did so. And as there were thousands who resorted to no place of public worship, he went after them into their own wilderness, "to seek and save that which was lost". When he was called away, others went into "the highways and hedges, to compel them to come in." And, by the grace of God, their labour was not in vain. The scene is already changed. Kingswood does not now, as a year ago, resound with cursing and blasphemy. It is no more filled with drunkenness and uncleanness, and the idle diversions that naturally lead thereto. It is no longer full of wars and fightings, of clamour and bitterness, of wrath and envyings. Peace and love are there. Great numbers of the people are mild, gentle, and easy to be entreated. They "do not cry, neither strive," and hardly is their "voice heard in the streets"; or indeed in their own wood, unless when they are at their usual evening diversion, singing praise unto God their Saviour.

That their children, too, might know the things that make for their peace, it was some time since proposed to build a house in Kingswood; and, after many foreseen and unforeseen difficulties, in June last the foundation was laid. The ground made choice of was in the middle of the wood, between the London and Bath roads, not far from that called Two-Mile-Hill, about three measured miles from Bristol.

Here a large room was begun for the school, having four small rooms at either end for the schoolmasters (and, perhaps, if it should please God, some poor children) to lodge in. Two persons are ready to teach, so soon as the house is ready to receive them, the shell of which is nearly finished; so that it is hoped the whole will be completed in spring, or early in the summer. It is proposed, in the usual hours of the day, to teach chiefly the poorer children to read, write, and cast accounts; but more especially (by God's assistance) to "know God, and Jesus Christ, whom he hath sent." The older people, being not so proper to be mixed with children, (for we expect scholars of all ages, some of them grey-headed) will be taught in the inner rooms, either early in the morning, or late at night, so that their work may not be hindered.

It is true, although the masters require no pay, yet this undertaking is attended with great expense. But let Him that "feedeth the young ravens" see to that. He hath the hearts of all men in His hand. If He puts it into your heart, or into that of any of your friends, to assist in bringing this work to perfection, in the world look for no recompense; but it shall be remembered in that day when our Lord shall say "Inasmuch as ye did it unto the least of these My brethren, ye did it unto me."

By June 1740 the building must have been open, for without further comment, Wesley records that he preached there.* It comprised "a fine hall for preaching" as well as smaller rooms used by the masters of the school, but just how it was used we do not know beyond what Wesley tells us. It certainly served the Wesleys as a centre for their work in the district, and when a year later Charles Wesley and his converts among the colliers were repelled from the sacrament at the Bristol churches, he led them to the school-chapel and there consecrated the elements for them.†

Collaboration with Whitefield in regard to the colliers' school was however shortlived. Whitefield did not share with the Wesleys the Arminian theology of the High Church party to which they belonged, and his Calvinism became more outspoken. Controversy flared up in 1741, and hard things were said on both sides. Finding Wesley firmly in control of the colliers' school in Kingswood, Whitefield was inclined to lay claim to it—had he not laid the first stone, collected funds for it, and so forth? To this Wesley retorted that whilst his friend had been in America, the whole burden had fallen upon him, he had bought the land himself and had to pledge his own credit, that he could fairly claim that the school was his, not Whitefield's. The friction soon passed, and Whitefield's subsequent actions showed that he conceded the point.‡

---

* Wesley says that he preached "at Kingswood School". Both Wesley and Whitefield referred to the colliers' school at this time as Kingswood School, hence much of the subsequent confusion. The separate identity of the later boarding school and its claim to the title are established by the steps taken by Wesley in 1748 (see pp.21ff). His *Short Account of Kingswood School*, 1749, does not refer at all to the colliers' school.

† Charles Wesley's *Journal*, August 27, 1739, and April 12, 1741. His *Journal* for the period makes numerous references to the work at Kingswood.

‡ See Tyerman's *Whitefield*, Vol. 1, pp.474–5; and for Wesley's reply, *Letters*, Vol.I, p.355, "Now my brother, I will answer your main question. I think you can claim no right to that building, either in equity or in law, before my demise. And every honest lawyer will tell you the same. But if you repent of collecting the money towards it I will repay it as speedily as I can; although I now owe more than two hundred pounds on account of Kingswood School only."

The breach with Whitefield was reflected in Wesley's relations with their youthful lieutenant in Bristol, John Cennick. Caught up in the excitement of 1739, Cennick had, at Whitefield's suggestion, joined Wesley in Bristol. He had become an active lay preacher, and had begun to exercise some supervision over the varied activities in Bristol and neighbouring Kingswood when Wesley was elsewhere.

It has long been supposed that he was the first master at the colliers' school. Whitefield had suggested it before the school had actually been built, and a letter Cennick wrote to Wesley in August 1740 seems to imply it. Would Wesley approve, he asked, of the appointment of one William Spencer "as a sort of usher under me to your school at Kingswood". Clearly at this time Cennick regarded himself as, in some sense, either in charge of the school, or suitable for it. But this has to be reconciled with the categorical statement by Wesley in his letter to Whitefield of April 27, 1741 that Cennick "never was so (i.e. schoolmaster) at all".*

It would seem therefore that the oft-repeated statement that Cennick was the first master at the colliers' school at Kingswood must be abandoned, for we have Wesley's explicit statement to the contrary. However this may be, Cennick was an important figure in the life of the community at Kingswood, and the source of much unhappy friction. No more than Whitefield did he share the Arminian outlook of the Wesleys, and by 1741 he found himself preaching the message of the revival in a form that was anathema to them. They parted, and hard words were used by Wesley in regard to the incidents of the breach. But Cennick had proved himself an able and zealous evangelist, and continued active in the district in association with those who shared his views.† With encouragement from Whitefield he began to build

---

* *Letters*, Vol. I, p. 356. Cennick's letter is given in full in a note by Dr. Frank Baker, W.H.S., XXVIII, p.149.

† At Tytherton, a quiet village in Wiltshire, not far from Chippenham, Cennick built in the early 1740's a chapel and school which still survive, and which may closely resemble Wesley's first buildings at Kingswood. The mellow red-brick block comprises a lofty central chapel, with additions at either end, partly residential, partly designed to accommodate a small school. An engraving of Cennick as a young man of considerable presence hangs within the chapel, which is still used by the Moravian community.

The visitor may easily be misled as to the dating of the building by a memorial plaque on the front face, which relates to the removal of certain tombstones. The traditional dating of the chapel to 1744 is borne out by an inscription in an obscure position on the wall at the back of the premises.

in Kingswood another and rival society room and free school for the colliers.* It still stands by the main road in Kingswood, and bears an inscription stating that it was erected by George Whitefield and John Cennick, A.D. 1741. It was opened as a school in 1743. Before long, however, Cennick allied himself with the Moravians, and became a leading figure among them. By 1746–47 he was encouraging them to take over his societies in Kingswood, a development that Wesley must have viewed with mixed feelings. His subsequent story lies outside our scope, but the presence in the district of religious societies other than Wesley's is a factor of which we have to take account. It may help to explain the constant criticism to which Wesley's later school in Kingswood appears to have been subjected.

By 1744 things had apparently settled down and Wesley was able to record his satisfaction with the school. In this year too he wrote to a correspondent again defending his claim to call the school-house at Kingswood his own house—"for I bought the ground where it stands, and paid for the building of it, partly from the contributions of my friends . . . (and) partly from the income of my own Fellowship."†

When therefore he decided in 1746 to set up an ambitious boarding school the "proper situation" was found at the scene of his labours in Kingswood, and the new school was built on land immediately adjoining the earlier buildings.

His school for the colliers continued to exist at least for a while alongside the new school, but it was apparently conducted on quite a modest scale. In a *Journal* entry of March 14, 1749 he mentions "Four schools" in Kingswood—the boys boarded in the

---

* This school of Cennick's was also sometimes described in letters of the period as Kingswood School, e.g. in a letter from Whitefield to Cennick, June 8, 1741; and in *Selected Trevecka Letters* 1742-7, p.219. Great care is therefore needed to avoid confusion either with Wesley's colliers' school, or with his later boarding school.

† *Letters*, Vol.II, p.199, and see also IV, p.196. For further references to Wesley's title to the land see an interesting note by the Rev. H. J. Foster, W.H.S., Vol.III, p.68, *et seq.* The whole area had long been a battleground for would-be possessors, most of whom were landowners whose property abutted on to the wood, An attempt to disturb the title by a member of the Creswick family of Hanham Hall came to nothing. Another landowner, a Mrs. Archer, tried in 1752 to establish title to the land on which Wesley had built the school, though she wanted to "do him no injury". She did not wish to disappoint so laudable a work as that which Mr. Wesley had set on foot.

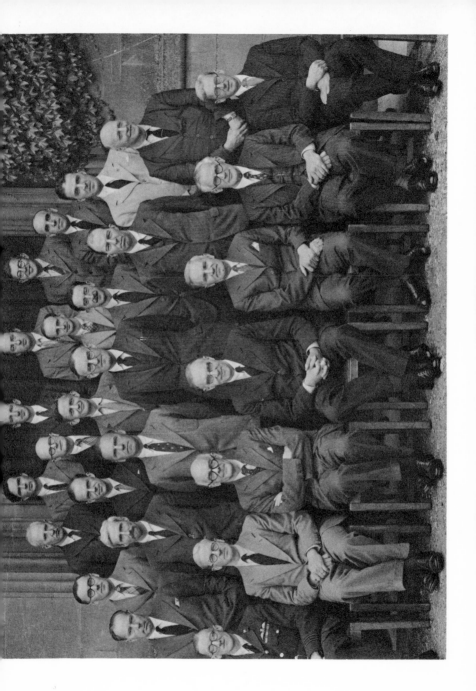

THE STAFF
OF 1959

LATEST ADDITIONS
The Sixth Form block under
construction 1969–70

A. L. CREED
Headmaster 1959–70

new House, the girls boarded in the old, and the day scholars, the
boys taught by James Harding, the girls taught by Sarah
Dimmock. After 1749 there is no further mention by Wesley of
the colliers' school. We know that a school or schools for colliers'
children existed in 1803, two of the smaller rooms attached to the
Chapel being used for the purpose, but whether it had had a continuous history is not certain.* Soon afterwards it was altogether
discontinued. The original large school room or "fine hall for
preaching"—it is Cennick's phrase—became the chapel both of
the local Methodist society and of the later Kingswood School.
Various references to it will be found in the text. It was succeeded in 1843 by a much larger building, the present Methodist Church in Kingswood.

* *History of Kingswood School,* 1898, p.23.

R

APPENDIX II

"One or two tracts . . ."

WESLEY had long been deeply interested in education. He had been for some years a conscientious tutor at Lincoln College, Oxford. Whilst still there in 1732 he had elicited from his remarkable mother a letter describing in vivid detail the methods adopted by her in the upbringing of her children in the parsonage at Epworth.* When in 1735 he was setting sail for Georgia he found time to write to his elder brother Samuel, recently appointed master of Blundell's school at Tiverton, reminding him of the dangers of the unexpurgated classics.

Among the books which he and his friends had with them on the vessel bound for Georgia was a copy of *Pietas Hallensis,* an account by the well-known German pietist August Hermann Francke (1663–1727) of his educational activities in Halle. It had recently been translated into English, and published by the S.P.C.K. The concrete embodiment of Francke's ideals in a substantial Georgian-style building was boldly figured by way of frontispiece and may well have made its impact on Wesley.

On the voyage out and in Georgia Wesley was thrown too into close contact with the Moravian Brethren, from whose practices he later on borrowed freely. Among the Moravians interest in education was strongly developed, and the works of their well-known and widely travelled Bishop Comenius (1592–1671) were held in high esteem. The provision of schools for the children of their community held a foremost place in their religious life.

When, therefore, after his return to this country and his profound religious experience in the spring of 1738 Wesley and his friend the Rev. Benjamin Ingham visited Germany they planned to see something both of Francke's activities, though he himself was no longer alive, and of those of the Moravians. They first made their way, via Jena, to Halle. There they gained admit-

---

* *Journal,* Vol.III, pp.34–9. Also conveniently reprinted in full in F. C. Pritchard, *Methodist Secondary Education,* 1949, pp.20–6. Her precepts related, however, rather to the little child than to the child of school age.

tance to the great Orphan House which, with its associated schools, loomed so large in *Pietas Hallensis*—that amazing proof, as Wesley called it, that all things were still possible to him that believeth. Wesley's account may be read in his *Journal*:*

> There is now a large yearly revenue for its support, beside what is continually brought in by the printing office, the books sold there, and the apothecary's shop, which is furnished with all sorts of medicines. The building reaches backward from the front in two wings, for, I believe, a hundred and fifty yards. The lodging chambers for the children, their dining room, their chapel, and all the adjoining apartments, are so conveniently contrived and so exactly clean as I have never seen any before.

Some six hundred and fifty children, he was told, were wholly maintained there, and three thousand taught. Nevertheless, Wesley's account is consistent with his having been somewhat disappointed.

Wesley and Ingham then went on to the famous Moravian settlement at Herrnhut, not far from Dresden; and there Wesley found what he regarded as a truly Christian community, in the midst of which was an orphan house or school. He took notes of the rules : †

> . . . the larger children rise at five. (The smaller between five and six) After a little private prayer they work till seven. Then they are at school till eight, the hour of prayer; at nine those who are capable of it learn Latin; at ten, French; at eleven they all walk; at twelve they dine all together, and walk till one; at one, they work or learn writing; at three, arithmetic; at four, history; at five, they work; at six, sup and work; at seven, after a time spent in prayer, walk; at eight the smaller children go to bed, the larger to the public service. When this is ended, they work again till at ten they go to bed.

These rules have often been thought to have been the model for Kingswood; but, as we shall see, we must not too quickly take it for granted that he looked no further.

Back in this country Wesley began to establish schools for the poor as part of his missionary activities; schools in Bristol and

---

* *Journal*, Vol.II, p.17.
† ibid., p.51.

Kingswood were among the first, followed by the orphanage at Newcastle. He soon recoiled however from what he regarded as the extravagances of his Moravian friends, and separated from them. Ingham, on the other hand, continued in his admiration of their activities, and encouraged them to assist him with the work of evangelism in Yorkshire. A small school had been begun by the Brethren in London in 1741. It was later moved to Broadoaks in Essex, where Richard Viney and his wife acted as superintendents.* It went finally to an estate at Fulneck in Yorkshire that Ingham was commissioned to buy for them in 1743; and there Fulneck School has flourished ever since.† We know from the Moravian records that the school at Broadoaks was conducted on lines that recalled Herrnhut—diet, discipline, no holidays, "soul edifyings"; and although Wesley makes no reference to this project of the Moravians in his account of Kingswood, he visited their settlement in Yorkshire in April 1747. This was before the school was moved there, but he may well have heard about their plans. He was much impressed by what he saw. "We walked to the New House of the Germans", he wrote. "It stands on the side of a hill, commanding all the vale beneath, and the opposite hill. The front is exceeding grand, though plain, being faced with fine, smooth white stone."

Of the influence of the Moravians' example on Wesley's project at Kingswood there can therefore be little doubt. The theme of an education guarded from the world's corrupting ways was fully explicit in the works of Comenius. Censorship of books, full and continuous employment whether in work or play, it is all there. We can indeed catch an echo of the very words of Comenius. His numerous works included, besides the oft-quoted *Great Didactic*, a lesser-known treatise entitled *Paradisus Juventuti Christianae Reducendus*, in which he confuses the spiritual aim of the school with that of a paradise as a place that may be made a happy one for boys, and indulges also in many forced analogies

---

* Richard Viney's diary, W.H.S., Vol.XIV, p.19. In 1744, when Viney had parted from the Moravians, Wesley told him that he had thoughts of beginning an "Œconomy", partly a boarding school, partly an orphan house, and partly a working house for poor people, which he thought Viney might superintend, but that he could not then proceed with it.

† For a history of Fulneck School see *Through Two Centuries*, by R. M. B. Hutton, 1953.

between the school and the first Paradise.* This must surely have been one of the tracts that fell into Wesley's hands, for the text books which Wesley would write for his school would carry the dedication *In Usum Juventutis Christianae.*

Moreover, on seeing the school opened he is reputed to have exclaimed, *"Behold Paradise opened in the wild!"*†

The theme, however, of an education guarded from the world's corrupting ways was by no means confined to its German and Moravian exponents. Interest in the provision of an environment for children which should preserve them in the innocence of their baptism had been widespread on the continent for more than a century. In France the "Little Schools" of Port Royal had caused a considerable stir in the middle of the seventeenth century. Although they had lasted but fifteen years before they were suppressed, the teachers who had been dispersed had devoted their lives to propagating their principles, and in their works are to be found passages anticipating in striking detail the regime which Wesley would inaugurate at Kingswood.

In the dormitories the beds were so arranged that the master could see all the children from his own. The children rose at 5.30 and the day began with prayers; then came school work, at 11 they went to the refectory, and during the meal there was a reading. When they left the refectory they went into the garden for recreation, and since the garden was large and full of thickets and glades they were forbidden to go without permission outside a space which had been marked out. The masters took their exercise in the same place without ever losing sight of their pupils. At 1 o'clock they all went into the big schoolroom until 2; at 2 they went back to their room to learn poetry. At 6 they had supper, and the recreation which followed this lasted until 8. At 8.30 came prayers and bed. The master in charge of each room was present; thus he was the last to go to bed and the first to get up. On Sundays the Superior used to catechise and give instruction, and they then went to the parishional High Mass. Their only free time was in the afternoon, and this was spent playing in the garden, or sometimes in going for walks to houses in the neighbourhood.‡

* S. S. Laurie, *John Amos Comenius: His Life and Educational Works,* 1887.

† *History,* p.24.

‡ Summarized from one of the most informative of the writings of the Port Royalists, known as *Supplement au Necrologe de Port Royal,* 1735; quoted H. C. Barnard, *Port Royalists on Education,* 1918, p.133.

The parallels are in some respects so close that it seems fair to conclude that we have here much of the model for Wesley's Kingswood. The attentive reader will notice details lacking in the rules of the Moravian school at Herrnhut which has often been assumed to have provided Wesley with his model.

A little book that must have been another of the tracts to which Wesley referred as falling into his hands was the work of a French Protestant, Pierre Poiret, to whom some further reference will be found in Appendix III. Its title was *Les Principes Solides de la Religion et de la Vie Chrétienne, appliqués a l' éducation des Enfans*. It had enjoyed a wide circulation in several languages. On this Wesley set to work in 1743, "extracting" as was his wont; and imparting to the author's reflections a vigour lacking in the original. This Wesley printed to follow on immediately after a short catechism; all schools had their catechisms, short and vivid, heaven and hell, and the plan of salvation; Wesley's included also a section dealing with the manners of the ancient Christians. The whole he published in 1745 under the title *Instructions for Children*. A Latin version for use at Kingswood followed in 1748. It is the opening catechetical section, rather than Poiret's *Principes Solides,* that gives its flavour to Wesley's tract—

Quo vadunt impii post mortem? In infernum.
Cujuscemodi locus est infernus? Infernus est specus tenebrosa ac profunda, plena sulphure ignito.
Quomodo impii tempus terent in inferno? Flendo & plangendo & stridendo dentibus.

To this composite tract Wesley gave the widest publicity. He was ever insisting on it, impressing on parents the urgency of instructing their families with its help. It would and did therefore figure largely in his own Christian family at Kingswood.*

Alongside Poiret Wesley placed the Abbé Fleury; indeed in praising *Instructions for Children* (Works, XI, p.339) and saying that he knew nothing in the English language to equal it, he

* Green's statement in his *Wesley Bibliography*, p.174, that *Instructions for Children* was "literally translated" from Poiret's work discussed above is scarcely accurate, and has perhaps misled others. The catechism is not to be found in *Les Principes Solides*. See article by M. Jean Orcibal, *Les Spirituelles françaises et espagnols chez John Wesley et ses contemporains*, in *Revue de l' Histoire des Religions*, 1951.

seems to imply that it was extracted from Fleury quite as much as from Poiret. Fleury is the well-known French ecclesiastical historian, Claude Fleury, 1640–1723, author not only of shorter and longer catechisms but of a monumental ecclesiastical history.* It is relevant that it was from the latter that Wesley extracted another tract, *The Manners of the Ancient Christians,* on which he placed an emphasis at Kingswood comparable almost to that on the *Instructions for Children.* In Fleury's work were to be found a statement of the Christian life and creed before it had been split into divisions, and a description of the habits of the early Christians, their prayers, reading of the scriptures, fasting and so on. Not only would the children study *The Manners of the Ancient Christians,* but the rules of the school would conform as far as practicable to the ways of the early Christians. If they fasted on Fridays, so would the school.†

One further important influence on Wesley's thinking, of a very different kind, remains to be discussed. In the latter years of the seventeenth century Milton and others had followed Comenius in formulating lofty, if somewhat impracticable, ideal systems of education. In 1690 Locke had followed them up with his more prosaic, yet provocative and still very readable, *Thoughts concerning Education.* Here will be found the clue to much of Wesley's wording, and when it came to drafting the *Short Account of Kingswood School* Wesley must have taken Locke down from the shelf. The parallel is in many places too close to be accidental.

"Vice," Locke had written, "if we may believe the general complaint, ripens so fast nowadays, and runs up to seed so early in young

---

* Not to be confused with the even better known Cardinal A. H. Fleury (1653–1743).

† An English translation of the first two volumes of Fleury's work had appeared in 1721. Wesley's choice of Fleury's work for such prominence in the curriculum is of more than passing interest. It was to appeal a century later to J. H. Newman. When, dissatisfied with the Church of his day, Newman searched about for a sure guide, it was to Fleury that he turned. Translations of Fleury's work on the early centuries followed one upon another in the formative years of the Tractarian movement, with prefaces by Newman. "I was fond of Fleury", he wrote later, "because it presented a sort of photograph of ecclesiastical history without any comment on it. In the event that simple representation of the early centuries had a good deal to do with unsettling me in my Anglicanism." But that is another story. Here it is sufficient to notice the relationship in which Fleury's work stood to both Wesley and Newman.

people, that it is impossible to keep a lad from the spreading
contagion, if you will venture him abroad with the herd, and trust
to chance, or his own inclination, for the choice of his company at
school. By what fate vice has so thriven amongst us these few years
past, and by what hands it has been nursed up into so uncontrolled
a dominion, I shall leave to others to enquire. I wish that those
who complain of the great decay of Christian piety and virtue
everywhere, and of learning and acquired improvements in the
gentry of this generation, would consider how to retrieve them in
the next."

Locke had set his face against effeminacy. "Let his bed be
hard, and rather quilts than feathers", he had written. So Wesley:
"All the beds have mattresses on them, not feather beds; both
because they are more healthy and because we would keep them
at the utmost distance from softness and effeminacy." Locke had
advocated simplicity of diet—"if my young master needs have
flesh, let it be but once a day, and of one sort, at a meal. Plain
beef, mutton, veal, &c. without any sauce than hunger, is best";
his simple breakfast and supper were to be "very sparingly
seasoned with sugar, or rather none at all". Locke too looked
askance at play—"how any one's being put into a mixed herd
of unruly boys and there learning to wrangle and trap, or rook
at span-farthing, fits him for civil conversation, or business, I do
not see". Play meant not cricket or football, but cards and dice.
It was vanity and riches that had given cards, dice, and drinking
so much credit in the world. But a gentleman might with advantage be trained in manual arts like gardening and carpentry, the
one affording him exercise when the weather keeps him from the
other. "A lazy listless humour that idly dreams away the days is
of all others the least to be indulged or permitted in young
people."* Locke, Wesley believed, should be read with
discrimination. Young students might read his *Essay on Human
Understanding* with a judicious tutor, who would "confirm and
enlarge what is right in it", and guard them against what is wrong
in it, "avoiding the immoderate attachment to him" which was
so common amongst his readers.

If Locke was an important source for Wesley, Milton was much
less so. It is true that in the *Plain Account of Kingswood School*
Wesley refers to Milton's "admirable treatise on Education" as

* For some further examples of the parallel phraseology see A. H. Body,
John Wesley and Education, pp.56–61.

if it had influenced him considerably. Milton thought that every youth should begin and end his education in the same place, and Wesley took the point in defending the provision of an academic course at Kingswood. But this is almost all. Milton starts indeed with the famous dictum that the end of learning is "to repair the ruins of our first parents by regaining to know God aright", but he is soon changing his ground and defining as a generous education that which fits a man to perform justly, skilfully and magnanimously all the offices, both private and public, of peace and war. The value of the great classical authors is common ground with Wesley, but with a quite different emphasis. The exercise which he recommends for his youth is the exact use of his weapon—to guard, and to strike safely with edge or point; military exercises are to be encouraged, and there looms ahead the becoming renowned and perfect commanders in the service of their country. It is a very different world from Wesley's.

To complete the picture and set Wesley's initiative in its context it is necessary also to take into account the quite extensive alternative provision available to those who did not hold with the ways of the public schools or of the grammar schools which in varying degrees emulated them.

It was quite possible to proceed to Oxford and Cambridge either through attendance at one of the private classical schools maintained by individuals, mostly clergymen of the Church of England, or by recourse to one of the many dissenting academies.

The newspapers of the period carry many advertisements of these private classical schools, and it was in itself in no way unusual for a clergyman to establish and maintain such a school.* "Send your boys", Wesley advised his friends, "not to any of the large public schools (for they are nurseries of all manner of wickedness) but to a private school kept by some pious man who endeavours to instruct a small number of children in religion and learning together."

One such school had been established in Salford in 1735 by the Rev. John Clayton, and deserves special notice here, for not only is it an example of a classical school of the period, but it may well have influenced Wesley. Clayton had been a

---

* Nicholas Hans *New Trends in Education in the Eighteenth Century,* 1951.

notable member of the Holy Club in Oxford, and Wesley had shared his enthusiasm for the restoration of the practices of the pre-Nicene or Apostolic Church. He had become a prominent High Churchman in Manchester. The school that he had established was large and successful, had an excellent library, and sent students regularly to the universities.† How far Clayton went in attempting to instil "religion and learning together" we do not know, but it would be surprising if he did not, for he called his school St. Cyprian's. It was he who at Oxford had suggested to Wesley that the members of the Holy Club should observe the fasts of the early Church on Wednesdays and Fridays.

The classical schools led, like the public schools, to the universities of Oxford and Cambridge. For many this route was barred by the religious tests imposed in 1662, and for all such the dissenting academies—part school, part college— offered an alternative education, where the curriculum often emphasised mathematics and the new sciences as the basis of a modern education. The important part played by the dissenting academies in the evolution of education in this country has often been described. It possesses much interest on its own account, but its relevance to the story of Wesley's Kingswood is less than has sometimes been supposed. Wesley in 1748 was no dissenter, and his school at Kingswood would conform to the pattern of the classical schools, and not to that of the dissenting academies.

The picture is complicated, however, by the fact that some of the dissenting academies helped to provide an educated ministry, not only for the independent and presbyterian congregations, but also for the Church of England. Many of the men prominent in the religious world of the day—Archbishop Secker, for example, and Joseph Butler, the Bishop of Bristol—had been trained at a dissenting academy.

One such academy was maintained at Northampton by the well-known and widely respected Dr. Philip Doddridge. Wesley visited it in September 1745, and the fact that this was less than a year before he laid the foundation stone of the New House at Kingswood may well be significant. He was also in the following

---

* ibid., p.132. In one respect, however, Wesley and Clayton differed sharply, for Clayton went so far as to welcome the Pretender in the streets of Manchester when he and his followers arrived there during the Forty-Five. For this Clayton incurred grave censure. Wesley never wavered in his support of the Hanoverian monarchy.

year in correspondence with Doddridge about lists of books. (See Appendix III).

Distinct again from both the classical schools and the dissenting academies were a number of schools maintained by the Quakers and other denominational bodies; and some degree of analogy may, not surprisingly, be traced between some of these schools and Wesley's Kingswood.

It had been well said by M. Jean Orcibal in his perceptive study of Wesley's theology that his originality becomes, paradoxically, all the more striking as the variety and breadth of his sources are revealed.* Something to the same effect might well be said of his synthesis of so much from so many sources in his model school at Kingswood.

---

* M. Jean Orcibal in *A History of the Methodist Church in Great Britain*, (ed. Davies and Rupp), Vol. I 1960, p.110.

APPENDIX III

The "advanced course" and the books placed by Wesley in the library at Kingswood

FROM the very beginning of the school Wesley had in mind a course more advanced than that printed in the Short Account of 1749. He was, we know, much concerned about the best course of reading for his young preachers. He had earlier, in the days of the Holy Club at Oxford, published his own father's *Advice to a Young Clergyman,* with its racy commendation of Anglican theology of the preceding century.* In 1745 he visited, and no doubt became much interested in, the Dissenting Academy at Northampton maintained by "that amiable man", Dr. Philip Doddridge. In the course of 1746 Doddridge sent him, in response to a request, a long and detailed list of books, to help him with "that little collection of books which you seem desirous to make for your preachers". There were books on Logic, Metaphysics, Ethics, Jewish Antiquities, Civil History, Natural Philosophy, Astronomy, Natural and Revealed Religion. When he came to Practical Divinity, Doddridge said he would not presume to mention to Wesley the divines of the Established Church, but the Puritans and the "divines of the separation" might be less well known to him. In both Wesley's father's list and in Doddridge's we recognize many titles that were to appear at Kingswood.†

When, therefore, in 1748 the New House at Kingswood was ready and Wesley brought to his Conference his proposals for it, they provided not only for a model school, but also for an academic or advanced course, intended for those who wished to prepare for the ministry.

---

* Reprinted in Jackson's *Life of Charles Wesley,* as an Appendix in Vol. II.
† For Doddridge's advice in full see *Arminian Magazine,* 1778, p.419. His extensive library is now housed in New College, London.

Q.29. After they have gone through the school, what do they learn the first year?

A. The Hebrew Bible and the Greek Testament, with Franke's *Manducatio*. The Apostolic Fathers. Tertullian. Pearson on the Creed: abridge it. Aldrich's *Logic,* and Sandn W.'s *Sermons.* Bishop of Meaux, *Introduction to History.* Puffendorf's *Introduction.*

It is no more than a sketch, but provision on similar lines was made for a second, third, fourth and even a fifth year.*

Wesley, however, "suspended" this part of his scheme for Kingswood (see page 10), although the occasional student was evidently encouraged to spend a period reading at Kingswood, or to use the list of books as a guide for his own reading.†

The advanced course at Kingswood was revived in 1768, when the expulsion of the Methodists at Oxford stung Wesley into action. He republished the *Short Account of Kingswood School,* with an addendum which differed radically from the sketch of 1746 :—

N.B.—The following method may be observed by those who design to go through a course of academical learning.

FIRST YEAR

Read Lowth's *English Grammar*; Latin, Greek, Hebrew, French Grammars; Cornelius Nepos; Sallust, Cæsar; Tully's *Offices;* Terence, Phaedrus; Æneid; Dilworth; Randal; Bengel; Vossius; Aldrich and Wallis's *Logic;* Langbaine's *Ethics;* Hutchinson on the Passions; Spanheim's *Introduction to Ecclesiastical History;* Puffendorf's *Introduction to the History of Europe*; *Moral and Sacred Poems*; Hebrew Pentateuch, with the Notes; Greek Testament— Matthew to the Acts, with the Notes; Xenophon's *Cyrus*; Homer's *Iliad*; Bishop Pearson on the Creed; Ten volumes of the *Christian Library*; *Télémaque.*

SECOND YEAR

Look over the Grammars; read Velleius Paterculus; *Tusculan Questions; Excerpta; Vidæ Opera; Lusus Westmonasterienses; Chronological Tables*; Euclid's *Elements*; Wells' *Tracts*; Newton's

---

* See *Bennet Minutes,* W.H.S. Publication No. 1, p.57.

† cf. advice to Samuel Furly, then 22 years old, March 30, 1754, *Letters* Vol.III, p.117.

Principia; Mosheim's *Introduction to Church History*; Usher's *Annals*; Burnet's *History of the Reformation*; Spenser's *Faerie Queene*; Historical Books of the Hebrew Bible; Greek Testament, *ad finem;* Κύρου 'Αναβασις; Homer's *Odyssey*; twelve volumes of the *Christian Library*; Ramsay's *Cyrus*; Racine.

THIRD YEAR

Look over the Grammars; Livy; Suetonius; Tully *De Finibus; Musae Anglicanae*; Dr. Burton's *Poemata*; Lord Forbes's *Tracts*; *Abridgement of Hutchinson's Works; Survey of the Wisdom of God in the Creation*; Rollin's *Ancient History*; Hume's *History of England;* Neal's *History of the Puritans;* Milton's *Poetical Works;* Hebrew Bible—Job to the Canticles; Greek Testament; Plato's *Dialogues*; Greek Epigrams; twelve volumes of the *Christian Library*; Pascal; Corneille.

FOURTH YEAR

Look over the Grammars; Tacitus; Grotii *Historia Belgica;* Tully *De Naturâ Deorum; Prœdium Rusticum; Carmina Quadragesimalia; Philosophical Transactions abridged;* Watts's *Astronomy,* etc.; *Compendium Metaphysicae;* Watts' *Ontology;* Locke's *Essay;* Malebranche; Clarendon's *History*; Neal's *History of New-England*; Antonio Solis's *History of Mexico*; Shakespeare; rest of the Hebrew Bible; Greek Testament; Epictetus; Marcus Antoninus; *Poetae Minores*; end the *Christian Library*; *La Fausseté de les Vertues Humaines; Quesnell sur les Évangiles.*

Whoever goes carefully through this course will be a better scholar than nine in ten of the graduates at Oxford and Cambridge.

Many of the books placed by Wesley in the library at Kingswood are still there, and are among the school's most cherished possessions. It must be remembered that the school had at its disposal also Wesley's editions or excerpta of many of the authors on whom he placed the greatest stress, and others, particularly the writings of the Puritan divines, had been given a prominent place in the Christian Library.

A fair proportion of the Divinity now on the shelves is such as might have formed part of his father's library at Epworth, and many of the volumes carry seventeenth-century dates. Thus Bishop Pearson *On the Creed*, his father had said, ought to be in every clergyman's study—"all the world allows him to have been of almost illimitable sense, piety and learning". The Arminian or High Church tradition is represented not only by an early Latin translation from the Dutch of the works of Arminius, but by others who, like him, opposed the Calvinists, and looked to a united Church; by Grotius, who admired the Church of Laud above all others, and his disciple Le Clerc; and by Stillingfleet, whom few save Grotius had equalled, so Wesley's father had said. Stillingfleet's *Irenicum: a Weapon Salve for the Church's Wounds* was one of two books which are known to have changed Wesley's views with regard to Church order, and led him to believe in a Church constituted on a broad and comprehensive basis tolerant of different parties within its communion. His comment in the Kingswood copy, "I think he fully proves his point", with the date 1760 is a significant (and hitherto unpublished) annotation. The great Reformers are noticeable by their absence; no Luther, and Calvin is represented only by a copy of the Geneva Bible with his preface. But there was room for some of the mystics who were at this time much read and whom M. Poiret had done much to introduce into England.* The Kingswood copy of Madame Guyon is marked "Half right, half wrong, 1777". Malebranche's once famous work with its theme that God is the first cause of all changes in bodies and souls had many admirers in England as well as on the continent. The copy at Kingswood is no doubt that to which Wesley referred in his letter to Joseph Benson in January 1768.

Wesley's wider interests are also well represented. In Natural History there are well-known works by Ray and Derham. We find also Newton, and Linnaeus, and works on medicine and electricity, including Benjamin Franklin's early observations.

The books in the library today may be compared with a list compiled in 1782 by Cornelius Bayley when a master at the school. Comparison shows that a number of volumes have disappeared, and that others were added at some date sub-

---

* This vogue for the mystical writers and the works of the metaphysician Malebranche comes out very clearly in the contemporary letters and papers of John Byrom, who taught the Wesleys shorthand; see *John Byrom, Selections from his Journals and Papers,* edited Henri Talon, 1950; and also the authoritative article by M. Jean Orcibal, *Les Spirituelles françaises et espagnols chez John Wesley et ses contemporains,* in *Revue de l' Histoire des Religions,* 1951. Three volumes of Poiret's own *Divine Œconomy* are among the books in the school library.

sequent to the compilation of his list. The loss is not surprising, for it is said that two whole cartloads of old books which left Old Kingswood in 1851 never reached Bath. Others may have been removed for what were felt to be sufficient reasons. Not surprisingly the works of the extravagant mystic, Madame Bourignon, are among those that have gone. A more unfortunate loss is that of St. Cyran's *Instructions Chrétiennes* which appears in Bayley's list, the elusive source of Wesley's oft-reprinted and influential *Christian Reflections*. The existence of a copy of the *Instructions Chrétiennes* in the library at Kingswood, as shown on Bayley's list, is cited by M. Orcibal as proof that it was indeed Saint Cyran's work that Wesley translated.

The foregoing is but a very cursory comment, and much more might be said. An important article on Wesley's reading by Dr. Frank Baker appeared in the *London Quarterly and Holborn Review* in April and July 1943.

R

APPENDIX IV

The appeal for the preachers' sons at the school

THE APPEAL is quoted in the text (pp.54–6) in the earliest published form that has come down to us. The dating of the appeal is important in relation to the history of the school, for it has often been wrongly assumed to date from the foundation in 1748, and the school's history distorted in consequence. Moreover the wording was revised from time to time. The successive editions as they appear in the *Large Minutes* are printed in parallel columns in Vol. I of the valuable octavo edition of the *Minutes of Conference* published in 1862. The opening exhortation to all parents to send their children, and the injunction to the preachers to refute all lies were repeated in the editions of '70 and '72, omitted in '80 and '89. The difficulty then was the number of applicants. The reference to the thirteen or fourteen poor children in para. 6 is also omitted in the later versions. A late version is printed in Wesley's *Works,* and has often been quoted in accounts of early Kingswood.

Myles in his *Chronological History* made two efforts to date the appeal; the first, as we have seen, associating it with the first reference to a collection for the school in 1756; and stating (on page 100) that it dated from 1763. This is the right date, but the version he quotes is a late one. By his own day the school was so definitely a school for the sons of the preachers that it was easy for him to ante-date the appeal. He deserves our sympathy; he had to cope with a mass of pamphlets of all kinds published and republished with or without alterations throughout the whole course of early Methodism, and he did his best. But the subsequent uncritical acceptance of his dating has led to confusion about the story of the school.

In paragraph 5 of the edition of 1763 Wesley speaks of the lies of every kind which were plentifully invented and handed about "even by some of our preachers". What these lies were does not appear. In the early fifties there had been "bitter evil speaking". Was it perhaps to be found in the families of those boys whom Wesley had "sent away"? But the cry of "Popery" was often raised in Bristol, not only against Wesley, and it is possible that Wesley's insistence on regular fasting and frequent communion, and the administration of the latter at Kingswood— and perhaps, too, the frequent singing heard within its walls— may have given rise to the suspicion that the school had Papist sympathies. The cry of "Popery" was often launched against the Methodists with less impressive evidence than this.

NOTE ON SOURCES

THE STORY of Kingswood School cannot be understood apart from that of early Methodism, and there is no short cut to an understanding of the latter. On the contrary, there is a formidable literature; and since bibliographies are numerous and easily accessible (e.g. that included in the first volume of the new *History of the Methodist Church in Great Britain,* edited Davies and Rupp, 1965) there is little need to reproduce such a list here. In them will be found listed the Standard editions of Wesley's *Journal* (8 vols) and of his *Letters* (8 vols), his *Works* (14 vols) and the most important biographies, not only of John Wesley, but of Charles Wesley, George Whitefield, and Lady Huntingdon. These have to be related to the minutes of the early Conferences. The various volumes of *Minutes* issued in the eighteenth century and still often found on old bookshelves are confusing to the unwary. They were put in order, and the chronology made intelligible, in the first volume of the octavo edition of 1862. This useful volume seems to have escaped authors of the Kingswood History of 1898. Green's *Wesley Bibliography,* listing all Wesley's own publications is also indispensable.

Moreover, since the last *History* was written much further material has been published in the *Proceedings* of the Wesley Historical Society. Almost all of the annual volumes contain references to Kingswood, or to persons connected with it, though only a few of these can be found by reference to the entry Kingswood School in the otherwise most useful index issued by the Society. A set of the *Proceedings* can be consulted at the Methodist Archives in City Road, London, where also is gathered together much other information of interest to the student of early Kingswood. A further source for the early period, only recently made available and often quaintly illuminating, is to be found in the extracts so far published from the Trevecka letters. References to these volumes will be found in the text.

The most reliable reference to the school in a secondary source is that to be found in the *Life of Wesley* by Coke and Moore, 1792. Myles' *Chronological History of the People called Metho-*

dists, 4th edition, 1814, contains a valuable appendix about the school. A useful account of early Methodism which escapes most bibliographies is an essay by Élie Halévy in *Revue de Paris,* 1906, entitled *La Naissance du Methodisme en Angleterre.* In this early work, antedating his better known references to Methodism, Halévy deals vividly with the movement in Bristol and neighbouring Kingswood.

Two works by old boys of the school discuss the different strands that went to the making of Wesley's ideas on education, A. H. Body's *John Wesley and Education* (1936) and F. C. Pritchard's *Methodist Secondary Education* (1949); and to both of these the present writer is indebted. A more recent book, *Pity my Simplicity,* by Paul Sangster, 1963, touches on Kingswood in discussing the wider topic of the religious education of children 1738–1800.

For the nineteenth century much help is given by the *History of Kingswood School,* by Three Old Boys, 1898. At that time interest in old Kingswood of the first half of the nineteenth century burned bright, and steps were fortunately taken to collect reminiscences and publish them in the *Magazine.* These are invaluable. A list of many of them can be found on p.182 of the *History.*

Summarised accounts of the school, many of which are to be found in secondary authorities, should be used only with extreme caution. About few schools—if any—have misstatements been made more frequently or with greater assurance. That it was founded for the children of the Kingswood colliers (occasionally said, and with some excuse; for the story is, as explained in the text and Appendix I, confusing); that it was founded for the sons of Wesley's preachers (definitely not true, though Wesley did later say that it existed 'on purpose' for them); that it was a total failure, and presumably perished (most frequently, and most inexcusably; this is an unchecked inference from Wesley's outspoken criticisms of the staff and management widely publicised in his *Journal*). It would be easy to compile an astonishing list of misstatements by otherwise reputable authors and historians, and scarcely a month passes without renewed currency being given to one or other of them.

INDEX

of persons, places, churches, colleges and schools. Titles of books and tracts are also, in general, included. Those, however, which occur only in Wesley's Short Account, *or in his list of books (e.g. pp.42–3), or in the list in Appendix III, are not included.*